Theatrical Unrest

CW01081452

What is it about theatre, compared to other kinds of cultural representation, that provokes such a powerful reaction? *Theatrical Unrest* tells the compelling tales of ten riots whose cause lay on stage. It looks at the intensity and evanescence of the live event and asks whether theatre shares its unrepeatable quality with history.

Tracing episodes of unrest in theatical history from an Elizabethan uprising over Shakespeare's *Richard II* to Sikhs in revolt at Gurpreet Kaur Bhatti's *Behzti*, Sean McEvoy chronicles a selection of extreme public responses to this inflammatory art form. Each chapter provides a useful overview of the structure and documentation of one particular event, juxtaposing eyewitness accounts with newspaper reports and other contemporary narratives.

Theatrical Unrest is an absorbing account of the explosive impact of performance, and an essential read for anyone interested in theatre's often violent history.

Sean McEvoy teaches English at Varndean College in Brighton and at Murray Edwards College, Cambridge. He has written a number of books on the theatre, including *Shakespeare: The Basics* and *Ben Jonson, Renaissance Dramatist*.

Theatrical Unrest

Ten riots in the history of the stage, 1601–2004

Sean McEvoy

Routledge
Taylor & Francis Group

LONDON AND NEW YORK

First published 2016
by Routledge
2 Park Square, Milton Park, Abingdon, Oxon OX14 4RN

and by Routledge
711 Third Avenue, New York, NY 10017

Routledge is an imprint of the Taylor & Francis Group, an informa business

British Library Cataloguing-in-Publication Data
A catalogue record for this book is available from the British Library

Library of Congress Cataloguing-in-Publication Data
Names: McEvoy, Sean, 1959–
Title: Theatrical unrest: ten riots in the history of the stage 1601–2004 / Sean McEvoy.
Description: Milton Park, Abingdon, Oxon ; New York : Routledge, 2016. | Includes index.
Identifiers: LCCN 2015031614| ISBN 9781138914308 (hardback) | ISBN 9781138914315 (pbk.) | ISBN 9781315690933 (ebook)
Subjects: LCSH: Theater—Political aspects—Europe. | Riots—Europe—History. | Theater and society—Europe. | Theater audiences—Europe—History.
Classification: LCC PN2570 .M38 2016 | DDC 792.094—dc23
LC record available at http://lccn.loc.gov/2015031614

ISBN: 978-1-138-91430-8 (hbk)
ISBN: 978-1-138-91431-5 (pbk)
ISBN: 978-1-315-69093-3 (ebk)

Typeset in Times New Roman
by Book Now Ltd, London
Printed and bound in Great Britain by
Ashford Colour Press Ltd, Gosport, Hampshire

Contents

Illustrations

Acknowledgements

I would especially like to thank Daphne Wall, who has translated many of the French sources used in Chapters 4 and 9, and who first brought to my attention the 1933–4 production of *Coriolanus* in Paris. I would also like to thank Conor Muldoon for his advice and his careful reading of Chapters 7 and 8, and Professors David Nash and John Kerrigan and Dr Clare Wilkinson-Weber for helpful suggestions. Barry Houlihan at the James Hardiman Library at NUI Galway was most supportive. As ever, the support and patience of my wife Nicky and my daughter Julia have been invaluable.

Introduction

In December 2004 there was trouble in Birmingham. Some young men amongst a large crowd of Sikhs attacked a theatre while a play was in progress. They believed that what was on stage insulted their religion. Dominic Dromgoole, the director of the Oxford Stage Company at the time, was not outraged at this apparent assault upon artistic freedom, but excited:

> Here's an incident to shut the pundits up. Every tired old ageing punk who drones on at self-defeating length about the death of theatre – its marginalisation and irrelevance to the modern world – can put this in their pipe and smoke it.
> When was the last time we had riots and arrests at the unveiling of a spring schedule for a television channel? … Theatre … is live and chancy and hot. It creates rumblings … Theatre asks for this trouble. It has to.
>
> (Dromgoole 2004)

Dromgoole went on to list the honourable roll call of theatrical violence in the cause of liberty. It is a long history. He did not mention that theatrical rioting and disorder have not in fact always been deployed in a liberal cause, as the events in Birmingham demonstrate. But whatever the motivation, the history of theatre riots can tell us something interesting and important about the nature of the theatre.

Almost all of the violence and disorder described in this book can be described as political. That is to say, it was carried out by groups of people who were taking action to produce an impact upon the public realm. Perhaps the assembly of a large number of people together always tends to produce an atmosphere which heightens emotions; at any rate these violent deeds were not motivated by merely individual sentiment. In every case they were inspired or provoked by a play, or by an actor's performance, or by the works of a playwright writing for a live audience. What is it then, about the nature of theatre to make it so politically inflammatory? Riots have been provoked by cinema and by live music, but there does not seem to be quite the same history of public troublemaking as that provoked by the stage (which includes ballet and opera, though they are not dealt with in this book).

The playwright Edward Bond, whose own work has often depicted and examined the roots of violence, puts it this way:

> The stage does not go inside the mind as easily as novels and music can. But it can demonstrate social relationships between people more concretely than other arts. All theatre is political – [Noel] Coward's as well as [Bertolt] Brecht's – and theatre always emphasises the social in art. The audience judges in the same complex way that it judges in ordinary life. But it is given this advantage: it may look at things it would normally run from in fear, turn from in embarrassment, prevent in anger, or pass by because they are hidden, either purposely or innocently. So audiences respond with all the faculties of their consciences that determine their social and private lives.
>
> (Bond 1978: xii–xiii)

Bond's point is that the theatre is 'concrete', that it 'demonstrates social relationships' in a way which makes the audience judge 'in the same complex way that it judges in ordinary life'. This would explain how the emotions and attitudes audiences feel towards fictional representation can transfer to 'real' situations outside the theatre. It is also, as he points out, significant that these fictional representations can make us confront matters which are normally hidden, or which we would wish not to encounter. But this account omits a crucial quality which is unique to art forms which are performed live (including, of course, music, opera and dance) and which is shared with the events of off-stage life: evanescence.

As in 'real life' the moment of theatrical performance is unrepeatable (I use quotation marks here because what is happening on stage is also, of course, alive and unfolding in historical time; it is also 'real'). The text of a novel or the frame in a film remains a constant each time it is read or viewed. The delivery of a line in a play is never exactly the same from performance to performance, even if the same actor has delivered it a hundred times before. It is always unrepeatable. The presence of the audience makes the delivery of the line a live act of communication between humans in a way which is radically different from our experience of reading or of watching mediated action on a two-dimensional screen. And it is always *historical*: it is never in the realm of the imagination outside time, that golden realm where the English renaissance writer Sir Philip Sidney thought true art dwelt (Sidney 1966: 24). Sidney was not, it seems, an admirer of the theatre. Theatre shares its unrepeatable quality with history. It unfolds uniquely, moment by moment, and cannot be replayed.

The experience of watching live performance can thus have an intensity, a requirement for our attention which other less ephemeral art forms do not possess. Yet together with the intensity which it shares with live experience there is *also* the awareness that what we are watching is not 'real', but a fiction devised for our pleasure. No-one has ever really 'suspended their disbelief' in the theatre because we cannot un-know what we know about the theatrical experience: it is not in fact 'real'. As such we are also always aware of *process*, in a way which is not always the case in 'real life', as Bond observed. We are aware of the actors as actors, of the stage, and of whatever *mise en scène* there might be: costume, props, set, lighting. This awareness of process not only encompasses our recognition that we are watching an actor in role. It can provoke a more abstract awareness. Crucially, it also includes our grasp of the way in which theatre, with some notable exceptions, explores the how and the why of how things happen to humans in social relations with each other. Theatre almost always has an element of live social and political critique. The whole process of putting on a play is to say: look, things need not be as they are; and look, this is how things come to be as they are. The theatre of its nature shows us what is not, but also shows us what might be. These ideas are present in the earliest plays that we have. In Aristophanes' play *The Frogs* (405 BC), the ancient Athenians, in a desperate situation in their war with Sparta, need to bring back a great tragic dramatist from Hades because he will have the wisdom 'to save the city' (Aristophanes 1964: 208). The theatre is, of its very nature, part of the 'real' political realm, of which violence has always been a part.

The anthropologist Victor Turner has examined how any piece of live theatre originates in the social and political moment of its creation at a particular time and in a particular place; how it is created by and performed for particular people, and is always imbued with the social forces inherent in that moment. He has also described how it operates in turn upon that moment, influencing and developing current social and political forces:

> The stage drama, when it is meant to do more than entertain – though entertainment is always one of its vital aims – is a metacommentary, explicit or implicit, witting or unwitting of the major social dramas of its social context (wars, revolutions, scandals, institutional changes). Not only that, but its message and its rhetoric feed back into the *latent* processual structure of the social drama and partly accounts for its ready ritualization. Life now becomes a mirror held up to art, and the living now *perform* their lives, for the protagonists of a social [off-stage] drama, a 'drama of living', have been equipped by aesthetic [on-stage] drama with some of their most salient opinions, imageries, tropes and ideological perspectives … Human beings learn through experience, though all too often they repress painful experience, and perhaps the deepest experience is through drama; not through social drama, or stage drama (or its equivalent) alone but in the circulatory or oscillatory process of their mutual and incessant modification.
>
> (Turner 1985: 300–1)

The very structures of dramatic narrative itself – conflict leading to crisis, a series of 'redressive actions' to attempt to address that crisis, leading often to some reintegrating resolution (Schechner 1988: 187) – have become models for how we 'perform' our 'real' lives in an 'infinity loop-model' where the theatre informs our lives and is informed by it (Schechner 1988: 188–91). This feedback-loop between the on-stage and the off-stage world 'is not in an endless, cyclical, repetitive pattern; it is a spiralling one ... Individuals can make an enormous impact on the sensibility and understanding of members of society' (Turner 1985: 301). Plays can change the world, and move the spiral upwards in a socially progressive way (but also do the opposite).

If riot, war and revolution are part of what Turner calls 'social drama', it should be no surprise that violence will then also break out in and around what he calls 'aesthetic drama' as part of that feedback-loop. However, Turner's definition of drama makes no distinction between on-screen and live performance. We still need to account for the specific incendiary potential of live theatre.

It also needs to be stated that the intense and evanescent quality of theatre can convey a special, almost metaphysical status upon the stage in Western culture. This factor is of significance. In a celebrated and influential essay, the critic Walter Benjamin noted that works of art traditionally possessed an 'aura'. What has caused this aura to 'wither' in the modern world, he wrote, is the process of 'mechanical reproduction' (Benjamin 1999: 215). Benjamin is particularly thinking of film. It is clear that live stage performance, by its very nature, cannot be mechanically reproduced. It can of course be filmed, but at that point it becomes another art form altogether. Live stage performance preserves its aura. Benjamin goes on to propose that

> We know that the earliest art works originated in the service of a ritual – first magical, then of a religious kind. It is significant that the existence of the work of art with reference to its aura is never entirely separated from its religious function ... This ritualistic basis, however remote, is still recognizable as secularized ritual even in the most profane forms of beauty.
>
> (Benjamin 1999: 217)

The survival of its ritualistic origins is most evident in the nature of theatre. In his presentation of what he believed to be the different kinds of theatre, the director Peter Brook identified the 'Holy Theatre' as 'the stage as a place where the invisible can take a deep hold on our thoughts' (Brook 1972: 47). Brook believes that the theatre ought to be a place where we seek the ritual and ceremony which permit 'the outer forms' of what we value in society ('goodwill, sincerity, reverence, belief in culture') to 'take on real authority' (Brook 1972: 51). Whereas Edward Bond believes that the theatre should be a place where what the powerful wish to keep hidden is made visible, Peter Brook is talking about a hidden, deeper spiritual reality in our lives which the theatre brings to light.

Furthermore, anthropologists have found in the theatre an aura which is closely analogous to, if not an instance of, the sense of the sacred felt by those who attend religious ritual. Victor Turner also argued that theatre and religious ritual perform the same functions in society. Theatrical performances are liminal, that is 'they constitute a threshold between secular living and sacred living. They take place in separate spaces and at separate times and places otherwise reserved for work, food and sleep' (Abercrombie and Longhurst 1998: 46). As Turner puts it, the function of rituals such as theatre was to place members of a society 'in a limbo that was not any place they were in before and yet any place they would be in, then returned them, changed in some way, to mundane life' (Turner 1986: 25 cited in Abercrombie and Longhurst 1998: 46). Turner also considered that it was this transformational experience at the threshold between the secular and sacred space which gave communities an opportunity to re-examine their values and beliefs, to 'probe a community's weaknesses, call its leaders to account, desacralize its most cherished values and beliefs, portray its characteristic conflicts and suggest remedies for them' (Turner 1982: 11 cited in Abercrombie and Longhurst 1998: 47). What happens on stage doesn't stay on stage.

It is also necessary in ritual that there should be a distance between performance and audience, which in traditional Western theatre became the division between the stage and the auditorium. The stage has retained that residual sacred aura, but so, in a different degree, has the place in which the audience experience the performance. Much of the violence described in this book concerns a fight for control of these 'sacred' spaces, and also for the meanings of the ritual actions which take place there, even in spaces beyond the theatres where they are produced. The idea of the theatre as a sacred space in a secular society, a location with an aura which bestows upon its statements a peculiar, even oracular authority, has allowed the theatre to become a potentially inflammatory space against which the power of rational argument seems inadequate. In such conditions violence has become a response. It could be that it is this combination of the theatre's quasi-sacred political function in political culture with the aura that surrounds the performance space, its participants and symbols, which makes live performance so potentially incendiary. A similar 'aura' can surround certain sporting venues, which can also be the site of violence, of course. It is also significant that radical political theatre has often sought to stage theatre in the street, in the space of its opponents, disrupting the streets used for display by those in power by inserting onto those streets the privileged space for thought and critique that is the stage.

This might perhaps sound a very long way from what theatre actually is in early twenty-first century Britain. There has been, it seems, a long process whereby audiences have become more and more docile, perhaps connected with the increasing division of the audience environment from that of the stage. In the nineteenth century the rise of stage spectacle followed by the darkening of the auditorium encouraged audiences to observe, not to respond (Blackadder 2003: 10–11). Baz Kershaw has described this as 'a shift in most Western theatres from *patron*, to *client*, to *customer*' (Kershaw 2001: 135; his italics). Kershaw argues that audiences today have become the acquiescent customers of a brand (the play) whose only permitted response to the action is to applaud the actor-celebrities whose authority over them they validate by attending, and at the same time applauding themselves 'for money so brilliantly spent' (Kershaw 2001: 144). There is now enormous cultural pressure on all audience members to applaud the play, and more and more to offer a standing ovation. In these conditions 'the theatre has become increasingly irrelevant to communities and to politics' (Kershaw 2001: 136). Yet Kershaw believes that this is a historically contingent phenomenon, and he playfully sets out conditions in which the audience for traditional theatre might escape becoming no more than cheer-leaders for a slickly marketed product. It could be that in these conditions for the foreseeable future theatrical unrest will take place around the theatre, not in it, and not amongst the audience, as the case of *Behzti* shows (see Chapter 10). Even those who do not attend the theatre can be affected by its aura, its unique cultural and political status. As Kershaw admits, the British theatre retains its inflammatory capacity.

There are two kinds of theatrically inspired violence discussed in this book. In the first kind the rioting is directly related to the content of the plays themselves. Prime examples of the former are the reactionary protests in the Abbey Theatre in Dublin against the depiction of Irish womanhood in *The Playboy of the Western World* (1907) by J. M. Synge or by Sean O'Casey's depiction of Irish nationalism in *The Plough and the Stars* (1926). I write about those plays in Chapters 7 and 8. The aura which can arise in a live performance of a high-prestige play in circumstances of great political tension can also energise an audience to direct their violence against opponents outside the theatre, as can be seen in the case of the pro-fascist production of *Coriolanus* in Paris in 1933–4, as I describe in Chapter 9, or in the case of the 1795 London performance of Otway's *Venice Preserv'd* (Chapter 2). A violent aesthetic objection to the style and content of a play can also be an indication of hidden politically revolutionary forces at work in wider society, as in the case of Victor Hugo's *Hernani* in Paris in 1830 (Chapter 4). Alternatively, the congruence between the 'social drama' of the political moment and the 'aesthetic drama' of the performance can break down, and the play can fail to bring about the desired violence, as in the case of the 1601 production of Shakespeare's *Richard II* (Chapter 1). My first chapter establishes the incendiary power of theatre in the intentions of those who would seek to use it to provoke violence, but also shows how theatrical violence must spring from the right alignment of political and theatrical power, even if those two forces are always mutually engaged and inter-reacting in any performance.

There have been theoretical explanations offered for the kind of disturbance which greeted certain live performances such as the Abbey Theatre riots in 1907 and 1926 (see Chapters 7 and 8) and the 'Battle of *Hernani*' in Paris 1830 (see Chapter 4). In these cases, it has been argued, the violence arises from a discrepancy between the wider cultural expectations which an audience bring to the theatre and the actual experience of the play they see. In the first sustained attempt to apply critical theory of 'reception' to audience experience, Susan Bennett suggested in 1997 that 'the spectator comes to the theatre as a member of an already constituted interpretative community and also brings a horizon of expectations shaped by … pre-performance elements' (Bennett 1997: 139) such as their own personal cultural and political backgrounds and their own previous experience of theatrical events. Bennett calls this the 'outer frame' of the two intersecting matrices which constitute the audience's experience:

the outer frame contains all those cultural elements which create and inform a theatrical event. The inner frame contains the dramatic production within a particular playing space. The audience's role is carried out within these two frames, and, perhaps most importantly, at their points of intersection. It is the interactive relations between audience and stage, spectator and spectator which constitute production and reception, and which cause the inner and outer frames to converge for the creation of a particular experience.

(Bennett 1997: 139)

Neil Blackadder has suggested that Bennett's model can be adapted to explain what happens when an audience are 'scandalized': 'in the terms of this theory, when scandalized audience members protest against a performance, the interactive relations in which they participate do not bring about a convergence at all but instead a discrepancy, a non-intersection between two frames' (Blackadder 2003: xiv). Blackadder goes on to consider how according to the reception theorist Hans Robert Jauss a work of significance in literary history will establish its aesthetic value to the extent to which it distances itself from 'the horizon of expectations of its audience' and their 'familiarity of previous aesthetic experience'. In fact the smaller the distance is between the expectations of the audience about the nature of the work of art and the work of art itself 'the closer the work comes to the sphere of "culinary" or entertainment art' (Jauss cited in Blackadder 2003: xv). Jauss's idea that a work which defies its audience's expectations is some kind of advance in artistic terms seems to be based on the optimistic notion of a continuing development in an art form through history. The plays that provoke their audience to dissent are those which advance the art form. As I argue in Chapter 4, it is not entirely persuasive that the audience's reactions to *Hernani* can be explained by the fact that they were not ready for the next great step forwards in theatrical art. Yet the reception theory model has even been taken up by cognitive scientists in an attempt to explain *The Playboy of the Western World* riots (Chapter 7) in terms of 'cognitive dissonance' (Swettenham 2006).

But it is far from clear that reception or reader-response theory, which is derived from literary study, is well suited to comment usefully on the phenomenon of audience disturbances in the theatre. 'Reader-response theory' can be defined as the notion that

far from being pregiven, meaning is produced by readers working in conjunction with the structures of the text, and in accordance with reading strategies and interpretive conventions that bind readers together into interpretive communities and put them in possession of an internalized literary competence that allows them to respond appropriately to the texts they encounter.

(Macey 2000: 324)

It does not seem obvious that reception or reader-response theory is a particularly useful way of approaching the kind of powerful emotional reactions amongst audiences we are dealing with here. The 'text' of a theatre performance is not a series of marks on a page, nor is it a screen of two-dimensional images to be interpreted to produce an internal mental impression which may be the grounds for an emotional reaction. The experience of watching a play is a matter of responding to real bodies talking and emoting in the same real specific time and space as the audience, an experience which goes beyond the conventions we all acquire in order to interpret works of art. It is true that in the kind of plays discussed in this book we know what we are watching is a fiction. It is also true that in even the most naturalistic productions there are acting conventions operating which distinguish the on-stage actions and speeches from the same actions and speeches off-stage, not least in the fact that they are taking place on the special area that is the stage itself. But our response is not a matter of 'reading' signs to produce an internal impression of what is being depicted, our response is to the bodies and words of the actors as physically present, alive, in three dimensions contemporaneously and evanescently to our own lives. This is not the case with reading texts or watching screens.

The 'interpretive communities' in the theatre are also very different from readers. A specific audience does bring to the theatre expectations about plays and the art form in general, but as far as the specific meaning of a given play is concerned a crucial part of their response has not been built up communally over time and place through a long process, but is concentrated in one space; it is dynamic in its reaction; it is instantaneous rather than reflective and immediately influenced by the actions of others and therefore potentially much more flammable. This is not the case with readers of fiction. As Marvin Carlson points out, the reader can just put the book aside if displeased. Audiences also have the power (especially through laughter) to find a meaning or intention in a play which was never the purpose of the actor or director (Carlson 1989: 85–6). In such a case, crucially, audience response can then change the nature and quality of the performance itself, which never can happen with art forms presented on paper or screens (Freshwater 2009: 15). It's also important to point out that the genuine, sub-discursive erotic response to the bodies and words and performers which is so often present can be a factor in theatrical violence (see below, pp.40–1) and is also a factor which reader-response approaches do not take into account. Audiences do produce meaning, certainly, but when 'scandal' occurs it is not solely or even principally because of the clashing of conceptual interpretive frames in terms of reception theory.

Another idea about what might license violent audience reaction is based on the idea of the unspoken contract in liberal political theory applied to the relationship between performers and audience. Originating in the work of Elaine Scarry, in this case 'spectators and actors alike give up freedom of movement and speech – the former sitting quietly, the latter following the prescribed course of the play – to receive artistic, psychological, or material rewards' (Dallett 1996: 323). If the actors break their side of the contract by not providing the pleasurable benefits the audience expect, the spectators are absolved from their side of the bargain and no longer need to sit quietly. But there are two problems with this. Firstly, audiences are quite capable of noisily disrupting a performance in order to express their pleasure or agreement (as happened in the Irish popular theatre in Synge's time, see below, p.127), and even to hold the play up with continued applause which interrupts 'the prescribed course of the play' (Dallett 1996: 323). This was common in the eighteenth and early nineteenth century. But secondly – and this applies to all historical periods – an implicit contract is no contract at all. This is also a major objection to the liberal political notion of the 'social contract' as well. Neither literary theory nor liberal political philosophy can account for the wild power to inspire violence which theatre can possess.

But there are also disturbances created by people who have not even seen the play. A space whose status is not the site of normal experience is central to all but modern avant-garde theatre, and the battle has sometimes been about control of that space, not the interpretation of an unseen play. Those young Sikhs who attacked Birmingham Repertory Theatre in December 2004 because of the representation of rape and murder in a Sikh temple in Gurpreet Kaur Bhatti's *Behzti* felt that the play was challenging their own sense of a sacred place usurped by the stage. I discuss this incident in the book's final chapter.

Others have sought to invoke the theatre's quasi-religious power in support of their own political desires. The contest here is about ownership of the meaning of the central symbols of the ritual. An example of the second case would be the huge crowd of campaigning trade unionists celebrating Shakespeare's birthday on Primrose Hill in London in 1864, an assembly which drew repressive violence from the Metropolitan Police, as I explain in Chapter 6. The planting of an English oak on this spot in memory of Shakespeare had a force beyond the merely political for those marchers who wanted a fairer, more democratic Britain. Those who seek to enlist to their cause the power granted by the aura of theatrical art have often had to fight against those who wish to deny their reading of the theatrical experience, and wish to claim that authority for themselves. Moments in plays, whole plays, or even individual actors can come to represent a particular political position. Sometimes a violent contest arises over this issue. A dispute whether a British actor of known anti-American views had the right to play Shakespeare on the public stage in New York in 1849 was the cause of the bloody Astor Place riots. I describe these events in Chapter 5. For early modern audiences, the theatre was also a distinctive place: a location where the ghosts of history could walk the stage again with a political warning for the present. The Essex conspirators attempted to exploit this idea, as I explain in Chapter 1. In Western cultures, from the days of the Christian martyrs through the Reformation to the present day, religious conflict has often led to violence, and the contest over the sacred space can be seen as a continuation of such a conflict.

There is also, I believe, a historical narrative which can be discerned in what exactly is being fought over in the violence being described in this book, a narrative which suggests something interesting about the developing position of the theatre in Britain and Ireland (and perhaps also in the United States of America).

When, in 1601, the Essex rebels thought that they could use a production of *Richard II* to signal and inspire an uprising against Queen Elizabeth I, they seemed to think that the theatre was so central to the common, national political and cultural process that it could not fail but help their cause. Given the fiasco that ensued when the rebellion itself began and failed to draw any popular support, it appears they may have been mistaken. It seems, however, that in nineteenth- and twentieth-century France the Parisian theatre did possess this cultural and political centrality when one considers the role of the 1830 production of *Hernani* and the 1933–4 staging of *Coriolanus* at the Comédie-Française at a time of critical events of great national significance. French audiences were also ready to respond violently to provocative, avant-garde work which shocked conventional sensibilities such as Alfred Jarry's *Ubu Roi* in 1896 (Blackadder: 2003: 41–68; Fell 2010: 90–4).

In Britain the very position of the theatre always seems more conflicted and contested in national life. From the beginning there was hostility in England to the theatre as an ungodly institution, as a place where wickedness was acted out on stage and licentiousness encouraged in the audience. Again, the idea of the stage and the auditorium as physical locations to be fought over by those wishing to assert political power seems important here. Even before the closing of the theatres by Parliament during the Civil War and Commonwealth (1642–60) it was far from unknown for Protestant apprentices to attack the London playhouses. In March 1613 the new Phoenix Theatre in Drury Lane was attacked by a huge crowd of young men during a performance. The actors defended the building as best as they could; one apprentice was shot through the head and killed, and many others were badly hurt. Many of the players were also hurt, and the rioters succeeded in cutting up costumes, burning books and furniture and vandalising much of the playhouse. Some even got on the roof and started to rip the roof tiles off. They may have destroyed the theatre entirely had not the justices of the peace and the sheriff assembled a large enough force to drive the attackers away (Wickham *et al.* 2000: 628–9). The rioters' motives are not recorded, but anti-theatrical sentiments were encouraged by Puritan preachers who saw the theatre not only as a place where sinful behaviour was modelled for the audience but also where they themselves were satirised (and perhaps their identity socially constructed, even from their point of view) in a politically damaging way (Lake 2002: 582).

After the restoration of the monarchy in 1660 the King attempted to keep firm control over the theatre, only permitting companies under royal patronage to perform in London (see p.42). But royal power in Britain in the eighteenth century was nowhere near as absolute as it was in France, and opposition to the monarchy found its way into the playhouses. In the turbulent years which followed the French Revolution of 1789, the clash between two different London companies, one supporting the King's reactionary ministers, and the other opposing them, is the background for the rioting which followed the 1795 production of Otway's tragedy *Venice Preserv'd*.

Class conflict then made the theatre itself a battleground from this time onwards. As Britain industrialised, an affluent middle class came into being, and there also arose a working class which sought political rights and a share in the nation's wealth and culture. One response of the powerful was to seek to exclude as many upstarts as possible from an institution which remained, at least nominally, under royal and aristocratic control. The Old Price riots of 1809 (Chapter 3) can be seen as the beginning of the process: the end of theatre as a place of national conversation, and the beginning of a class-based division between 'high' and 'popular' culture. In the decades which followed changes to ticket prices and to the architecture of the theatre, combined with the effective ending of the restrictive royal monopoly over the theatre in 1845, ensured that working people became more marginal in 'respectable' London theatres, while at the same time new, popular theatrical forms such as melodrama and music hall developed the class divide in culture which persists to this day, so far as theatre and opera are concerned. The events at Astor Place in New York in 1849 cannot be separated from this narrative of the wealthy seeking to monopolise access to a theatre space of their own, although other political factors were clearly present as well.

Once the socially respectable had gained physical possession of the theatre buildings, however, a struggle continued, and continues over the right to interpret and possess key cultural symbols which are part of theatrical presentation. The conflicts over who owned Shakespeare – and whether he was a radical or revolutionary – during the 1864 Tercentenary celebration to mark his three-hundredth birthday were not about a particular play or production, but about what Shakespeare as a cultural icon signified in class-divided Victorian Britain. When W. B. Yeats and Lady Augusta Gregory declared they had founded Ireland's national theatre in Dublin they were also claiming that their vision of Irish nationalism and nationhood was the authentic one. The people who came to disturb the productions of both Synge's *The Playboy of the Western World* in 1907 and O'Casey's *The Plough and the Stars* in 1926 were not responding to the experience of seeing either play themselves, but protesting against what they had heard to be depictions of Irish rural life and Irish womanhood in one case, and those who had fought and died in the struggle for Irish independence in the other. It was a struggle over representation, over symbols. The Sikhs who attacked Birmingham Rep in 2004 were angry about the representation of the Sikh priesthood, but also in dispute about the use of a sacred text on stage which transformed that space into somewhere holy. To the liberal defenders of *Behzti*, the protestors were infringing a sacred space of their own, the stage, where freedom of expression had to be defended against all comers and all claimants.

In this way the history of theatre riots might then be seen to reflect wider cultural developments, where the virtual and representational have acquired more power than the physical in the way societies conduct themselves politically. Those who control the meanings of images and stories current in a society control that society. Theatre, by its very nature, is a difficult art form to control, but perhaps the most dynamic and potentially dangerous.

This book does not set out to be a comprehensive account of all major theatrical disturbances in Western Europe and the USA no matter what their causes. It seeks to focus on those riots where much was at stake politically or culturally, rather than when the violence was apparently more personal or a settling of private grudges. Such trouble was not uncommon in the eighteenth century. There was just such a brawl at the Lincoln's Inn Theatre in London in 1721 which required the intervention of soldiers. Violence and kidnappings took place in a Dublin theatre over several nights in 1740, when students from Trinity College defended the theatre from the friends of a Mr Kelly, who had had his nose broken by Thomas Sheridan when he climbed on stage and insulted an actress (Moody 1958: 14–16). Sometimes audiences have disrupted a play simply because they feel they have wasted their money on something inept and patronising. This seems to be the case with the trouble which marked the first night of Henry James's disastrous *Guy Domville* in 1895. It was also the case when a would-be radical group called Living Theatre performed *Paradise Now!* on the Berkeley campus of the University of California in February 1969. The directors explained that the audience for this play would 'suddenly discover that they are no longer the "privileged" class to whom the play is "presented" but are needed by the actors for the very accomplishment of the play' (cited in Dallett 1996: 329). The actors mingled with the audience in the theatre, and in the street outside, haranguing them with political slogans, carrying each other and leaping into each others' arms from a height, chanting revolutionary slogans, and eventually 'stripping partly or completely, forming a body-pile and caressing one another in the "Rite of Universal Intercourse"' (Dallett 1996: 329). Many of the audience of Berkeley students were veterans of the student protest movement and regarded the performers from Living Theatre as charlatans. To chants of 'Bullshit! Bullshit' they disrupted the performance, and demanded their money back from the box office.

There is perhaps a tendency amongst those who love the theatre to long for audiences who are not passive and who will engage actively, emotionally and even physically with the performers rather than sit mutely and only respond with conventional applause at the end. Theatre riots can seem then to be examples of theatre at its most powerful. As Helen Freshwater writes

> the enthusiasm for stories of riots and disturbances in the theatre can sometimes give the impression that audiences of old did little *but* riot. The attraction for theatre enthusiasts is obvious: theatre riots suggest a bygone age when theatre was a venue for public debate and dialogue where audiences could express themselves without social inhibition and effect social change. As a result theatre buffs tend to recall them with affection and some nostalgia.
> (Freshwater 2009: 25–6)

Freshwater points out that audiences can be powerfully affected by the theatre without showing it actively. But the picture of the uninhibitedly responsive, socially progressive theatre audiences of the past suggested here doesn't tally with the audiences of this book. Half of the disturbances described in what follows can be seen as resisting social change, not effecting it. It's the visceral, inflammatory power of the theatre, its aura of a kind of sacredness which theatrical violence springs from, not its innate capacity for social progressivism. This inflammatory power can be destructive, but ultimately I think the theatre retains the power 'to save the city'. That is why the theatre is worth fighting for. The theatrical riot, even if uncommon today compared to previous centuries, reveals something central about the nature of theatre itself.

References

Abercrombie, Nicholas and Brian Longhurst (1998), *Audiences: A Sociological Theory of Performance and Imagination* (London: Sage).

Aristophanes (1964), *'The Frogs' and Other Plays*, trans. David Barratt (Harmondsworth: Penguin Books).

Benjamin, Walter (1999), 'The Work of Art in the Age of Mechanical Reproduction', in *Illuminations*, trans. Harry Zorn (London: Pimlico), 211–44.

Bennett, Susan (1997), *Theatre Audiences: A Theory of Method and Analysis*, revised edition (London: Routledge).

Blackadder, Neil (2003), *Performing Opposition: Modern Theater and the Scandalised Audience* (Westport CT: Praeger).

Bond, Edward (1978), *A Note on Dramatic Method*, published with *The Bundle* (London: Methuen).

Brook, Peter (1972), *The Empty Space* (Harmondsworth: Pelican Books).

Carlson, Marvin (1989), 'Theatre Audiences and the Reading of Performance', in Thomas Postlewait and Bruce A. McConachie (eds) *Interpreting the Theatrical Past: Essays in the Historiography of Performance* (Iowa City IA: University of Iowa Press).

Dallett, Athenaide (1996), 'Protest in the Playhouse: Two Twentieth-Century Audience Riots', *New Theatre Quarterly*, 12, 323–32.

Dromgoole, Dominic (2004), 'Theatre's Role is to Challenge Religion' http://www.guard ian.co.uk/stage/2004/dec/20/theatre.religion (accessed 20/7/15).

Fell, Jill (2010), *Alfred Jarry* (London: Reaktion Books).

Freshwater, Helen (2009), *Theatre and Audience* (Basingstoke: Palgrave Macmillan).

Kershaw, Baz (2001), 'Oh for Unruly Audiences', *Modern Drama* 44 (2), 133–54.

Lake, Peter (2002), with Michael Questier, *The Antichrist's Lewd Hat: Protestants, Papists and Players in Post-Reformation England* (New Haven CT and London: Yale University Press).

Macey, David (2000), *The Penguin Dictionary of Critical Theory* (London: Penguin Books).

Moody, Richard (1958), *The Astor Place Riot* (Bloomington IN: The University of Indiana Press).

Schechner, Richard (1988), *Performance Theory*, revised edition (London: Routledge).

Sidney, Philip (1966), *A Defence of Poetry*, ed. J. A. Van Dorsten (Oxford: Oxford University Press).

Swettenham, Neal (2006), 'Categories and Catcalls: Cognitive Dissonance in *The Playboy of the Western World*', in Bruce McConachie and F. Elizabeth Hart (eds) *Performance and Cognition: Theatre Studies and the Cognitive Turn* (London: Routledge), 206–22.

Turner, Victor (1982), *From Ritual to Theatre* (New York: PAJ Publications).

—— (1985), *On the Edge of the Bush: Anthropology as Experience*, ed. Edith Turner (Tucson AZ: University of Arizona Press).

—— (1986), *The Anthropology of Performance* (New York: PAJ Publications).

Wickham, Glynne, Herbert Barry and William Ingram (eds) (2000), *English Professional Theatre, 1530–1660* (Cambridge: Cambridge University Press).

Chapter 1

Raising the dead

The Essex Rebellion of 1601
and Shakespeare's *King Richard II*

One afternoon in the summer of 1601 the greatest actor in England stood at the front of the stage at the Globe Playhouse and looked his whole audience squarely in the eye.

Richard Burbage played all the lead roles in Shakespeare's company and was at ease and at home. From his central position, if he gazed over his right shoulder and scanned leftwards, looking up and down, he could meet the gaze of three thousand spectators crammed into the amphitheatre. They surrounded him in an arc of some 270 degrees and were ranked in three levels, from the pit to the upper gallery nine metres above him (Gurr 1992: 128). Burbage, in the role of Prince Hamlet, addressed his audience.

'I have heard', he began, perhaps with a faint chuckle, 'that guilty creatures sitting at a play...' (perhaps he paused again here, and the caught the eye of an individual in the pit or in the middle gallery, to the amusement of those around the unfortunate spectator) '...Have by the very cunning of the scene/ Been struck so to the soul that presently/ They have proclaimed their malefactions' (2.2.520–4).[1] There may have been laughter. There may have been some teasing between friends amongst the audience. But some playgoers may have recalled some recent events, of deadly seriousness, when the theatre's supposed power to inspire its audience to reflection and then action had been an important element of an attempted *coup d'état* aimed at Queen Elizabeth herself, led by Robert Devereux, Earl of Essex. They would have recalled a notorious performance earlier that year of Shakespeare's *Richard II* commissioned by the insurgents as a provocative signal for their rebellion.

Queen Elizabeth I never married. In the final years of her reign there was considerable disquiet over who would be her heir. Elizabeth was the last of the Tudors, and many feared that without a clear successor to the throne England might be plunged back into the civil wars which marked the decades before her grandfather, Henry VII, seized the throne in 1485. Now any conflict might quickly become a savage religious war. On the mainland of Europe the struggles between Catholics and Protestants had been, and would continue to be, bloody and protracted. Essex had been the Queen's favourite but when he fell from power he also became a standard-bearer for some who were disaffected with the declining Queen and felt that a strong warrior-leader might be the answer to England's problems. Essex's second-in-command was Henry Wriothesley, Earl of Southampton, and former patron to William Shakespeare. In *Hamlet* – written at about the time when Essex's rebellion occurred – Shakespeare would explore both rebellion against a monarch and the power of theatre to inspire political action. The rebels themselves had sought to employ an earlier play of his, *Richard II*, to their particular ends.

In *Hamlet*, the later scene where a company of actors, the 'Tragedians of the City', perform *The Murder of Gonzago* at the court of King Claudius of Denmark, is where Shakespeare examines the power of the stage to provoke political violence: the very issue at the heart of the story of *Richard II* and the Essex Rebellion.

In the first Act of *Hamlet* the Prince is visited by the ghost of his recently dead father, who claims that he was murdered by his brother Claudius, who is now king. At the end of the second Act, which is when Hamlet talks to the audience about the reactions of the guilty spectator, Hamlet is still afraid that the ghost may be a demon sent to trap him. He therefore asks the actors who have recently arrived at the court to re-enact on stage the murder of his father precisely as described by the ghost. Hamlet makes his intentions for Claudius clear to the audience: 'I'll observe his looks/ … if he but blench,/ I know my course' (2.2.528–30). He also shares his plan with his friend Horatio.

Thus when *The Murder of Gonzago* (or 'the *Mousetrap*', as Hamlet calls it, 3.3.205) is performed on stage, the audience in the theatre auditorium are not only watching the on-stage play, but are also watching (along with Hamlet and Horatio) King Claudius for *his* reaction to the events of the play. But the off-stage audience are also paying close attention to Hamlet's reactions to Claudius's reactions. 'The very cunning' of this scene in *Hamlet* is designed to make the audience ask themselves about the effect that watching *Hamlet* is having upon them. Having been induced into these reflections, the 1601 audience may well have been especially self-aware when two later scenes plausibly re-enacted certain recent events in the life of the recently executed Earl of Essex. The Globe audience would also recall how the very company they were watching, the Lord Chamberlain's Men, had been implicated, through that performance of *Richard II*, in the failed rebellion that ended in Essex's execution. They would note that the 'Tragedians of the City' in *Hamlet* are on a provincial tour because of a ban on plays brought about by 'the late innovation' – a provocative line which is often taken to refer to Essex's rebellion itself: 'innovation' in 1601 could have the sense of 'revolution' (2.2.302; Shakespeare 2006: 259).

Teasingly, *Hamlet* offers no clear endorsement of the theatre's capacity for genuine moral and political impact. Even if modern directors have often made the King's guilty reaction to the on-stage murder obvious, Claudius offers not a word in response to *The Murder of Gonzago*. As the play progresses, Hamlet feels the need to spell out the key events to the king ('he poisons him i' th' garden for his estate … You shall see anon how the murderer gets the love of Gonzago's wife'; 3.2.226–7). But, plausibly embarrassed by the Prince's constant disruptions, the

King merely calls for lights and leaves the stage, never to mention the play again, not even when he admits to the audience in soliloquy soon afterwards that he did indeed kill his brother Old Hamlet (3.3.39–41). Shakespeare's script allows Horatio no corroboration of Hamlet's belief that the King's reaction to the play has convicted Claudius beyond doubt (3.2.250–2).

In refusing to confirm that Claudius's secret guilt is flushed out by watching his crime re-enacted on stage Shakespeare is subtly undermining 'a common-place of the age' (Shakespeare 1936: 189). Modern editors of the play cite the case, amongst others, of a woman in King's Lynn in Norfolk, who had confessed to the murder of her husband after attending a tragedy, *Friar Francis*, in which a wife committed a similar crime. The incident is mentioned in a play which Shakespeare's own company had performed as recently as 1599, *A Warning for Fair Women* (Shakespeare 1982: 482; 2006: 60, 278).

In *Hamlet* it is not initially a play, but a ghost, risen from the dead, who reveals the murder to the Prince and provokes violent action. But the theatre itself was a place where the dead could walk again in order to provide guidance, admonition and provocation to the living. These were arguments used by contemporary writers who sought to defend the theatre against its Puritan opponents. Not only did the Puritans believe (correctly) that the theatre was a place where drunkenness and prostitution flourished, but they also condemned playhouses for providing spectacles of sin and immorality which would encourage spectators to emulate what they saw. One defender of the theatre, Thomas Nashe, claimed the opposite: that one of the virtues of the playhouse was its capacity to bring great men out of the grave in order to provide an inspiration to martial deeds for audiences in 'these degenerate, effeminate days of ours'. In his *Pierce Penniless his Supplication to the Devil* (1592) Nashe writes of the history plays then fashionable. These dramas displayed the English heroes of the Hundred Years' War against France alive on stage once more. In particular, Nashe considers the representation of Sir John Talbot, Earl of Shrewsbury, the distinguished warrior who appears in Shakespeare's *King Henry VI Part One*:

> How would it have joyed brave Talbot, the terror of the French, to think that after he had lain two hundred years in his tomb, he should triumph again on the stage and have his bones new embalmed with the tears of ten thousand spectators at least (at several times), who in the tragedian [actor] that represents his person, imagine they behold him fresh bleeding!
>
> (Nashe 1972: 113)

Talbot is only an 'imagine[d]' presence on the stage, but he is sufficiently present to enjoy his triumph and to have his wounds soothed ('embalmed') by the tears of the audience. The actor here becomes a kind of living ghost come back from the dead.

In considering the idea that the early modern theatre could have a direct influence on the actions, violent or otherwise, of those watching, it is worth pausing to look at how they saw the relationship between what happened on stage and what happened in the auditorium and beyond. In the early modern theatre the audience did not think of the on-stage world as a separate universe regarded at a distance by detached observers. Neither did the actors pretend that the audience were not present, as if their world ended at the front of the stage. When the Globe audience listened to Richard Burbage playing Hamlet that afternoon in 1601 they did not 'suspend their disbelief' and somehow believe that they were watching a real prince in distant Denmark. The evidence we have suggests that the audience were constantly aware that they were watching Richard Burbage performing Hamlet, but at the same time felt that the figure of Prince Hamlet was in some sense really present amongst them, and talking *to* them (Kiernan 1996; Weimann 2000; Hawkes 2002). Not only when characters spoke in soliloquy on the early modern stage were they directly addressing the audience. Recent scholarship has persuasively argued that all performers on the early modern stage regarded the audience as people whose approval their character required – both as actors, and as characters in the play. As Bridget Escolme puts it, 'Shakespeare's stage figures have another set of desires and interests, inseparable from those of the actor. They want the audience to listen to them, notice them, approve their performance, ignore others on stage for their sake' (Escolme 2005: 16). Actors on stage are liminal figures like ghosts, half-in and half-out of the audience's reality.

If this sounds a little paradoxical and mystical to the modern ear – that there is no real divide between the on-stage and off-stage world, and that the actor is both fully themselves and fully in role at the same time – we should not forget that for many in England, very possibly including Shakespeare, the world-view of Catholic humanist thinking was still very influential. In this way of understanding reality rationalism fought with a more ancient way of thinking which saw nothing to be simply itself. One thing could exist in the material substance of another in the guise of something else, or even be a sign of something else altogether at the same time. After all, the many Catholics in England believed (and still believe) that the communion bread and wine were both food and drink *and* the body and blood of Christ *and* a sign of the divine sacrifice that brought salvation.

The power of theatrical ritual to 'deny rigid boundaries', including the divide between the visible and the mystical (or merely represented) worlds, can be seen in the well-known anecdote about Christopher Marlowe's play *Dr Faustus* (1592). Faustus has learned how to summon devils in order to barter away his soul. During one performance, according to William Prynne, 'in Queen Elizabeth's days (to the great amazement both of the actors and spectators)' the show was interrupted by 'the visible appearance of the Devil on the stage' (Hopkins 2008: 51). From that time onwards Edward Alleyn, when he played the role, always wore a cross on stage in case he were successful in conjuring a real devil who would come to claim his soul.

More scientific and rationalist ways of seeing the world were certainly present and would eventually triumph, yet the old ways of thinking were still clearly extant. The theatre was a place where the old needs were met, where the devil and the departed could really be present in some sense. Stephen Greenblatt has argued that since the suppression of Catholic ritual by the Protestant state in the 1530s the theatre itself became a place where popular longings and needs to connect with the dead, for whatever reason, found some emotional fulfilment.

For the state church now denied that the living were able to aid the dead by their prayers, and claimed that ghosts out of purgatory were no more than a papist superstition. The presence of the ghost in *Hamlet*, Greenblatt writes, 'immeasurably intensifies a sense of the weirdness of the theatre, its proximity to certain experiences that had been organized and exploited by religious institutions and rituals' (Greenblatt 2001: 253). The theatre summons up the dead. But why would a ghost wish to return?

In the first scene of that tragedy Horatio addresses the ghost of Hamlet's father, and offers a reason why it was believed a ghost might come back to this world:

> If thou art privy to thy country's fate –
> Which, happily, foreknowing may avoid – O, speak!
> (1.1.124–5)

The dead have a special knowledge which, if it can be accessed, can save the nation from political disaster. Their appearance in the world of the living can also be ominous, marking the imminence of a crisis. In the 1604 Second Quarto version of the play, this is the interpretation which Horatio himself puts on the ghost's appearance, recalling how just before Julius Caesar's assassination 'the squeaking dead did gibber in the Roman streets' (Shakespeare 2007: 2000).

So when, on the afternoon of Friday 6 February 1601, certain lords who were known to be close associates of the Earl of Essex went to Shakespeare's Company, the Lord Chamberlain's Men, at the Globe Playhouse and asked for a special performance of the play 'of King Harry the IV, and the killing of King Richard the Second', they were deliberately summoning certain ghosts from two hundred years previously, who might be seen as 'privy to' their 'country's fate', so that England, 'happily, foreknowing may avoid' it. Essex's political opponent, the royal minister Francis Bacon, later declared that the instigator had been Essex's henchman Sir Gelly Meyrick, who hoped 'to satisfy his eyes with the sight of that tragedy which he thought soon after his lord should bring from the stage to the state, but that God turned it upon their own heads'. Under interrogation Meyrick said it was another of the Essex faction, Sir Charles Percy, who had arranged the performance (Bate 2009: 258). The play was staged the following afternoon, Saturday 7 February. On the Sunday morning Essex led his followers into the streets of London in a botched attempt to take control of the Court through force, to place himself in a paramount position of influence and to take vengeance on his enemies. At his subsequent trial for High Treason the indictment read that Essex had been 'so often present' at the playing of this tragedy in the past, 'with great applause and giving countenance and liking to the same' (Chambers and Williams 1933: 174–6). Almost all scholars believe that play to have been Shakespeare's

Richard II.[2] It is even possible that Essex's prosecutor and personal enemy, Sir Robert Cecil, had seen the Earl applauding the play in a performance arranged by Meyrick in 1598 at the Earl's home at Essex House on the Strand, a location in London but outside the walls of the city (the location of his house is still remembered in the London street name, Essex Street) (Bate 2009: 265).

Shakespeare's play tells the story of a vain and vacillating heirless monarch who had been on the throne a long time. Richard insults the honour and seizes the patrimony of a politically astute and noble warrior, Henry Bullingbrook, the son of the King's uncle, the Duke of Lancaster. When Bullingbrook returns from exile the nobles and commons abandon their allegiance to the king and flock to him. Despite the fact that Bullingbrook never explicitly confesses an ambition to take the throne, King Richard's forces melt away and the King is thrust aside. Bullingbrook becomes King Henry IV and resolves to go on crusade to unite his people.

At least, that seems to be the way in which Essex must have seen the play. Shakespeare's portrayal of the two antagonists is much more even-handed than the above account would suggest. Richard is conveniently murdered by someone seeking to ingratiate himself with the new regime, but dies heroically. As Henry ascends the throne the Bishop of Carlisle makes a terrifying and, as the audience would know, accurate prophecy of the civil wars which will rack England as a consequence of Bullingbrook's usurpation:

> And if you crown him, let me prophesy
> The blood of English shall manure the ground,
> And future ages groan for this foul act.
> Peace shall go sleep with Turks and infidels,
> And in this seat of peace tumultuous wars
> Shall in with kin and kind with kind confound.
>   (*Richard II*, 4.1.130–5)

To many contemporaries Essex was seen as a latter-day Bullingbrook and Queen Elizabeth was Richard's counterpart. In February 1601 the 67-year-old Elizabeth had been on the throne for forty-three years. The exchequer was practically bankrupt after a long and inconclusive war with Spain. Ireland was in open rebellion. There had been a series of disastrous harvests in the summers of 1594–7. King James VI of Scotland looked to be the most likely successor to the unmarried and childless Queen, but the possibility of a return to the civil wars for the succession which had caused so much devastation in the fifteenth century remained a serious threat. Elizabeth herself was indecisive in the face of a series of crises.

As for the Earl of Essex, he saw himself as a young and vigorous man of action. He had at one time, in the late 1580s, been an intimate of the Queen, enjoying her favours both politically and personally (although there is no conclusive evidence that they were ever lovers; despite contemporary gossip) (Harrison 1937: 23ff.; Lacey 1971: 43ff.; Duncan-Jones 2009: 120–1). He had become one of the

Figure 1.1 Robert Devereux, Second Earl of Essex. An engraving made in 1601, the year of his fall, proclaiming the Earl to be 'her Majesty's Lieutenant and Governor General of the Kingdom of Ireland'. A serenely confident Essex turns a commanding eye on the viewer, easily controlling his rearing horse while holding out for our view the baton which proclaims him 'Earl Marshall of England'. Listed first amongst his titles is 'Viscount Hereford', also a title held by Bolingbroke in Shakespeare's *Richard II*. His special status as Knight of the Garter is proclaimed in his arms (with coronet) at the top right of the picture. War being waged on both land and sea form the background to the martial hero's depiction. The three feathers on the horse's headgear might provocatively seem to echo the badge of the Prince of Wales, the title of the heir to the Kingdom. At any rate the caption, in two lines of Latin hexameter poetry, is most enthusiastic: 'Here is your noble Earl of Essex. How we rejoice that he is here as leader in our affairs'.

principal English generals in various expeditions in the war against the Spanish. On campaign Essex had been a showman, equipping his personal troops in a distinctive tangerine and white uniform, and even challenging the governor of Rouen in 1592 to meet him in single combat to determine whose cause in the war was 'more just' and to prove that Essex's 'mistress', the Queen, was 'more beautiful than yours' (Lacey 1971: 49, 90). But Essex's aristocratic *virtù*, his playing the role of the noble knight-at-arms, was not an asset in early modern warfare. It was a rashness that shaded into outright military incompetence. This was especially evident in the naval expedition to the Azores islands of 1597. Thanks to Essex's squabbles with the principal general, Sir Walter Raleigh, the campaign failed in its prime objective of seizing the Spanish treasure fleet on its way home from the Americas. After this failure the Earl continued to suffer from violent swings of mood and emotion, perhaps the result of syphilis, which made him an even less attractive political figure to the Court (Lacey 1971: 201–2).

Yet Essex, like Bullingbrook in *Richard II*, remained popular with the people. His increasing awareness of royal displeasure, combined with a certain glamour, made him a magnet for all those who saw themselves as enemies of the late Elizabethan regime, as well as for adventurers who saw in him a chance to mend their desperate fortunes by attaching themselves to his ambition. Essex's own Puritan beliefs made him a figurehead for certain preachers who saw him as a champion for religious views which had been excluded from the Elizabethan mainstream. His apparent belief in religious toleration, on the other hand, made him attractive to those Catholic gentry who sought to improve the position of the old religion in England: nine of the gunpowder plotters of November 1605 who sought to blow up the King and Parliament together were involved in Essex's rising in February 1601 (Guy Fawkes himself was not present) (Lacey 1971: 273). Essex has also been associated with radical opponents of absolute rule in England, as a precursor of the parliamentarians who would challenge Elizabeth's Stuart successors, James I and his son Charles I, who believed that their right to rule was absolute because God-given. In 1598 he challenged royal absolutism in a letter to Lord Egerton, Keeper of the Great Seal: 'What, cannot princes err? Cannot subjects receive wrong? Is an earthly power or authority infinite? Pardon me, pardon me, my good lord, I can never subscribe to these principles' (Lacey 1971: 213, full text of letter in Harrison 1937: 199–201). Essex was all things to all malcontents.

Elizabeth and her ministers had no doubt about the danger of the popular association of the Queen with Richard II and of Essex with Bullingbrook. When the historian Sir John Hayward published his *First Part of the Life and Reign of King Henry IV* in February 1599 he dedicated his book to the Earl of Essex. The clumsy Latin dedication contained the words *magnus siquidem es, et presenti iudicio, et futuri temporis expectatione* ('Since indeed you are great both in present opinion, and in the expectation of future time') (Harrison 1937 214–15, 267; Palmer and Palmer 2000: 112). Was Essex aiming at the crown itself? Three weeks later the Archbishop of Canterbury ordered the dedication to be removed from all copies. The scandalous history now became much in demand, and a second edition of 1,500 copies was printed at Easter with an 'epistle apologetical' in which Hayward sought to explain himself. But it did little good; at Whitsun all copies of the book were called in and burned. In July Hayward was arrested and put in the Tower where he remained until Elizabeth's death in 1603. In the August after Essex's rebellion the antiquary and Tower of London archivist William Lambarde was presenting to the Queen a catalogue of his records at Greenwich Palace, including some from the reign of Richard II. Elizabeth is reported to have remarked to him, 'I am Richard II, know ye not that?' (Chambers and Williams 1933: 176).[3]

As for the political intentions of Shakespeare's *Richard II*, which was probably first performed in late 1595, there is no evidence to suggest that Shakespeare designed the play to pass any comment on Essex directly (Shakespeare 2002a: 15–16). All that it had in common with Hayward's book seems to be that both used the same sources. Alternatively it is also very plausible that Hayward used Shakespeare's play as one of *his* sources (Bate 2009: 276–9). That did not stop the play being adopted by Essex and his followers, and others, to their own particular ends. The three 'Quarto' (inexpensive, unbound) editions of *Richard II* printed between 1597 and 1598 sold very well (Harrison 1937: 215). It has been claimed that one scene in the play was far too politically explosive to be published when the text came to the printers in 1597 (Paterson 1989: 78; Shakespeare 2002a: 10): the scene in which Richard is deposed by Bullingbrook (*Richard II* 4.1.148–315). This scene does not in fact appear in printed versions of the play until the fourth edition of the individual text of the play, which was published in 1608. It is in truth unclear whether this scene was suppressed in the 1597 and 1598 Quartos, or was added rapidly for this 1601 performance, or was added much later before being printed in the 1608 Quarto. On the one hand Richard's embarrassingly self-obsessed behaviour in this abdication scene might be taken to make the taciturn and calm Bullingbrook seem more monarchical, but it has also been claimed that the abdication made the play 'less subversive, turning a desposition into an abdication' (Bate 2009: 257). Nevertheless, the sight of a weak, effeminate monarch being replaced by a noble military strongman cannot but have a powerful political resonance in the political situation of February 1601.

The events which led to Essex staking all on a desperate attempt to seize control of the government as a latter-day Bullingbrook began with his failure to put down the rebellion in Ireland of Hugh O'Neill, Earl of Tyrone, in 1599. For three hundred years English kings had sought to extend their rule over Ireland, with varying but limited success. Ireland remained almost entirely Catholic when England became a Protestant country in the 1530s, and thus the cause of a new anxiety for the English government. In the late 1590s Irish resistance to English rule grew in strength both militarily and politically. Essex obtained the Queen's commission to lead an army against the dangerous O'Neill. It is possible that Elizabeth was deliberately setting up her waning favourite to fail against an able and well-armed opponent. In any case, having ignored most of the Queen's orders and concluded a truce with the Irish forces, Essex was still politically astute enough to realise that he had to make sure that his version of events was the one that the Queen heard first. Once news of events reached England Essex knew that his enemies at court would not be slow to present an account of his ineptitude in his absence. With a small group of attendants he left Dublin on the evening of 24 September 1599 and raced towards the Queen. Early on the morning of September 28 he arrived unannounced and strode into the Queen's private bedroom at Nonsuch Palace in Merton, just south of London (Lacey 1971: 238–41).

The Queen was alone, not yet dressed and without the wig and elaborate make-up which transformed her into her iconic public self. A contemporary account by Rowland Whyte talks of the Queen 'being newly up, her hair about her face'. Essex strode 'boldly to her Majesty's presence, she not being ready, and he so full of dirt and mire that his very face was full of it' (cited in Shapiro 2005: 300). She had thought that Essex was still in Ireland. She had no idea whether this muddied, booted and armed nobleman was in fact at the head of force which had overpowered her guards, seized the palace and arrested her advisers.

It is not clear whether *Hamlet* was completed either before or after September 1599, but most scholars attribute the latter date (Shapiro 2005: 307 argues for 1599; for a later dating see Shakespeare 2006: 59; 1982: 13). Whatever the truth, the ghostly shadow of this critical moment and its symbolic revolutionary potential appear in this play ('it's next to impossible to grasp today how great a taboo Essex had violated', writes James Shapiro, 2005: 300). Hamlet's impassioned interview with his mother in her private apartment (her 'closet'; 3.4.) must have recalled this moment to the audience. In this scene Hamlet stabs the King's chief minister Polonius as he hides, overhearing, behind a wall hanging. In a strange echo of this moment at Essex's trial, Elizabeth's Secretary of State Robert Cecil stood unseen behind a curtain in Westminster Hall, only to emerge at a crucial point in the proceedings (Harrison 1937: 307; Lacey 1971: 306).

The nightmare of the armed coup launched into the heart of the palace by a young nobleman occurs twice in the play. First of all Polonius's son Laertes leads a crowd of Danes crying 'Choose we! Laertes shall be king' (4.4.103) into the royal apartments, only for Laertes, once alone, to be won over by the super-calm response of Claudius, full of royal authority even with a sword at his throat. Then in *Hamlet*'s final scene Prince Fortinbras of Norway arrives '*with Drum, Colours and Attendants*' (s.d. 5.2.311) as Claudius, Gertrude, Laertes and Hamlet all lie dead or dying, just in time to seize power for himself. If *Hamlet* was indeed completed or amended after Essex's irruption into Elizabeth's private chamber, then the anxious ghost of this moment rises again, either as a warning, or to be exorcised.

The Queen behaved with as much self-possession in the face of Essex that morning as Claudius does when confronted by Laertes (Harrison 1937: 249–51; Lacey 1971: 242–6). When it became clear that Essex had come to ask her to listen to his excuses for his failure to achieve victory in Ireland, and that he was making no demands upon her, armed or otherwise, she played for time and suggested that they should talk again later in more suitable circumstances. An hour later, at eleven, they spoke again in private. Once she was in possession of all that she felt she needed to know about the situation, she was ready to act. At a third meeting that day Elizabeth made her accusations of his incompetence and his dereliction of duty, and dismissed him scornfully, never to see him again. After an appearance before the Queen's Council on September 29, Essex was a few days later put under arrest and taken to York House, what was once Cardinal Wolsey's old palace in Westminster, now the residence of one of Essex's friends, the same Thomas Egerton, Lord Keeper of the Great Seal.

Essex remained in custody until August 1600. In October came the disastrous news that Essex's principal and essential source of income, a monopoly of the tax paid on the importation of all sweet wines into the country, was not being renewed by the Queen. The Earl, just like many of his followers, was massively in debt and he was now facing ruin. This seems to have been the moment when violent action became a viable, perhaps the only way, of restoring Essex's fortunes. Detailed preparations for a *coup d'état* began to be made.

Plans were laid, but were not completely in place, when the crisis came in February 1601. The performance of *Richard II* was perhaps a signal for the uprising to begin, or perhaps the revival of this old play was intended as a public statement to the people of London that the Essex faction felt now was the time for action against what was seen, in a familiar trope of the time, as the regime of the modern Richard II. But perhaps the play's unexpected revival was also seen by the authorities as a sign that danger was imminent. At any rate, a few hours after the play ended the Queen's Privy Council took the action that was to precipitate violent conflict in the streets of London the following morning. For a moment at least, Elizabeth's regime would be in serious danger, once the ghosts of Richard and Bullingbrook had spoken their message to their London audience.

On the evening of Friday 6 February a party of Essex's lieutenants met Augustine Phillips of the Lord Chamberlain's Men, the company of actors that ran the Globe Playhouse. According to Phillips's later testimony the group consisted of Sir Charles Percy, Sir Jocelyn Percy and Lord Monteagle. Sir Charles was the brother of the scientist Earl of Northumberland (Chambers and Williams 1933: 175–6). He had been knighted not by the Queen but by Essex himself as Elizabeth's deputy in the field in France in 1591 (Lacey 1971: 60). He was a known devotee of the theatre who would no doubt take delight in the appearance on stage of the character of his ancestor Harry Percy ('Hotspur') in *Richard II* (Bate 2009: 259). Lord Monteagle was a Catholic who had also been knighted by Essex, in 1599 in Ireland. He would survive the rebellion and live to betray the gunpowder conspirators four years later. His reward then would be a rich pension from the state (Palmer and Palmer 2000: 167). The actor whom the noblemen met was famous as a singer and dancer, but also one of the seven shareholders in the Globe Playhouse, which had only opened in Southwark in 1599 (Gurr 1992: 44). Phillips was a successful businessman who had bought an estate at Mortlake

(Palmer and Palmer 2000: 192). Other members of the Lord Chamberlain's men were present too, but we do not know their names.

Shakespeare was another shareholder in the company and had dedicated his narrative poems *Venus and Adonis* (1593) and *Lucrece* (1594) to the Earl of Southampton, the man who was now Essex's second-in-command. There has been speculation that Southampton was Shakespeare's close friend (or even ex-lover) and that their relationship smoothed the way for this special performance. But such a hypothesis remains guesswork. Those who have sought an imaginative reconstruction of Shakespeare's life from limited evidence have speculated about his role in these events with unfounded confidence (Quennell 1969: 166–7; Levi 1988: 100, 120: Duncan-Jones 2001: 79–81). The twentieth-century scholar John Dover Wilson, for example, wrote that 'it is at once difficult to see how Shakespeare escaped being mixed up in all this, and impossible to believe that he approved of it' (Wilson 1932: 102). But it is most likely that any association Shakespeare might have had with Essex's closest colleague had ended in 1594 (Shakespeare 2002b: 15). There is no evidence that Shakespeare was at the meeting with Essex's men that Friday evening.

Essex's lieutenants had a special request: that the Lord Chamberlain's men would put on the play 'of the deposing and killing of King Richard the Second' the following afternoon. In his testimony to the examining judge on 18 February Phillips mentioned neither the fact that they would have had to change their planned performance nor the political significance of their request. If he was to escape implication in the plot, pleading ignorance of that significance was no doubt a wise move. The reason he gave, initially, for turning down their request was that they would lose money. Phillips told Monteagle and the Percies that the play was 'so old and so long out of use that they should have small or no company at it'. *Richard II* had presumably been out of the repertory since 1596. But the noblemen offered Phillips and his company 'forty shillings more than their ordinary to play it'. It is not quite clear what 'their ordinary' means, but forty shillings – £2 – was an attractive inducement on top of their takings for the show. The Lord Chamberlain's main rivals, the Lord Admiral's Men, were averaging gallery takings of £20 a week in 1597: about £3 a performance (Gurr 1992: 71). They 'played it accordingly' (Chambers and Williams 1933: 175–6).

Whether there was much of an audience the following afternoon we do not know. There would have been little or no rehearsal time for a play 'so long out of use'. It is perhaps testimony to the remarkable memories possessed by actors on the early modern stage that they were able to recall and perform a five-year-old play, or at least relearn it in time. The company would not have had the same actors as in 1596 in any case: beyond the major roles men and boys were hired to perform on a casual basis. But Richard Burbage, probably in the role of the King, must have remembered these lines to summon up the ghost of Henry Bullingbrook, describing how Richard's nemesis had gone into exile as the darling of the London crowd:

Ourself and Bushy, Bagot here and Green
Observed his courtship to the common people.
How he did seem to dive into their hearts
With humble and familiar courtesy,
What reverence he did throw away on slaves,
Wooing poor craftsmen with the craft of smiles
And patient underbearing of his fortune,
As 'twere to banish their affects with him.
Off goes his bonnet to an oyster-wench.
A brace of draymen bid God speed him well
And had the tribute of his supple knee,
With 'Thanks, my countrymen, my loving friends',
As were our England in reversion his,
And he our subjects' next degree in hope.
                              (*Richard II*, 1.4.22–35)

These lines, spoken by the King, are not devoid of the suggestion that Bullingbrook's popular touch was a politic affectation. But to the conspirators they must have represented the way they believed that Essex would be greeted as he rode through the streets on his way to Whitehall Palace to oust those advisers such as Robert Cecil who had corrupted the Queen's mind and made the Earl lose her favour.

King Richard's speech does seem to describe how Essex had left London on his way to Ireland on 27 March 1599, when crowds followed and cheered the Earl for over six kilometres crying 'God save your lordship' and 'God preserve your honour' (Lacey 1971: 218). During the summer of that year Shakespeare had imagined the Earl's triumphant return in somewhat ambiguous language in the prologue to the fifth Act of *Henry V*, when he compared Essex's anticipated return to that of Bullingbrook's son Henry after his great victory over the French at Agincourt in 1415:

Were now the general of our gracious empress,
As in good time he may, from Ireland coming,
Bringing rebellion broachèd on his sword,
How many would the peaceful city quit,
To welcome him? Much more, and much more cause,
Did they this Harry.
                              (*Henry V*, 5.0.30–5)

Is the rebellion 'broachèd' on Essex's sword the skewered corpse of O'Neill's insurgency or the opening up of a civil conflict in England? (To 'broach' is to drive a tap into a beer barrel). Just how welcome would the latter really be to the city?

The precise impact of that Saturday afternoon performance of *Richard II* has excited much academic interest. It also provoked Elizabeth's ministers into action.

We know that the Privy Council met in emergency session that evening and summoned Essex to appear before them that night. Essex would be faced either with submission or with the necessity of declaring his intentions before he was fully ready. But was the fact of the performance really a serious threat to state? How powerful was the playhouse as a political force in early modern England?

Some have argued that theatre as art form was held in such low esteem that it was never recognised as of any political influence at all: Essex's faction was out of touch with reality in thinking that a performance could be politically provocative (Yachnin 1997: 16). Others have suggested that the theatre was an instrument of state power: the stage was a place where sedition and subversion were allowed because the audience would identify with the on-stage rulers; the theatre could thus contain 'the radical doubts it continually provokes' (Greenblatt 1985: 45). But at least on the surface the theatre was of great political significance. The fact that all plays had to receive permission from the monarch's Master of the Revels to be performed can be considered recognition of the subversive danger of the stage. The theatre's Puritan opponents, who included influential London churchmen, preached that the playhouse was a school of profanity, lewdness and sedition and should be closed down (see below, p.47). The playwright Ben Jonson was imprisoned twice and interrogated once for writing drama which offended the government (Donaldson 2011: 111–13, 206–13, 190–2).

In this particular case Jonathan Bate has discounted the role of the performance of *Richard II* that afternoon as playing a major political role, suspecting those who make the claim of being 'ideologically minded' (Bate 2009: 281–2). He argues that it was the summons for Essex to appear before the Privy Council – which arrived after the play was performed – which precipitated the action. The rebellion was a hurried reaction to the threat of arrest conceived that evening (Bate 2009: 255). In any case, he proposes, it was Hayward's book that was seen at the trial as evidence of treasonous conspiracy, not primarily Shakespeare's play, which instead was seen as an invocation of Hayward's book, 'fusing the play with the prose history' (Bate 2009: 280). *Richard II* was just the 'signature play' of the Essex faction, analogous to the 'tendency of modern political parties to choose a theme song for their election campaign and play it at their rallies' (Bate 2009: 275). But as Katherine Duncan-Jones points out, if they just needed to cheer up their supporters they could easily have had the play performed indoors in Essex House, as had been done previously: 'the decision to commission a performance by the Lord Chamberlain's Men at the Globe suggests a deliberate intention to include the ordinary citizens of London in the favourite recreations of Essex and his conspiratorial circle' (Duncan-Jones 2009: 125). If the country's leading theatrical company had no political significance, why was one of James I's first acts on his accession two years later to take Shakespeare's company 'under his own personal patronage and protection' (Duncan-Jones 2009: 126). Certainly Elizabeth felt that it was the public performance of 'this tragedy' that had been a threat to her by a man who both forgot God and his own benefactors (Chambers and Williams 1933: 177).

So, even if the performance of *Richard II* failed to motivate the people of London to rise up against the Queen, 'the impact of the spectacle itself should not be underestimated'. The critic Margaret Healey writes that 'the political significance of staging the deposition and killing of a king … lay not in the play's explicit approval or condemnation of it – it [*Richard II*] does neither – but rather in the offering of it as a real possibility' (Healey 1998: 29). The staging of *Richard II*, it can be argued, made possible the real overthrow and killing of a monarch half a century later, when Charles I was overthrown and executed as a tyrant in 1649.

Whatever the wider issue of cultural history, and even if it were mere coincidence that the emergency meeting of the Council took place the evening after the performance, the resuscitation of *Richard II* at a time when the author of a book on the same topic was in prison for his alleged promotion of sedition could not but be seen as provocative. Hamlet says that it is the function of theatre to show 'the very age and body of the time his form and pressure' (3.2.17). Hamlet's image is of a piece of wax which takes the imprint of contemporary events. But here, as in many of the other moments in the theatre which this book discusses, the theatre seems to be a place where the whole body of the time becomes compressed into a single moment, existing in a unique realm which is both imaginary and acutely alive, a place where anything is possible. The huge energy contained in that compressed moment can inspire and inflame people to extreme actions. That may well have been the conspirators' hope: that even if the people had not seen *Richard II*, the audacity of brandishing such a symbolic provocation would induce them to flock to his banner. Essex did believe he was the people's favourite. He was of course mistaken.

The summons from the Council came but Essex sent the messenger away. A second emissary was also dismissed. He was worried. He had heard rumours of two different plots against his life that day, one saying that Sir Walter Raleigh and Lord Brooke would stab him as he slept that night (Bate 2009: 250). The Earl resolved to act the following morning, and summoned his supporters to Essex House.

When at ten in the morning a government delegation (which included Egerton, and the Lord Chief Justice of England) arrived in the courtyard of Essex House they were faced with an unruly and abusive crowd of the Earl's faction. Essex promptly but politely put the government delegation all under arrest, held hostage while Essex said he would 'go into London and take order with the Mayor and Sheriffs for the City, and be here again within this half hour' (Harrison 1937: 286).

Essex believed that the people of the city would show the same loyalty as Bullingbrook had received. He believed, for some reason, that one of the city's Sheriffs, one Smyth of Fenchurch Street, had a thousand armed men belonging to the city volunteer militia, the 'Trained Bands' who could be mobilised at a moment's notice to support him. Consequently, when his forces tumbled into the Strand, shouting 'To the Court! To the Court!' Essex countermanded them. Instead of turning west towards Whitehall Palace, at that moment guarded by a handful of the Queen's soldiers, Essex and his curious mob of gallants, adventurers, dissidents and desperadoes headed east for Temple Bar and the City of London.

There were about two hundred of them, armed only with pistols, swords, rapiers and daggers. As they made their way down Fleet Street Essex called out 'For the Queen! For the Queen! A plot is laid for my life'. He beseeched the people to arm themselves and rally to his cause, but they merely stared at him. When they reached St Paul's he encountered the huge crowd who had gathered to hear the weekly sermons at the cross in the churchyard and who were now making their way home. But the Londoners merely smiled and waved back at Essex's parade. The Earl made his way to Sheriff Smyth's house in Fenchurch Street only to find that the Sheriff had already slipped away to find the Lord Mayor, denying any knowledge of Essex's plot, and still less any promise of armed men who would support the insurrection.

When leading the Queen's army Essex's inability to seize the initiative had led to military failure in the past. Now it would cost him dear. For three hours Essex remained in Smyth's house in Fenchurch Street. In great agitation and unsure what to do next he sweated so much that he called for a change of shirt. He then ordered food for his officers and ale for his men, stolen from the Sheriff's kitchen.

The Queen's Privy Council had meanwhile begun to gather its forces and take action. A barricade of coaches was formed across the road from the City to Whitehall at Charing Cross. Robert Cecil's brother Lord Burghley, accompanied by a herald and a dozen horsemen, was riding through the city proclaiming Essex a traitor and offering a pardon to all who would abandon him and seek the Queen's mercy. A chain was drawn across the roadway at Ludgate, and a hastily armed force of the Bishop of London's retinue was assembled there under the command of the Earl of Cumberland and an experienced old officer who happened to be present, Sir John Leveson. This small force consisted of some armoured pikemen and some musketeers. At the same time three hundred infantry and sixty cavalry were rapidly assembled and set off from Whitehall under the command of the Lord Admiral of England. This was Charles Howard, Earl of Nottingham, who had led England's navy against the Spanish Armada thirteen years before. Nottingham had also been the patron of the theatrical company which was the rival to Shakespeare's. Until 1593 Christopher Marlowe had been its principal dramatist (Palmer and Palmer 2000: 123–4).

As the news of the government's reaction spread Essex's men began to melt away. Still with his napkin round his neck, Essex ran out into the street declaring that he was only acting for the Queen and the City; that he had armed himself to defeat a gang of atheists in the pay of Spain. In Gracechurch Street he finally met Sheriff Smyth, who had been in contact with both the Mayor and the Council. The Sheriff told Essex to accompany him to the Mansion House to make his surrender, but in reply Essex asked Smyth to join him and charged off to try to get back to Essex House in the Strand. At least there he had some hostages to bargain with.

But at Ludgate he was met with a small military force drawn up in battle order. The Bishop of London's musketeers were drawn up in the gateway, their fuses smouldering and ready for action. Behind them stood armoured pikemen, presenting their six-metre-long spears in a steel-tipped hedge in front of the gunmen. At first Essex bluffed that he had permission from the Mayor to pass the gate. Leveson was not taken in, but demanded corroboration from the Mayor himself. A nervous stand-off ensued. Then one of Essex's frustrated gallants discharged his pistol at the defenders. Essex's men, desperate to see some action, attacked, vainly hacking at the pike shafts with their rapiers. They were halted when the musketeers returned fire. It seems as if the soldiers were under orders to shoot at the Earl himself. Essex was not wounded, but his page was killed. Two bullets passed through the crown of the Earl's felt hat. Two unlucky spectators were hit and mortally wounded. Then the Bishop's pikemen pushed forwards and the spirit of the rebels failed them. Essex's men ran away towards the river at Queenhithe, leaving the Earl's father-in-law, Sir Christopher Blount, lying in the street with a face wound.

Once in a boat on the Thames it would still have been possible for Essex and his lieutenants to have escaped downriver and to have found a ship to take them out of England, but they still did not seem to have appreciated the depth of their peril. When they returned to Essex House the Earl found that the hostages had been released by one of his own officers, Sir Ferdinando Gorges, who was now desperate to save his own neck. They also learned that the Lord Admiral's forces would soon be upon them. Not long after that the Queen's artillery would arrive and their situation would be totally hopeless.

Essex set about burning his papers, diaries and lists of his friends and supporters. He also threw onto the fire a small black bag which he always wore about his neck. It was said to contain a secret undertaking from King James VI of Scotland, the man who would succeed Elizabeth on the throne of England two years later.

Darkness was now falling. When the siege of Essex House began there was some exchange of fire and some casualties. Soon the royal forces broke into the courtyard. Sir Robert Sidney, once one of Essex's friends, came forwards to demand surrender. After some negotiations, led by Southampton for the rebels, it was agreed that the women in Essex House would be let out and the defenders be given an hour to refortify the gates after their exit. Nottingham's concession suggests that he knew that given enough time the resolution of the rebels would falter. He was right. At first Essex was determined to die sword in hand rather than meet death as a criminal on the scaffold. But soon enough Southampton appeared on the roof again asking for nothing more than civil treatment for all the rebels, a fair trial and permission for Essex's favourite Puritan preacher to attend him in prison. Out came the rebels one by one in the darkness to kneel before the Lord Admiral and to present their swords in surrender (Harrison 1937: 286–93; Lacey 1971: 290–7).

Six weeks later, at dawn on Ash Wednesday, Essex walked onto a scaffold inside the walls of the Tower of London. As a nobleman he was to be beheaded, not ritually disembowelled, castrated and hacked into four pieces, – the traitors' fate which befell two of his less aristocratic lieutenants, Sir Gelly Meyrick and the ex-Oxford professor Henry Cuffe. The great majority of his followers, including Southampton, escaped execution. Interestingly, no action was taken against the Lord Chamberlain's Men, who had in fact performed before the Queen the previous evening. Essex, however, was ready for death. He was wearing a bright-red waistcoat and began a long prayer as he prepared for the end. He was still praying aloud when the axe struck the first time. It took three blows to sever the Earl's head. He was thirty-three years old.

During this last prayer Essex hoped that 'it would please the everlasting God to send down His angels to carry my soul before His Mercy Seat' (Harrison 1937: 325). In 1778 the Shakespeare scholar Edmund Malone claimed that 'Lord Essex's last words were in our author's thoughts' when he wrote Horatio's prayer for the dead Hamlet: 'Goodnight, sweet prince,/ And flights of angels sing thee to thy rest!' (5.2.308–9; cited in Shapiro 2010: 42). Malone was probably the first critic to attempt to interpret the plays as coded authorial biography, but this dubious tendency has continued ever since. It led John Dover Wilson in 1932 to proclaim that the character of Hamlet is 'remarkable … portraiture' of Essex himself; 'everything is there': Dover Wilson describes a witty, theatre-loving, gallant but dangerously impetuous man in his thirties, who is brave and intelligent, but also cruel and touched with insanity. The contradictory and puzzling nature of the character of the Danish Prince has exercised the pens of critics since the beginning of English literary criticism. The enigma is solved, wrote Dover Wilson, when we realise that 'Hamlet's mystery is the mystery of Essex'. Shakespeare rewrote *Hamlet* following the rebellion and execution 'as an everlasting memorial to his friend' (Wilson 1932: 105–7).

For Dover Wilson, Essex lives on in every performance of the tragedy. This is surely a simplistic and romantic reading of the play for which there is absolutely no evidence beyond the text. But we do not have to accept this to recognise that there are moments in the play that must have reminded its original audience of the events of Essex's fall. The memory of Essex was briefly summoned into their consciousness, but without the political power that the conspirators hoped would radiate from the ghosts of King Richard and Bullingbrook when they walked the Globe stage the evening before the bloody fiasco of the Essex Rebellion.

The bespoke Saturday performance of *Richard II* demonstrates how closely the theatre was interwoven with politics in early modern London. It is also clear that political action and violence were rarely complete strangers at this time. The performance may have inspired Essex's lieutenants, but it did not inflame the people. Elizabeth's ministers perhaps appreciated that fact. The Earl greatly overestimated his political position in England. A play or theatrical event must have a wider political currency than Essex's *Richard II* if it is to provoke serious trouble on its own account. Later events upon the London stage would have both 'much more, and much more cause' (*Henry V*, 5.0.34) and a larger, more susceptible constituency, and would more effectively spark political violence in the streets.

Notes

1 All references to Shakespeare are to Shakespeare (2007) unless otherwise stated.
2 Worden (2003) has been one of a small number of scholars who suggest that the play may not have been Shakespeare's *Richard II* but a dramatisation of Hayward's history. Jonathan Bate argues convincingly that this cannot have been the case (2009: 468–70).
3 Jonathan Bate has challenged the reliability of the source which declared that Elizabeth was troubled by the identification of herself with Richard II in the theatre (Bate 2009: 281–6). Jason Scott-Warren (2012) has shown, however, that there are good reasons for trusting in the source's reliability and authenticity.

References

Bate, Jonathan (2009), *Soul of the Age: the Life, Mind and World of William Shakespeare* (London: Penguin Books).

Chambers, Edmund and Charles Williams (1933), *A Short Life of Shakespeare with the Sources* (Oxford: Clarendon Press).

Donaldson, Ian (2011), *Ben Jonson: A Life* (Oxford: Oxford University Press).

Duncan-Jones, Katherine (2001), *Ungentle Shakespeare* (London: Thomson Learning).

—— (2009), 'The Globe Theatre, February 7, 1601', in Byron Hollinshead and Theodore K. Rabb (eds) *I Wish I'd Been There: Twenty Historians Revisit Key Moments in History* (London: Pan Books), 120–33.

Escolme, Bridget (2005), *Talking to the Audience: Shakespeare, Performance, Self* (London: Routledge).

Greenblatt, Stephen (1985), 'Invisible Bullets: Renaissance Authority and Its Subversion, *Henry IV* and *Henry V*', in Jonathan Dollimore and Alan Sinfield (eds) *Political Shakespeare: New Essays in Cultural Materialism* (Manchester: Manchester University Press).

—— (2001), *Hamlet in Purgatory* (Princeton NJ: Princeton University Press).

Gurr, Andrew (1992), *The Shakespearean Stage 1574–1642*, third edition (Cambridge: Cambridge University Press).

Harrison, G. B. (1937), *The Life and Death of Robert Devereux, Earl of Essex* (London: Cassell).

Hawkes, Terence (2002), 'Hank Cinq', in *Shakespeare in the Present* (London: Routledge).

Healey, Margaret (1988), *William Shakespeare: 'Richard II'* (Plymouth: Northcote House).

Hopkins, Lisa (2008), *Christopher Marlowe, Renaissance Dramatist* (Edinburgh: Edinburgh University Press).

Kiernan, Pauline (1996), *Shakespeare's Theory of Drama* (Cambridge: Cambridge University Press).

Lacey, Robert (1971), *Robert, Earl of Essex: An Elizabethan Icarus* (London: Weidenfeld & Nicolson).

Levi, Peter (1988), *The Life and Times of William Shakespeare* (London: Macmillan).

Nashe, Thomas (1972), 'Pierce Penniless his Supplication to the Devil', in *'The Unfortunate Traveller' and Other Works*, ed. J. B. Steane (Harmondsworth: Penguin Books), 49–145.

Palmer, Alan and Veronica (2000), *Who's Who in Shakespeare's England* (London: Methuen).

Paterson, Annabel (1989), *Shakespeare and the Popular Voice* (Oxford: Basil Blackwell).

Quennell, Peter (1969), *Shakespeare: The Poet and his Background* (Harmondsworth, Penguin Books).

Scott-Warren, Jason (2012), 'Was Elizabeth I Richard II?: The Authenticity of Lambarde's "Conversation"', *Review of English Studies*, 64, 208–30.

Shakespeare, William (1936), *Hamlet*, ed. John Dover Wilson (Cambridge: Cambridge University Press).

—— (1982), *Hamlet*, ed. Harold Jenkins (London: Methuen).

—— (2002a), *King Richard II*, ed. Charles R. Forker (London: Thomson Learning).

—— (2002b), *The Complete Sonnets and Poems*, ed. Colin Burrow (Oxford: Oxford University Press).

—— (2006), *Hamlet*, eds Ann Thompson and Neil Taylor (London: Thomson Learning).

—— (2007), *Complete Works*, eds Jonathan Bate and Eric Rasmussen (Basingstoke: Macmillan).

Shapiro, James (2005), *1599: A Year in the Life of William Shakespeare* (London: Faber & Faber).

—— (2010), *Contested Will: Who Wrote Shakespeare?* (London: Faber and Faber).

Weimann, Robert (2000), *Author's Pen and Actor's Voice* (Cambridge: Cambridge University Press).

Wilson, John Dover (1932), *The Essential Shakespeare* (Cambridge: Cambridge University Press).

Worden, Blair (2003), 'Which Play was Performed at the Globe Theatre on 7 February 1601?', *The London Review of Books*, 10 July.

Yachnin, Paul (1997), *Stage-Wrights: Shakespeare, Jonson, Middleton and the Making of Theatrical Value* (Philadelphia: University of Pennsylvania Press).

Chapter 2

Passion and revolt

Thomas Otway, *Venice Preserv'd* and the 1795 Westminster riot

During the political unrest in Paris in May 1968 a famous graffito was painted on a wall: 'The more I make revolution, the more I want to make love. The more I make love, the more I want to make revolution'. The erotic aspect of theatre – the pleasure of watching attractive people talk of love and making love – has always been a significant part of the audience's experience. When the subject matter of a play combines eroticism with political insurrection in a manner where one feeds off the other, the impact on the audience can be powerful. In the case of Thomas Otway's 1682 tragedy *Venice Preserv'd* the entangled combination of the sexual and the revolutionary was to give this play a remarkable history, and one quite out of sorts with the author's original intentions.

On 14 April 1685 a 33-year-old man in obvious distress entered a coffee house on Tower Hill in London. 'Almost naked and shivering', he approached a man whom he recognised and asked for the loan of a shilling. The coffee-house customer was shocked at the desperate appearance of the beggar. He recognised him to be a London playwright who had once enjoyed fame and distinction. A guinea was offered and graciously accepted. Having purchased a bread roll, the playwright returned to the Bull tavern where he had been hiding from his creditors. However, in the words of Theophilus Cibber in his 1753 *Lives of the Poets*, 'as his stomach was full of wind by excess fasting, the first mouthful choked him, and instantaneously put a period [end] to his days' (cited in Ghosh 1932: 29–30).

There is another, equally romantic account of the last hours of Thomas Otway. According to Joseph Spence, Otway died in pursuit of the murderer of a close friend, one Blakiston, who had been shot: 'the murderer fled towards Dover, and Otway pursued him; in his return he drank water when violently heated, and so got the fever which was the death of him' (Ghosh 1932: 31).

The twentieth-century editor of Otway's works, J. C. Ghosh, cast doubt on both of these accounts, but the nature of Otway's brief and passionate life could not but help provoke such tales about him. His greatest play, the 1682 tragedy *Venice Preserv'd*, is also suffused with powerful melodrama and violent emotion.

Venice Preserv'd is usually regarded by historians as a royalist play, a drama which supported King Charles II in his struggle against parliamentary control over the royal succession. Curiously, however, *Venice Preserv'd* became in later

P Lely Pinx

Thomas Otway

Printed for the Booksellers the Corner in St Pauls Church Yard & In' Bowles at ye Black Horse in Cornhil London.

Figure 2.1 Thomas Otway. An engraving from about 1750 based on a mezzotint by the painter Peter Lely who died in 1680. Other engravings show a much more genial Otway, but this picture suggests a more brooding and insecure presence. Satirists mocked Otway for his corpulence (Ghosh 1932: 29).

years a rallying point for violent opposition to both monarchy and aristocracy. A performance was to become the occasion for an attack on the King himself, and the tragedy was eventually to be banned from the English stage. It is a prime example of the strange combination of the erotic and the political being an explosive mixture in the theatre.

Thomas Otway was the son of a Sussex vicar. He was born in the village of Trotton, near Midhurst, in 1652. After Winchester and Oxford, where he never took his degree, he was an actor on the London stage. The playwright Aphra Behn offered him his first role in her first play, *The Forc'd Marriage, or the Jealous*

Bridegroom (1670). Extreme stagefright made it a difficult opening night for him, one from which he never really recovered. John Downes, the prompter, wrote that 'he being not us'd to the stage; the full House put him to such a Sweat and tremendous Agony, [and,] being dash't, spoilt him for an Actor' (cited in Ghosh 1932: 12).

Otway cut a much more impressive figure in the theatre some years later. He was a member of the audience in the pit at the Duke's Theatre in Dorset Garden, where his own plays were performed. The French visitor Henri Misson gave a vivid account of a Restoration theatre's auditorium:

> The Pit is an Amphitheatre, fill'd with Benches without Backboards, and adorn'd and cover'd with green Cloth. Men of Quality, particularly the younger Sort, some Ladies of Reputation and Vertue, and an abundance of ladies that hunt for Prey, sit all together in this Place, Higgledy-piggledy, chatter, toy, play, hear, hear not.
>
> (Cited in Langhans 2000: 16)

Refreshment in this hectic environment was offered by 'orange wenches'. These young women not only sold oranges at sixpence a time but acted as paid messengers who would help arrange assignations between the gallants and the actresses. Not that they were always needed: Restoration audiences thought that the backstage area was as much their province as the front of house, and there was little to stop men visiting the female performers in their dressing room. Actresses had little chance to protect their virtue. A contemporary observer, Tom Brown, wrote that ''tis as hard a matter for a pretty Woman to keep herself Honest in a Theatre, as 'tis for an Apothecary to keep his treacle from the Flies in hot Weather; for every Libertine in the Audience will be buzzing about her Hony-Pot' (cited in Howe 1992: 33).

The most famous orange seller, Nell Gwynn at the Drury Lane Theatre, became an actress herself, despite her illiteracy. Later she became one of the King's mistresses. On this occasion in the pit at the Duke's Theatre, Otway saw an aristocratic gentleman beating an unnamed orange seller. Otway tried to make the nobleman show some restraint, but a row ensued. Swords were drawn. Both men were wounded, but the playwright had the better of it. His antagonist was John Churchill, the future Duke of Marlborough. In the following century Marlborough was to win major victories over the French army during the War of the Spanish Succession (1701–14). The grateful nation built Blenheim Palace in Oxfordshire for him.

The row with John Churchill in the pit at Dorset Garden was quite typical of the theatrical world in which Otway sought to make his living. When Charles II returned from exile in Paris in 1660 one of his first acts was to reopen the London theatres which had been closed by the Puritan city authorities since the outbreak of civil war in 1642. The new heartland of the London theatre was Covent Garden and the new 'West End', rather than the suburbs as in Shakespeare's time.

'Restoration' theatre saw professional actresses on the English stage for the first time, performing entirely in indoor, candlelit theatres patronised by the nobility. In a conscious rejection of the austere moralism of the Commonwealth years (1649–60), Restoration comedy was bawdy, scurrilous and satirical; Restoration tragedy emotional, high-flown and passionate. The mood of the theatre was in tune with the members of the King's court who patronised the stage. Charles II made no secret of his mistresses and of his love of pleasure. The generally overheated atmosphere of the writing was matched by the often rowdy, licentious behaviour of the audience, and indeed of the actors.

Otway's habit of recklessly throwing himself into daunting challenges was also true of his love life. After his failure in Behn's play he continued to act, but now also began to write for the stage. In 1675 his tragedy *Alcibiades* was performed. In the lead role was the age's finest actor, Thomas Betterton, who had also taken the principal part in Behn's *The Forc'd Marriage*. Betterton was also to play the lead, Jaffeir, in *Venice Preserv'd*. Author and actor seem to have become friends; at least, Otway died owing Betterton money. Also making her debut in the theatre was the seventeen-year-old Elizabeth Barry in the role of Alcibiades' sister Draxilla, and it seems that Otway's infatuation with Barry dates from this period.

The daughter of a royalist lawyer ruined after the civil war (Roberts 2014: 120), Barry grew to be a brilliant performer in both comic and tragic roles, and was to play Belvidera in *Venice Preserv'd*. She combined a natural authority on stage with a capacity to depict the most profound emotions with great power and pathos. The actor Colley Cibber, who saw Barry play Belvidera at the beginning of his career reflected much later (1740) on her abilities in his *Apology for the Life of Mr Colley Cibber, Comedian*:

> Mrs Barry, in characters of greatness, had a presence of elevated dignity, her mien and motion superb and gracefully majestic: her voice full, clear and strong, so that no violence or passion could be too much for her. And when distress or tenderness possessed her, she subsided into the most affecting melody and softness.
>
> (Cited in Roberts 2014: 133)

Critics also lauded her for staying in role and reacting to the speeches of others when she herself had no lines to speak. It seems that many other actors did not do as much on the Restoration stage.

In his passion for Barry, as in his challenge to Churchill, Otway was facing heavyweight opposition. Barry was the mistress of John Wilmot, Earl of Rochester. Her performance as Draxilla had in fact been disastrous, and she had been dismissed from the company. Rochester was a notorious gambler and a contemporary anecdote tells how he undertook, for a bet, to turn her into a good actor. He won his wager, and Barry's return to the stage as the Queen of Hungary in Orrery's tragedy *Mustapha* was triumphant. The sister-in-law of the King himself, the Duke of York's Italian wife Mary of Modena, is said subsequently to have engaged Barry to teach her English.

Rochester was a very attractive man. He was also a poet, a courtier and a rake. He lived life uproariously, as his writings reveal, and he had a sharp, cruel but very funny pen. Otway was red-faced, indigent, portly, not particularly clean and very fond of wine; he died owing a vintner £400. His suit was doomed. Barry owed the nobleman her success on the stage. Yet Otway was gallant to his rival in the unequal contest and dedicated two plays to Rochester in 1677. This did not, however, spare him from Rochester's wit. In the previous year Otway had had his first success on the stage with *Don Carlos*, a tragedy set in the court of King Philip II of Spain. Despite the acclaim Otway received, Rochester caustically refused Otway membership of the pantheon of great dramatists with these words:

> *Don C[arlos]* his [i.e. Otway's] Pockets so amply had fill'd
> That his *Mange* was quite cur'd, and his Lice were all kill'd.
> But *Apollo* had seen his Face on the Stage,
> And prudently did not think fit to engage
> The Scum of a Play-house for the Prop of an *Age*.
>
> (Ghosh 1932: 15)

We do not know if at this time Rochester knew of Otway's passion for Barry, which seems to have remained unconsummated and unrequited.

It was not a particular sense of chastity which led Barry to reject Otway's advances. Barry never married. She was also the lover of the playwright Sir George Etherege, and had affairs with the Earl of Dorset (a wild-living patron of poets) and with Sir Henry St John Bart. Barry's single status showed great strength of character but also made economic sense, for the wages of married actresses were paid to their husbands. Barry was, unusually, paid as much as a male actor (fifty shillings, £2.50 a week). By comparison Betterton, her frequent co-star, was paid even more, receiving £5 a week. Barry had no reliable male support, and she acquired a no-doubt undeserved reputation for avarice; but the contemporary rumour that she was actually a prostitute, for which there is no evidence, merely displays resentment at female professional success (Howe 1992: 27–33; 51–4; 113–19).

In 1697 some love letters of Otway's were published, which were later claimed to be those which he had sent to Barry. In them he tells of seven years of torment. Barry offered friendship, when he was desperate for her love:

> I ask for *glorious* Happiness, you bid me welcome to your *Friendship*, it is like seating me at your *Side-table*, when I have the best pretence to your *Right Hand* at the Feast: I *Love*, I *Doat*, I am *Mad*, and know no *measure*. Nothing but *Extreams* can give me ease, the kindest *Love*, or most provoking Scorn ...
>
> (Otway 1932: 478)

Otway's passion for Barry is more than evident in the roles he wrote for her, beginning with the role of Phenice in the tragedy *Titus and Berenice* (1677). It is the extremity of emotion, as well as a remarkably sustained erotic charge, which give *Venice Preserv'd* its distinctive character and made it a great favourite on the English stage until the mid-nineteenth century.

In *Venice Preserv'd* Otway tells of a failed conspiracy against the Venetian Republic in 1618. His hero, the virtuous Jaffeir, has married Belvidera, the daughter of a corrupt senator. Jaffeir's father-in-law disapproves of his daughter's match and uses his authority to seize Jaffeir's property. This provides the motive for Jaffeir joining a plot to overthrow the government by force. Jaffeir's co-conspirator, Pierre, on his part is enraged because his lover, the courtesan Aquilina, has taken another senator, Antonio, as a paying customer. The other conspirators are purely motivated by power-lust, rather than noble vengeance, and Jaffeir has to prove his loyalty by offering his wife as a hostage. Renault, the leader of the insurgents, attempts to rape her while she is in his custody. The appalled Belvidera persuades Jaffeir to inform the Senate of the plot before disaster strikes the city, but the authorities already have heard rumours and the conspirators are arrested. In custody, Pierre strikes Jaffeir for his betrayal of trust. At first the Senate promise Jaffeir that the conspirators' lives shall be saved, but when he hears that the rulers will break their word Jaffeir is overwrought with shame at breaking his oath and with grief for the loss of his friendship. He is on the verge of stabbing Belvidera, but relents. In the final act Belvidera reconciles her father to her husband's nobility, but it is too late: Jaffeir stabs Pierre as he is on the scaffold to save him from an ignominious death at the hands of the public executioner, then kills himself. Belvidera, crazed with grief, dies broken-hearted.

To a modern audience the intense action of *Venice Preserv'd* sounds over-wrought and melodramatic, but for over a hundred years the play was a fixture upon the London stage and was very highly regarded, enjoying as many revivals as Shakespeare's major tragedies. Oliver Goldsmith, the eighteenth-century dramatist, claimed that Otway was 'next to Shakespeare the greatest genius England has produced in tragedy' (cited in Otway 1969: xvii). The parts of Jaffeir and Belvidera were challenges for the very best actors to display their quality.

Its apparently ponderous theatricality can still work wonders today if carefully handled. The most recent British production, at the Glasgow Citizens Theatre in 2003, was highly effective. Philip Prowse directed and Greg Hicks took the role of Jaffeir. The *Guardian* critic Mark Fisher thought the production got it right: Hicks as Jaffeir was 'tough and relentless'. The dialogue also brought out the play's dramatic power: 'So speedy and intense are the exchanges that they leave no space for distraction: all that matters is the passion of the moment. If at the start of the play it can be an effort to keep up, by the end, it is nothing less than compelling'.

The *Guardian* reviewer also noted that the play is 'spiked with ribald overtones of sexual perversion' (Fisher 2003). Joseph Roach has noted that the audience attended the theatre in Restoration London to experience 'a variety of exciting incidents calculated to stir involvement: in tragedy a rising pulse of lurid violence, frequently erotic; in comedy a concatenation of intrigues and cross-purposes, always erotic' (Roach 2000: 33). *Venice Preserv'd* is indeed a particularly erotic piece of theatre. Jaffeir is several times frank about the nature of his passion for Belvidera, not least when he claims that 'I have known the luscious sweets of plenty, every night' (Otway 1969: 11). Belvidera is several times accompanied on stage by a phallic dagger which always seems to threaten imminent penetration. When pleading for her life at her husband's hands she calls on him to:

'pity these panting breasts, and trembling limbs,/ That used to clasp thee' (Otway 1969: 76); when begging in the final act to die with him, she invokes the time when 'melting kisses sealed our lips together,/ When joys have left me gasping in thy arms' (Otway 1969: 86).

There is also a masochistic homoerotic subcurrent in the friendship of Jaffeir and Pierre. In the final act Jaffeir has chosen to die so that he may remain loyal to his friend rather than live on with his wife. As he crawls on his knees and approaches the condemned Pierre, he claims that lashes from his friend are 'fitter for me than embraces'. In a speech whose subtext might bear scrutiny, Pierre replies:

> Dear to my arms, though thou hast undone my fame,
> I cannot forget to love thee. Prithee, Jaffeir,
> Forgive that filthy blow my passion dealt thee …
> (Otway 1969: 92)

The threatening dagger finally penetrates Pierre, who cries out 'Now thou hast indeed been faithful' (Otway 1969: 95).

Otway wrote the emotionally and sexually overcharged speeches of Belvidera for the woman he desired, Elizabeth Barry. Perhaps the passionate outpourings which he put into the mouth of Betterton in the role of Jaffeir are some sort of expression of his frustrated feelings, and the text's extraordinary energy has its source in a thwarted but powerful desire. But critics have also found that the play depicts an explosive breakdown of the whole code of aristocratic values and its language – an eroticised deconstruction of the language and validity of a misogynistic patriarchal nobility (Canfield 2000: 109–10). In its imagery it dreams of a primal liberty for its deracinated protagonists, even as they take a masochistic pleasure in being enslaved by powerful social codes (Hughes 1996: 303). Somewhere in its twisted subconscious the play has revolutionary potential.

It may well be that the fevered, arousing erotic atmosphere of *Venice Preserv'd* in the context of an uprising against a corrupt government has been a factor in the capacity of the play to provoke violent unrest amongst its audience. The surface politics of the text itself are muddled and certainly neither egalitarian nor revolutionary. When first performed the play won the approval of Charles II, who attended its third performance. By April 1682 the King had seen off an attempt by Parliament to exclude his Catholic heir and brother, James, from being next in line to the throne, since Charles had no legitimate children. There had also recently been a hysterical popular reaction against a supposed Catholic terrorist conspiracy ('The Papist Plot'). The leader of the campaign against the Catholic threat and monarchical rule unfettered by Parliament was the Earl of Shaftesbury.

It is likely that Otway won royal approval in *Venice Preserv'd* by satirising Shaftesbury's known sexual predilections in the figure of the corrupt senator Antonio, which apparently included foot-fetishism and being spat upon. The play advocates loyalty to those in power, but there is no king-like patriarch in the Venetian Republic for the royalist to admire and die for. Belvidera's father Priuli is a bad and selfish parent who repents too late. Revolution remains a glamorous and tempting, if sinful, project.

It may well be that Tory tragedy in the Restoration theatre could not but reflect the loyalists' own reservations about the conduct of a monarch whose own lechery and lack of principle made him fall short of the Tory ideal. The play's celebration, in erotic terms, of revolutionary fervour made it a lightning conductor for radical sentiment when next the monarchy was seriously threatened.

So keen was the monarchy to keep the theatre under political control after 1660 that only two 'patent' theatre companies were permitted to stage serious plays. Originally they were the King's Company under Thomas Killigrew at Covent Garden (from 1663), and the Duke of York's company under Sir William Davenant, first at Lincoln's Inn Fields and then in a new theatre built by Sir Christopher Wren at Dorset Garden (from 1671). *Venice Preserv'd* was a staple of the London theatres throughout the eighteenth century, enjoying over 170 performances at both 'patent' theatres between 1703 and 1795. The century's greatest actor-manager, David Garrick, excelled in the role of Jaffeir at Drury Lane from 1748 until 1759 (Mackenzie Taylor 1950: 292–9).

The late-seventeenth- and eighteenth-century London audiences came as much to see the performance as the play itself. They would deliberately revisit productions of the same play in order to pass opinion upon how the 'points' – notable moments of tension and emotion – were played by different actors in different performances. Consequently, the words of those plays which appeared most frequently in the repertory became very well known indeed. The Tory credentials of Otway's tragedy were established from the beginning, but there came a time when the play, and one passage in particular, struck a resonance with radical revolutionary feeling in the capital. In Act One, Pierre inspires Jaffeir to join the conspiracy by asserting that

> our Senators
> Cheat the deluded people with a show
> Of liberty, which yet they ne'er must taste of.
> They say, by them our hands are free from fetters,
> Yet whom they please they lay in basest bonds;
> Bring whom they please to infamy and sorrow;
> Drive us like wracks down the rough tide of power.
>   (Otway 1969: 13)

Pierre's personal grudge behind these lines was ignored by those theatregoers who found this all too apt a description of England in the years following first the American, and then the 1789 French Revolution. Jaffeir agrees with his friend:

> JAFFEIR I think no safety can be here for virtue,
> And grieve my friend as much as thou to live
> In such a wretched state as this of Venice,
> When all agree to spoil the public good,
> And villains fatten with the brave man's labours.

> PIERRE We have neither safety, unity nor peace,
> For the foundation's lost of common good;
> Justice is lame as well as blind amongst us;
> The laws (corrupted to their ends that make 'em)
> Serve but for instruments of some new tyranny
> That every day starts to enslave us deeper.
> (Otway 1969: 14)

The new American Republic, created after the victory over British forces in the War of Independence (1775–83) offered a model of a democracy on classical lines, at least in as much as the vote was denied to women and slaves. But the freedoms it offered stood in stark contrast to George III's England. Repression and state violence were the government's response to popular demands for the 'common good' to be understood in a more democratic way. There was widespread clamour for a recognition that the commonwealth of Britain was not entirely the property of a corrupt and unaccountable aristocracy, an oligarchy barely restrained by a House of Commons which was in no way representative of even the male middle classes. This was Britain's own corrupt 'Senate'.

The country was industrialising rapidly. There was social dislocation caused by rapid urbanisation and the growth of both a new working class and of a new and prosperous bourgeoisie. The French Revolution acted as an inspiration for radicals, but the long and costly wars, first in America and then against revolutionary France (from 1793), produced increased taxation, poverty and hunger. Draconian laws were put in place; a network of government spies and agents provocateurs was put in place to counter the reformists, some of whom found in Pierre's words an inspiration to revolt.

John Thelwall was one of the founders, in 1792, of the London Corresponding Society, an organisation of artisans dedicated to parliamentary reform, and in particular to the extension of the vote to working men. Thelwall deliberately sought to use *Venice Preserv'd* for radical ends. In 1795, on the first night of a new production at Covent Garden, Thelwall and his friends loudly applauded Pierre's sentiments in Act One and called for encores. After one more performance the production was closed by the authorities to avoid further outbursts. When Thelwall was subsequently arrested and tried for High Treason a government spy gave evidence of his actions during Otway's play as part of the case against him. Thelwall faced the ancient and terrifying punishment of hanging, drawing and quartering, but the trumped-up case against him failed (Barrell 2000: 567).

Venice Preserv'd had now been appropriated for the democratic and, indeed, republican cause, however. William Jackson, an Irish clergyman acting as a spy for the French revolutionary government, was found guilty in Dublin of High Treason. On his way to the dock for sentencing he whispered to his lawyers 'we have deceived the Senate'. These are the last words of Pierre, as he dies from the wound which Jaffeir has inflicted upon him to avoid the shame of death upon the scaffold (Otway 1969: 95). Jackson was using the play to announce that he was also mortally afflicted himself, having put arsenic in his own tea that morning. He collapsed and died in convulsions moments later (O'Toole 1997: 295–6).

Jackson had unsuccessfully tried to involve one of the age's great playwrights in his conspiracy. The Dublin-born Richard Brinsley Sheridan, author of *The Rivals* (1775) and *The School for Scandal* (1777) was not only the MP for Stafford, but, from 1778, sole owner and manager of Drury Lane Theatre. Sheridan had entered Parliament to argue for the cause of the American rebels. Now, in October 1795 Sheridan planned to stage a new, lavish production of *Venice Preserv'd* at a time of great political agitation. The high emotions of Jaffeir, Pierre and Belvidera in Drury Lane would soon spill out into the streets and lead to an assault upon the King himself.

The production opened on October 21, with John Philip Kemble in the role of Jaffeir. Kemble was to be at the centre of a major theatrical riot himself four-teen years later (see Chapter 3). On the afternoon of its second performance (26 October) the London Corresponding Society held a huge open-air meeting at Copenhagen Fields, just to the north-west of where King's Cross Station stands today. The organisers claimed that 200,000 people attended. There probably were fewer, but it was still a massive demonstration. The protestors called for the King to dismiss his ministers, end the war with France and extend the right to vote beyond the 3 per cent of the population currently entitled.[1] Sheridan's produc-tion of *Venice Preserv'd* at Drury Lane that evening became a continuation of the protest. Those lines which condemned the government of Venice, such as Pierre's 'cursed be your Senate! Cursed your constitution!' were 'enthusiastically applauded' (Otway 1969: 68).

Matters moved to a climax on the morning before the third performance, October 29. It was the day of the state opening of the new parliamentary session. King George III's speech setting out his ministers' political programme had been leaked the previous day. The King displayed shocking tactlessness, or simple political ineptitude. In the speech he praised his subjects for putting up with huge increases in the price of food, and proposed further increases in taxation. A very large crowd of protestors gathered to line the King's route from St James's Palace to the Houses of Parliament in the early afternoon. They chanted 'No king! No George', 'Peace, peace!' and 'Bread, bread!' Troops cleared a path for the state coach, but they could not prevent it being pelted with mud and stones, and several windows were broken. Just before the coach reached Old Palace Yard, in what is now St Margaret's Street, some kind of small missile penetrated the window. The King was immediately convinced he had been fired on by an assassin: 'that's a shot!' he is said to have exclaimed.

After his speech, George got back in one piece to St James's Palace, but not before his face had been sprayed with glass shards from an oyster shell hurled through his window. Once the King was safely at home the state coach was attacked and wrecked by the crowd on the way back to the Royal Mews (where Trafalgar Square stands now), and was only saved from total destruction by the intervention of the Horse Guards.

Despite the best efforts of the authorities, no evidence was ever produced that a shot of any kind had been fired, even though two arrests were later made and a £1,000 reward offered for any information that led to a conviction. It was nevertheless an incident which the government could use to discredit its opponents and would shortly employ as a pretext for the most repressive legislation. First, action had to be taken where possible against the King's enemies.

The scene at Drury Lane that night was a triumphant provocation. The performance of *Venice Preserv'd* began with a half-hearted rendering of 'God Save the King', played falteringly by half an orchestra after some royalists in the audience demanded it. But when the play began, as the royalist newspaper the *True Briton* reported, 'the applause from a Party in the Pit and Gallery was, as before, directed to those passages which make all honest men shudder!' A new silent scene had been added to this production. It showed a tableau of the conspirators being led to their execution, 'to the sound of tolling bells and muffled drums'. In Otway's text Pierre is the only condemned conspirator seen on the scaffold (Otway 1969: 94). In giving the other conspirators a dignified death ritual, rebels such as the would-be rapist Renault were turned into political martyrs dying in a noble cause.

Sarah Siddons, in the role of Belvidera, made herself the emotional centre of the production by the intensity of her acting. She took upon herself the responsibility for what happens to Jaffeir and Pierre, and her performance of Belvidera's guilt-stricken madness in her final scene was quite overwhelming. A later (1808) account of her performance recalled that 'her ravings, wild, terrible, desperate, were rendered more awful and impressive by the strong exertions with which her mind struggled from time to time to recover its balance, and the evanescent glimpses of reason which glimmered doubtfully through the darkness of the soul' (Mackenzie Taylor 1950: 195). When her life came to an end, 'the terrible agonies of her death closed a representation of suffering nature almost too real and too dreadful to be borne'. As Daniel O'Quinn has pointed out, the extreme pathos generated by Siddons's performance made the Senate, as represented by her father Priuli, all the more reprehensible. It is the Senate's duplicity in revoking its pardon for the conspirators that precipitates the play's catastrophe. For the Senate, the Drury Lane audience read Prime Minister William Pitt's government. Siddons's histrionic fury thus sharpened the play's political edge (O'Quinn 2004).

That night the passions that blaze in *Venice Preserv'd* kept London's political temperature at boiling point. A royalist pamphlet published the following year asserted that the production had been part of a conspiracy to provoke regicidal violence, which was certainly the view of government propaganda at the time. The opulence of the production was further evidence of its deliberately inflammatory nature: 'it was certainly not *chance* that directed the *patriotic* Patentee of Drury Lane theatre to *get up* with such uncommon splendour a play so disgraceful to *public morals*, and so inimical to order and government'. That the conspirators had French names such as Pierre and Renault only exacerbated the suggestion of treasonous intent. Something had to be done. On the following day the Lord Chamberlain's licence for the play was revoked and it was not seen again in London for seven years.

Venice Preserv'd still had the power to evoke republican demonstrations when revived in 1809 and in 1848, a year of revolutions on the mainland of Europe. An American version of the play by William Dunlap was banned in 1798 as disrespectful and seditious not of a monarchy, but a republic.

King George still needed to show that the London theatre was not enemy territory. On the following evening, on October 30, he visited the other patent theatre, Covent Garden, whose management were supporters of the Tory cause. The King deployed 800 troops and police to guard his route from the palace to the theatre, and swords were drawn and used on the hostile crowd. The audience that night was deliberately composed of loyalists, government officials and members of the security forces, yet the monarch was still hissed by some in the pit.

The performance that night was in fact Sheridan's own comedy *The Rivals*. It was certainly not an attempted royal gesture of reconciliation. Perhaps the intention was to assert the monarch's right to determine the political significance of whatever appeared on the London stage. In the final scene, when Joseph Munden, the actor playing Captain Absolute, explained his reason for fighting a duel with the words 'I serve His Majesty' (Sheridan 1967: 93), 'a great degree of clamour was excited' in the words of a loyalist newspaper. Since Absolute is actually fighting the duel in pure self-interest and as part of a plan to deceive both his lover and his father, it would seem that the loyalist crowd may also have been asserting their right to interpret parts of the drama out of context, and to impose their own reading.

A strange event occurred during the shouting and cheering at this point, for 'in the midst of it, the actor Mr Macmanus walked on the stage, no one knew why, and placed himself opposite the King's box. The noise then increased to an almost alarming degree, till Mr Macmanus retired; and then it subsided'. No-one knows why Macmanus crossed the stage out of turn to stand confronting the royal box. Was he about to make some petition to the King? Or to make a loyal declaration? For whatever reason, he did not speak. The government had demonstrated its power not only to close down those productions which provoked seditious reaction, but also to pack an audience with supporters and thus determine the meaning of whatever performance they wished. The power of the theatre had been put to silence, but not without an acknowledgement of that power. The state now went further. Its response to the events of 29 October 1793 was to bring in two repressive pieces of legislation: the Seditious Meetings Bill and the Treasonable Practices Bill. When passed, these Acts would savagely limit rights of assembly and freedom of expression (Barrell 2000: 554–69; Taylor 2002: 201–2).

The Elizabethan and seventeenth-century puritan opponents of the theatre had always condemned both the sexualised nature of the event and its capacity to stir up political passions. Philip Stubbes claimed, in the same sentence, that the theatre was the place to learn 'to become a bawd, unclean and devirginate maids, to deflower honest wives … to rebel against princes, to commit treasons' (Stubbes 1877: 144). The history of *Venice Preserv'd* would indicate that sex, politics and powerful acting can be an inflammatory mixture in the right historical moment. The years after the French Revolution were such a moment. It was a time when theatre and politics were fully intermingled, and even the issue of ticket prices could produce serious political unrest.

Note

1 http://www.nationalarchives.gov.uk/pathways/citizenship/struggle_democracy/getting_vote.htm (accessed 23/4/15).

References

Barrell, John (2000), *Imagining the King's Death: Figurative Treason, Fantasies of Regicide, 1793–1796* (Oxford: Oxford University Press).

Canfield, J. Douglas (2000), *Heroes and States: On the Ideology of Restoration Tragedy* (Lexington KY: University of Kentucky Press).

Fisher, Mark (2003), Review of *Venice Preserv'd*, The Citizens Theatre, Glasgow, *The Guardian* 30 September http://www.guardian.co.uk/stage/2003/sep/30/theatre2 (accessed 23/4/15).

Ghosh, J. C. (1932), 'Introduction', in J. C. Ghosh (ed.) *The Works of Thomas Otway*, vol. 1 (Oxford: The Clarendon Press).

Howe, Elizabeth (1992), *The First English Actresses* (Cambridge: Cambridge University Press).

Hughes, Derek (1996), *English Drama 1660–1700* (Oxford: The Clarendon Press).

Langhans, Edward A. (2000), 'The Theatre', in Deborah Payne Fisk (ed.) *The Cambridge Companion to English Restoration Theatre* (Cambridge: Cambridge University Press).

Mackenzie Taylor, Aline (1950), *Next To Shakespeare: Otway's 'Venice Preserv'd' and 'The Orphan' and their History on the London Stage* (Durham NC: Duke University Press).

O'Quinn, Daniel (2004), 'Insurgent Allegories: Staging *Venice Preserv'd*, *The Rivals* and *Speculation* in 1795', *Literature Compass*, 1 (1) http://onlinelibrary.wiley.com/enhanced/doi/10.1111/j.1741-4113.2004.00088.x/ (accessed 21/5/15).

O'Toole, Fintan (1997), *A Traitor's Kiss: The Life of R. B. Sheridan* (London: Granta).

Otway, Thomas (1932), 'Love Letters', in J. C. Ghosh (ed.) *The Works of Thomas Otway*, vol. 2 (Oxford: Oxford University Press).

—— (1969), *Venice Preserv'd*, ed. Malcolm Kelsall (London: Edward Arnold).

Roach, Joseph (2000), 'The Performance', in Deborah Payne Fisk (ed.) *The Cambridge Companion to English Restoration Theatre* (Cambridge: Cambridge University Press).

Roberts, David (2014), *Restoration Plays and Players* (Cambridge: Cambridge University Press).

Sheridan, Richard Brinsley (1967), *The Rivals*, ed. A. Norman Jeffares (London: Macmillan).

Stubbes, Philip (1877), *Philip Stubbes's Anatomy of the Abuses in England in Shakspere's Youth, A.D. 1583*, ed. Frederick J. Furnivall (London: New Shakespere [*sic*] Society).

Taylor, Anthony (2002), 'Shakespeare and Radicalism: The Uses and Abuses of Shakespeare in Nineteenth Century Popular Politics', *The Historical Journal*, 45 (2).

Chapter 3

'The Drama's laws the Drama's Patrons give'

The Covent Garden Old Price riots of 1809

For sixty-seven nights in the autumn of 1809 the audience of one of London's great playhouses hooted, jeered, stamped, danced, fought and performed acrobatics. They even improvised their own drama. They paid no attention, however, to what has happening on the stage. They did this because ticket prices had gone up, and they felt that in consequence their theatre no longer seemed a common national space, an arena in which all classes could share the same cultural experience. They constantly declared their intention to protest until the cost of tickets came down, and until the new arrangement of the auditorium was altered. This drama gripped the whole city. After two months of mayhem, the actor-manager John Philip Kemble capitulated: the Old Prices were restored.

In 1809 the spectre of revolution lurked in London. Britain was ruled by a wealthy and complacent oligarchy who resisted all attempts to widen the voting franchise beyond a tiny elite (see above, p.43). The country had been at war against revolutionary and Napoleonic France for sixteen years, apart from a short interval in 1802. Nationally, industrialisation and urbanisation were bringing squalor, poverty and exploitation for many, together with great opportunities for wealth accumulation for a few. Rapid social change made people wish for stability, and look with nostalgia on the recent past when, they thought, English people lived in harmony, showing deference to their betters and charity to their inferiors. Yet nevertheless a desire for democracy was rapidly growing in strength, especially in London.

There was a numerous and well-organised radical movement in the city in that cold autumn. Prices, particularly for coal, were rising swiftly. Lord Liverpool, the Tory Home Secretary during most of the trouble at Covent Garden, commented that 'one insurrection in London and all is lost' (Baer 1992: 240). Yet the sixty-seven nights of Old Price riots (or just 'OP riots' – the abbreviation soon stuck) never quite seemed to threaten the political status quo. It appeared to have been a carnival of protest, rather than a violent insurrection (although a certain amount of violence did occur). This was a riot about the abstract rights of an audience in the theatre, not directly about any particular play or performance; but it was also a larger political protest in a country where the stage had become central to national culture. In some ways, as we shall see, these rioters were also conservative activists of a kind, trying to preserve a vision of an England united in the playhouse, an ideal which was fading away in the turbulence of those years. Yet the desire to return to a pristine, uncorrupted past has often been a driving sentiment in revolutions, and the radical political potential of the OP rioters should not be discounted.

Covent Garden was one of the two 'patent' theatres (see above, p.42) which alone had permission to stage plays during the 'season' (which ran from September until the late spring). But there was also some competition from the unlicensed theatres, which found cunning ways of evading the legislation as far as possible. Drury Lane was its 'legitimate' rival. The Theatre Royal in the Haymarket had become a third patent theatre in the summer months since 1766, and by this time there were also patent theatres in Bath, Bristol and Liverpool. The first theatre at Covent Garden had opened in 1732, next to London's main fruit and vegetable market.

Georgian theatres were lit by hundreds of candles, and with so much canvas, cordage and inflammable fabric in use fire was a constant hazard. At four in the morning of 30 September 1808 a fire broke out in Covent Garden Theatre. Firemen and volunteers broke in to try to douse the conflagration in the galleries, but the roof fell in upon them. Thirty people died that night. All the costumes and scenery were destroyed, together with the archive of many of the composer Handel's manuscripts, and the organ he had once played there (Baer 1992: 1, 21; Thornbury 1887: 227–37).

The cost of rebuilding was originally estimated at £150,000, but Kemble had been insured for only a third of that sum. Aristocratic patrons were, however, on hand. The Duke of Northumberland came forwards with £10,000 and the Prince of Wales another £1,000. A substantial sum was also raised by public subscription at the cost of £500 a share. The Prince, gorgeously dressed as ever, laid the foundation stone for the new theatre on 30 December 1808, accompanied by parties of Freemasons. The Royal Life Guards lined the streets and a twenty-one gun salute was fired.

The theatre in Georgian London was crucial to the nation's culture, and like the nation its patent theatres were divided upon political lines. Covent Garden was the Tory theatre, and the royalist political establishment were quick to ensure that the playhouse was not silent for long. Drury Lane was associated with their liberal opponents, the Whigs. Both theatres were, and are, located in the borough of Westminster, then a centre of left-wing anti-government activism. Many more men than elsewhere had the vote in this part of London because it was one of the few boroughs to award the franchise to all who paid the poor rate, whether householders or not. Until 1806 its MP was the radical Charles James Fox. When he died, the Duke of Northumberland put up his own son as the unopposed candidate in the by-election that followed, disgusting the radicals by his display of aristocratic patronage: he ordered his servants to give out free food and beer to encourage the electors. Soon the seat was back in more radical hands in the form of Richard Brinsley Sheridan, the manager of the Whig patent theatre in Drury Lane (see above, p.44). Aristocratic and royal involvement in the new Covent Garden Theatre was thus provocative to the radical theatregoers and to residents of Westminster.

The architect was Robert Smirke, who also designed the neo-classical façade of the British Museum in Bloomsbury. The new theatre was also classical in concept, the inspiration being the Parthenon in Athens. There was a portico on Bow Street of fluted columns featuring allegorical statues of comedy and tragedy, with bas-relief panels showing scenes from ancient and modern drama, the Greek gods Athena and Dionysus (deity of the theatre), the Greek dramatist Sophocles and, of course, Shakespeare. The interior was also lavishly decorated. The lobby featured white-veined marble walls, red porphyry columns and rows of plaster classical statues. But it was the construction of the interior which was of particular significance. The whole building was larger, now seating up to 3,000 people, controversially decreasing the intimacy of the contact between the audience and the stage. The motto on the gilt proscenium arch which framed the part of stage where scenery was displayed read *Veluti in Speculum*, 'As in a mirror', but it was the lack of a clearly visible stage picture for the whole audience which would provoke the spectators to reflect on the reality of their status in the new theatre (Baer 1992: 22, 33; Downer 1966: 20–1).

A typical Georgian theatre featured horseshoe-shaped tiers of galleried seating around a central 'pit'. The seating in the pit, on the lowest auditorium level, consisted of backless wooden benches. These seats were cheaper than those in tiers above, to the sides and the rear of the pit. The cheapest accommodation of all was the upper gallery on the highest tier. Smirke's new theatre did away with the third tier of 'dress boxes' of the old theatre and replaced them with twenty-six private boxes, for which part of the auditorium there was a separate entrance and lobby. Each box, resplendent in white paint with gold and pink ornamentation, was available to be rented out for the whole season. Not only was this seen as a privatisation of a space hitherto regarded as commonly available on a daily basis; but also the design of the new boxes made it difficult for the rest of the audience to see the occupants within, if they chose to remain unobserved (auditoria were not darkened during performances as in modern theatres). Both factors were offensive to many theatregoers, especially to the aficionados in the pit, who felt that the theatre was a national institution where all classes were united in a common culture. To be able to see the reactions of everyone in the auditorium gave that experience a mutuality and sense of shared experience they valued highly. Prostitutes frequented the London theatres, and it was quickly suggested that the new boxes were designed to be no more than rented brothels for the wicked and wealthy.

The poky upper gallery above the boxes was now a long way from the action (26 metres) and was immediately given the title 'the pigeonholes'. The price for perching in this lofty nest remained unchanged, but those who watched from there were still aggrieved.

Despite the support of aristocratic patrons, the rebuilding costs had significantly exceeded expectations. The Duke of Bedford, who owned some of the land needed, had held out for the highest possible price, as had the owner of an adjoining pub, but the latter was a man condemned by a nineteenth-century writer as 'well skilled in driving a hard bargain. The more eager the Committee showed themselves to come to terms with him for his miserable pot-house, the more grasping he became in his demands for compensation' (Mackay 2011: 160). It seems that by opening night there was still a shortfall of about £164,000, including the debts from the old theatre.

But the new boxes – and, of course, price increases – would bring in perhaps £40,000 a season. Prices for a seat in the old-style boxes went up from six shillings to seven shillings (35p) and unreserved places in the pit from three shillings and sixpence to four shillings (20p). As Kemble was to protest in his defence, this was actually the first increase in the cost of theatre tickets at Covent Garden since the early eighteenth century (Baer 1992: 21–2, 27). There had been little, if any, inflation in the eighteenth century, but now suddenly the cost of living was rising substantially; the new prices were seen as one more demand on people's pockets. To make matters worse Drury Lane had also burned down during the rebuilding of its rival. In the autumn of 1809 Covent Garden had a monopoly of spoken theatre in London and its management were seen to be taking advantage.

But more than that, those angered by the new prices saw them as bringing market values into a public arena – the theatre – where they had no place. The playbills and press adverts for the performance of *Macbeth* which opened the new theatre on Monday 18 September 1809 expressed the hope that, as it were, its audience had been reading its Adam Smith, the founder of liberal, free-market economics, since the theatre hoped that the rationale for the new prices would be 'honoured with the concurrence of an enlightened and liberal public' (cited in Baer 1992: 22). But their audience saw it differently. The theatres were established under royal patent, and for many they functioned as a part of the unwritten British constitution, as a space where a common national culture found its expression under royal protection. The patentees had ownership of the building, but if the price they charged prevented public access to that space they were acting in an unconstitutional and indeed unBritish manner. The century-old price of theatre tickets made the new increase seem to be the junking of an ancient tradition of great cultural value. The theatre was a place where people of all social classes mingled to share a common art form whose concerns were both politics and domestic life, both tragic poetry and low comedy. A 1761 poem by Charles Churchill widely quoted by the rioters stated that 'The stage I choose – a subject fair and free,/ 'Tis your's – 'tis mine – 'tis public property' (cited in Baer 1992: 76). A letter by 'A. F.' to the *Constitutional Review* in October 1809 put the point in a more rhetorical manner, stressing the importance of the stage as a forum for the airing of political issues:

> theatres in a country under a monarchical form of government can never be considered as private property, but as a great national concern; as a powerful political engine, as a wheel without which the remainder of the state machinery would be incomplete: in fact, they form an absolutely constituent part of our political system.
>
> (Cited in Baer 1992: 76–7)

Particularly offensive was the idea that rich aristocrats should enter into a private contract with the licensees to allow them, for a single fee, to disappear from view into their private boxes and no longer be part of a common space where classes of different ranks shared a hierarchically divided but communal theatrical experience. Elaine Hadley puts it this way:

> Once the proprietors raised prices in the name of an inflationary marketplace, once the rich paid a single fee to disappear from view for an entire season, the source and amount of the profit became mysterious, depending on unseen market forces instead of common consent, and hidden in private books never open to the public view. These books, like the private boxes, concealed the economically determined social exchanges between aristocrat and proprietor that were replacing the public, deferential exchanges among all ranks.
>
> (Hadley 1992: 527)

It wasn't so much that class antagonism would motivate the OP rioters: they can be seen to have opposed the whole idea of class, of hidden market exchange creating stark division where there had been deferential unity. This smack of modernity offended their vision of a more gentle Englishness.

The early nineteenth-century theatre was not a space where the audience sat in another world apart from the fictional world of the stage. The auditorium was lit so that both actors and spectators could see each other. Audiences could be vocal in their response to what happened on stage, both to show displeasure and to indicate when they wanted a particularly fine moment played again. The fact that the audience would change at nine o'clock, when half-price admission was available and there would be an influx of voluble poorer spectators was yet another factor in the need for some negotiation between actors and audience. The auditorium was as much part of the performance experience as the stage itself, and under certain conditions the focus of the drama could plausibly be resited in the auditorium itself (Emeljanow 2003: 23): and this is just what the OP rioters did.

The changes to the theatre were the subject of many articles in the press prior to the opening night, and indignation was growing. A huge crowd had gathered outside the theatre on the afternoon of 18 September before the opening production of *Macbeth*. In the end only a quarter of those who had spent three or four hours in a crush of people in the Piazza and on Bow Street managed to get in. Excitement built; 'God Save the King' was sung and Kemble came forwards dressed in a tartan kilt and plaid. In the eighteenth century Shakespeare had generally been played in what we would call 'modern dress', but, as his friend the novelist Walter Scott wrote, he prided himself 'on improving, by all means which occurred, the accuracy of the dresses which he wore while in character' (Wells 2000: 33).

John Philip Kemble was fifty-two years old in 1809. He had a tall and stately figure, and moved on stage with precision and elegance. Macbeth, Shakespeare's Scottish lord who kills his king after supernatural promptings, had been the role in which he made his debut at Drury Lane in 1783, and again at the beginning of his tenure at Covent Garden in 1803. He had also played Jaffeir in the tumultuous 1795 *Venice Preserv'd* at Drury Lane (see Chapter 2). Scott considered that his more flamboyant predecessor, David Garrick, had surpassed him in the roles of Lear and Hamlet, but this role offered him the opportunity to demonstrate his 'minutely elaborate delineation' of emotions, and his ability to portray internal conflict. 'We can never forget', wrote Scott, 'the rueful horror of his look, which by strong exertion he endeavours to conceal ... on the morning succeeding the murder' of King Duncan (Wells 2000: 33–4). Kemble declined to have an actor play the blood-boltered ghost of Macbeth's victim Banquo in the banquet scene so that the audience could attend to his own expressions of terror and guilt. He was fortunate to have Lady Macbeth played by his sister, Sarah Siddons, reckoned to be the finest actress of her generation (see above, p.45). Though Kemble was genuinely admired by his audience, he nevertheless possessed a somewhat reserved, patrician air which was not to his advantage at this moment. A Roman Catholic who had originally trained to become a priest in France, he was always an outsider in the eyes of the patriotic Protestants of the pit.

Kemble knew he was likely to face some trouble when the theatre reopened. As recently as 1792 there had been disturbances at Drury Lane when the management had attempted to double the admission price for the upper gallery to two shillings (Baer 1992: 58–9). The theatre owners, who on that occasion were trying to recoup the costs of enlarging the auditorium, had been forced to back down. Both Covent Garden and Drury Lane had also capitulated in 1763 when they had to abandon plans to abolish the traditional half-price admission after the third act or at nine o'clock, whichever came earlier (McPherson 2002: 240–5). Kemble must have been apprehensive, for cries of 'Down with the pigeonholes! Old prices for ever!' could be heard backstage even before the anthem was played (Mackay 2011: 161).

On such occasions as this new prologues and epilogues were often written to introduce the new run of a play. Kemble's prologue for the night hoped that the audience would put up with the new prices in gratitude for the theatre's patriotic custodianship of this jewel in Britain's cultural crown:

> We feel with glory, all to Britain due,
> And British Artists raised this pile for you;
> While zealous as our patrons, here we stand,
> To guard the staple genius of our land.
> Solid our building, heavy our expense:
> We rest our claim to your munificence.
>   (Cited in Baer 1992: 19)

But not a word of this was heard. Instead, 'a roar of disapprobation ... a volley of hisses, hootings, and execrations, surpassing anything we ever heard' filled the theatre (Mackay 2011: 161). The hooting and shouting and stamping in fact drowned out the whole of *Macbeth*, apart from a few moments when the 'sublime acting' (Mackay 2011: 161) of Sarah Siddons in the role of Lady Macbeth distracted the rioting audience.

In the Georgian theatre there was generally a lighter play to follow the evening's main event, in this case the comedian Joseph Munden's short comedy *The Quaker*. The cacophony also continued through the afterpiece. Only then did the authorities take any action.

Bow Street Magistrates' Court was conveniently situated opposite the main entrance to Covent Garden Theatre (where it remained until 2006). Two Justices of the Peace, Mr Read and Mr Nares, accompanied by some constables, appeared on stage literally to read the Riot Act:

> Our Sovereign Lord the King chargeth and commandeth all persons, being assembled, immediately to disperse themselves, and peaceably to depart to their habitations, or to their lawful business, upon the pains contained in the Act made in the first year of King George, for preventing tumults and riotous assemblies. God Save the King!

By an Act of 1714, any group of twelve persons who did not disperse within an hour could be dealt with by force, and anyone arrested and convicted could face the death penalty. But Read and Nares were treated with contempt. The volume of the tumult increased, and there were cries of 'No Police in the Theatre'. A few token arrests were made, but the demonstration continued until two in the morning, when the crowd sang 'God Save the King' and 'Rule Britannia' and went home (Baer 1992: 19–20).

In fact at no time during two months of disturbances did the authorities order the suppression of the rioters, even when trouble spread into the streets around the theatre later that week and thirty-five local householders petitioned the Lord Chamberlain (Baer 1992: 91). In the first place there was very little actual damage to the theatre on that night or on any subsequent night. The government also seemed divided over whether repressive action was necessary or sensible. The deployment of police officers was generally regarded by the Tory administration as unBritish, and although there were soldiers in barracks nearby who appeared on the streets – but took no action – on 21 September and 16 October – their use was either regarded as excessive, or, it seems, unwise, since the soldiers' loyalty to their officers in this situation could not be guaranteed. There is also some evidence that a government spy, James Powell, was influential amongst the rioters and their supporters, and so the authorities had some kind of handle on events, or at least good intelligence of what the rioters may have been planning in any case. There was also some contention in government circles whether the whole matter was a private dispute between the management and their paying customers, or whether the state should intervene to close the theatre and deprive the patentees of their rights on the grounds that they had failed in their duty of providing theatrical entertainment which united the nation: but in that case the rioters would have won. The Attorney General, Sir Vicary Gibbs, summed up the government's dilemma in a letter to the Lord Chamberlain, Lord Dartford, the court official responsible for the theatre:

> The introduction of force into the House is a very delicate measure, and I very much doubt whether any civil force would be found for the purpose. To shut up the Theatre (with or without authority) would give effect to the object of the mob, and would be unjust to the proprietors unless they have been to blame, of which I can form no judgement.
>
> (Cited in Baer 1992: 98)

So action against the rioters was limited to individual civil actions brought before magistrates. There was no concerted effort at suppression of the riots (Baer 1992: 90–105). Perhaps they were a useful distraction from the government's own problems: in 1809 the British army was involved in a disastrous expedition to Walcheren in the Low Countries. It is possible that the government saw the Old Price riots more as noisy mischief-making than an insurgency, and if so they were not totally wrong.

Yet on the first night the wider political context of the protest was more than clear. When the King's son, the Duke of York, alighted from his carriage, he was met with ribald cries, calling him 'Dukey' and 'my Darling &c' (Worrall 2006: 60). The Duke (of nursery rhyme fame) had recently resigned as Commander-in-Chief of the British army; not because of any military failing, but because he had been accused of selling officer's commissions to men who had paid a fee to his mistress, Mary Anne Clarke. Clarke herself claimed in court that she had subsequently withdrawn her sexual favours from the Duke until the requests for the petitioners' commissions were granted. A distinct lack of deference towards a discredited aristocracy was also evident in the slogans on the banners smuggled in by the rioters and hung from the balconies on subsequent nights. On the third night banners read 'No private Rooms – Opposition, persevere and you must succeed – No snug Anti-rooms [sic] … No privileged orders in the third circle … No monopoly – No private accommodations before the curtain'. The following night one placard simply read 'No theatrical taxation'. As the historian David Worrall argues, aristocratic control over the theatre through the licensing and censorship system, and now through price rises and changes to the building itself, could be seen to be 'all part of a [wider] economy in which politics, morality and capital colluded as a cartel over dramatic representation' (Worrall 2006: 58–9). The last slogan echoed the sentiment which had been a founding principle of the recently established American Republic: 'No taxation without representation'.

On the second night, Tuesday 19 September, Gay's *The Beggar's Opera* was to be performed (Moody 1958: 20). This was the first occasion when the letters 'OP' became prominently displayed as the badge of the protestors, as placards and banners were put out in the theatre for the first time. The *Covent Garden Journal* reported that 'a paper, with the words "Old Prices" in extremely large letters was pinned to one of the front boxes, a lady furnishing the pins' (Baer 1992: 27). The

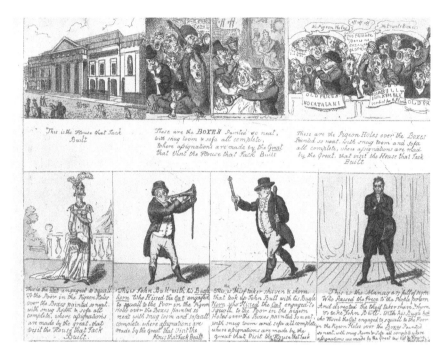

Figure 3.1 'The House that Jack Built'. A satirical print engraved by Isaac and perhaps George Cruikshank published on 28 September 1809. 'Jack' is John Philip Kemble, who is depicted bottom right standing disconsolate and baffled in the face of protest: 'This is the manager, full of scorn/ Who raised the price to the people forlorn'. Top left is the house itself, a sketch of the façade of Smirke's new Covent Garden theatre. Top centre the OP protestors, male and female, shout 'Off! Off!', twirl rattles, ring bells and play trumpets while in the box behind them 'assignations are made by the Great/ That visit the house that Jack built.' Top right shows the protestors crammed into the new 'Pigeon Holes' at the top of the theatre. Placards call for the removal of Catalani, bottom left, who is caricatured as a scrawny 'cat' who has been 'engaged to squall/ To the poor in the Pigeon Holes'. At bottom centre John Bull 'with his bugle horn' stands for the typical OP protestor, facing his opponent to his right, the mercenary 'Thief Taker' holding his staff of office and a cudgel.

play was ignored and hooted through once more, many in the pit turning their backs to the stage for the whole evening. At the end some advanced towards the stage, but constables appeared. The stage hands then opened the downstage trap-doors to present a hazard to any would-be invader (Moody 1958: 20). But most of the audience again stayed in their seats, this time hissing and calling out 'God Save the King – no Foreigners – no Catalani – no Kemble'.

Angelica Catalani was a beautiful and talented Italian soprano engaged by Kemble for the new season at no less than £75 a night. She had been a great favourite of London audiences when she had first sung three years earlier, but now she became a target for xenophobic sentiment. Catalani was married to a French officer, and she had antagonised the public when she had failed to sing 'God Save the King' properly at a concert in 1807 and then refused to sing at a charitable event for the Middlesex Hospital (Baer 1992: 212–14). What might seem mere reactionary prejudice needs perhaps to be seen in the context of some of the rioters viewing themselves as defenders of English liberty against both aristocratic repression and Napoleonic tyranny, and also as acting in defence of the theatre as a communal national institution. Catalani's marriage counted against her. There had been trouble before during the long wars with France when members of the audience had wanted French performers boycotted. In 1737 French comedians had been pelted from the Haymarket stage and their ambassador jeered out of the building (only to find that his coach had been vandalised) (Moody 1958: 15). The actor-manager David Garrick's house had been stoned after fighting broke out between his aristocratic supporters and violently patriotic 'Anti-Gallicans' when he employed some French dancers in a show called *Chinese Festival* in 1755 (McPherson 2002: 237–40). On the sixth night of the OP riots the same sentiment was abroad again. A placard was hung which read 'National Theatre: Fair Prices: English Drama: No Catalani'. Catalani was indeed later to be dismissed as Kemble's resolve began to crumble on 24 November (Baer 1992: 33).

On the third night Shakespeare's *Richard III* was performed, with the alcoholic George Cooke as the tyrant king (Moody 1958: 20). Before the performance began Kemble attempted to address the rioters and put what he saw as a rational case for the new prices, but was met with a clatter of sticks against wooden seats, overlaid with the sound of bells, bugles, trumpets and what was to become the symbolic weapon of the rioters: the wooden watchman's rattle (the same device which was to become a favourite of twentieth-century football supporters). By the Friday and Saturday nights, 22 and 23 September, frying pans, a gridiron, a pair of tongs, an octave fife and a dustman's bell were added to the 'rough music' which drowned out the play. Saturday also saw the first outing of the OP dance, which, according to the *European Magazine* of October 1809 was:

> performed with deliberate and ludicrous gravity, each person pronouncing the letters O.P. as loud as he could, and accompanying the pronunciation of each with a beat or blow on the floor or seat beneath him with his feet, a stick or a bludgeon.
>
> (Cited in Baer 1992: 28)

At the end of Saturday night an exhausted Kemble decided to close the theatre while, at his invitation, an independent committee produced a report on whether they felt the theatre management had a good case for the price increase.

Perhaps Kemble thought his aristocratic connections and an official report of the great and good would enable him to triumph over the desires of the London audience where others had failed. In 1760 David Garrick had held out for only two nights when he tried to end the practice of allowing half-price tickets to those who arrived at the end of Act Three of the main play for the evening. He had even been forced to refund the rioters' ticket money, and to suspend an actor who had prevented a rioter from setting fire to the scenery.

Kemble's committee looked at the proposals in purely economic terms and approved them. But this was to miss the moral and political motivations of the rioters. When the theatre reopened on 4 October with *The Beggar's Opera* the trouble continued (Doran 1865: 410). Banners proclaimed that the figures in the report were fixed, and there were also new claims on the protestors' placards of rampant immorality in the boxes.

Kemble now resorted to force. He brought in his own 'security': East End prize-fighters who had instructions to take action against those disrupting the play in the pit. The fact that many of these men were Jewish only aggravated those who felt that they were standing up for English tradition against foreign infiltrators. But the boxers could not silence or eject the protestors. In fact there were men in the pit prepared to take them on in a bare knuckle bout, cheered on by the audience as the fighting spilled over the wooden benches. All the time the play continued unattended to upon stage, with the real drama taking place in the auditorium. After six nights of fisticuffs the 'bruisers' were withdrawn. A triumphant banner appeared: 'And it came to pass that John Bull smote the Israelites sore!' (Doran 1865: 412). There do not seem to be reports of serious injuries. The level of physical restraint shown by all sides during these carnivalesque riots is remarkable.

After this pugilistic excitement the protests quietened a little. From 9 to 27 October the first two acts of the play began to be heard in relative peace, with the protests beginning when half-price admission was allowed and the composition of the audience became less well heeled. The theatre's income now began to decline as most of the people who came to riot were paying half-price for the privilege. The protestors may have been saving money on tickets, but those who came in at this point were often bedecked with the new OP paraphernalia, including fans, handkerchiefs and badges. Perhaps the theatre was also initially quieter because the protestors now took their complaints into the streets nearby, where, according to Thomas Tegg, a bookseller and publisher and a prominent man on what became the 'OP Committee':

> O.P. continually they roar,
> And write O.P. on every door:
> They chanted now the O.P. war,
> In Covent-Garden, Temple Bar;
> Nay, everywhere both near and far.

This seemed to have continued despite the Westminster magistrates having placed placards in the streets on 11 October threatening the prosecution of rioters. On 25 October twelve rioters were indeed indicted by the Westminster Grand Jury (Baer 1992: 28–32).

But two incidents at the end of the month inflamed matters and brought the disturbances towards their climax. First, on 30 October a popular Manchester actress, Mrs Clark, was hired to play Euphrasia in Arthur Murphy's *The Grecian Daughter* (Doran 1865: 413). A new prologue was written for the play that night and spoken by Cooke. The bibulous tragedian suggested that the rioters should now 'protect' the feelings of 'the gentle sex' and be quiet. This lame ruse was seen as a provocation, and the uproar rose again, reaching a climax that night at the on-stage death of Kemble's brother Charles in the role of Dionysius. More serious trouble was to follow the next day. James Brandon, the theatre's door keeper, arrested the barrister Henry Clifford in the theatre. Clifford was a well-known radical republican and a Catholic (Catholics had only been allowed to practise the law since 1792). A hostile cartoon by Thomas Gillray, published on 5 November, shows a saturnine Clifford holding a burning torch in front of the theatre, empty brandy bottles at his feet, with the satirical caption 'Counsellor O. P. ———— defender of our Theatric Liberties'. He had become seen as one of the leaders of the movement, and from this point the Westminster radicals were to play a prominent role in the turn of events. Later that night Magistrate Read at Bow Street dismissed the charges against Clifford and four other men, including a former member of the London Corresponding Society (see above, p.43), John Ridley, who was charged with standing on his seat, blowing a small trumpet and having the letters OP displayed in his hat. Clifford then brought a counter-suit against Brandon for false imprisonment (Baer 1992: 146).

The arrest of Clifford provoked a march by demonstrators on the premises of the newspapers known to oppose the OPs on 1 November. Then on Saturday 4 November Kemble's house at 89 Great Russell Street was attacked. Three hundred rioters assembled after the play, and cheering Clifford's name and singing OP songs they marched north. When they arrived in Bloomsbury they called for Kemble to come out and face them. When no response was made they booed and hissed, and flung mud, filth and coins, smashing some windows. Having failed to break the door in, the crowd moved on to Fleet Street and Chancery Lane, stopping hackney carriages and demanding to know whether the passenger was for OP or an NP – 'New Prices' (Baer 1992: 161).

The extent to which the OP riots can be seen as part of a wider conflict between conservatives and radicals in Georgian London is suggested by the focus on Kemble as the source of the conflict, as far as the rioters were concerned. It is also evident in the way in which the Westminster radicals who had once led the now illegal London Corresponding Society came to be seen as the leaders of their dispute. Indeed, it was prominent members of that group, with Clifford in the chair, who were to accept Kemble's eventual capitulation and bring the controversy to a close.

Kemble had dominated the London stage since his first appearance in 1782 and by 1809 was seen as an establishment figure both theatrically and politically. His statuesque posture and slow delivery was, for some, out of tune with a felt need for a more romantic and passionate style of acting, especially of Shakespeare, where Kemble's insistence on 'authentic' historical and national costumes was felt by some to be an authoritarian attempt to make a special claim, as Garrick had done, over the right to speak for the bard. Shakespeare was a central element of the theatrical repertoire and allusions to his plays were very common at this time in political and literary discourse of all kinds. The eighteenth century had established Shakespeare as a quintessentially English literary figure in response to the neo-classicism of French drama (Dobson 1992: 85ff.). Both radicals and conservatives sought to conscript him to their cause in a battle which still had many decades to run (see Chapter 6). Jonathan Bate has argued that the OP riots can in fact 'be seen as a battle for the possession of Shakespeare ... to remove cheap gallery seats and replace them with secluded boxes was to make Shakespeare less widely available, more exclusive – to appropriate him for the elite' (Bate 1989: 42). Bate also quotes James Boaden, a friend and biographer of Kemble, who stated that the riots were not so much about money but rather the 'absolute seclusion of a *privileged order* from all *vulgar contact*' (Bate 1989: 42, emphasis in original).

Shakespeare loomed large symbolically throughout the dispute. It began with a performance of *Macbeth* on 18 September and ended with *Hamlet* on 15 December. Allusions to Kemble as one of Shakespeare's tyrants were commonplace. On the first night the audience repeated back apposite lines from the Scottish tragedy to the actors, aimed at the management. On the fifth night an OP banner proclaimed 'Up with King George and down with King John [Kemble]' (Baer 1992: 162, 210). Thomas Tegg's poetic epistle on the 'OP War' compared Kemble to two treacherous tyrants, both Macbeth and Richard III. Kemble was not, however, only symbolically a right-wing figure. Boaden boasted that his friend was a keen royalist and a defender of the aristocratic principle (Bate 1992: 44, 63). As the Bastille fell in Paris in 1789 Kemble put on an adaptation of *Henry V*, Shakespeare's play about English nobility triumphing, with God's help, over their pernicious enemy, subtitled 'The Conquest of France'. Over the next three years he replayed the role; yet war with France did not actually come until February 1793. The great radical critic William Hazlitt felt that Kemble's greatest role, and one to which he was ideally suited, was Shakespeare's Coriolanus, the aloof patrician whose disdain for the people makes him unable to adapt to democratic peacetime politics (see pp.150ff.). It was the role Kemble himself chose for his farewell to the stage in 1817. In this production he orchestrated a crowd of 164 extras in one scene with perfect order and decorum (Bate 1992: 63). Bate notes that 'from 1789 onwards any "mob" would have overtures of the revolutionary crowd; Kemble's firm handling of the Roman plays served as an image of control, a proclamation that London would not go the way of Paris' (Bate 1992: 64).

The storming of Kemble's house could not then be allowed to become a theatrical fall of the Bastille. After observing a respectable Sabbath, when an OP crowd reassembled in Great Russell Street on Monday evening there were magistrates waiting with constables, and arrests were made when the crowd did not disperse (Baer 1992: 162). On Tuesday the Home Secretary ordered a group of thirty soldiers to be positioned outside the British Museum, next door to Kemble's house, at 6pm, and another thirty at the Savoy in the Strand, a couple of min-utes' march from Covent Garden. Sixty new constables were sworn in. There was thenceforth no more street violence of note.

On that same evening, 6 November, the annual dinner was held by the Westminster radicals to celebrate the acquittal of John Thelwall and others on the charge of High Treason following their demonstration of republican senti-ment during the 1795 production of Otway's *Venice Preserv'd* (see above, p.43) (Baer 1992: 125). It seems clear that even though local democratic activists such as Clifford, Tegg and the Charing Cross tailor Francis Place became important in the defence of those arrested and in the eventual resolution of the dispute, they were not its instigators nor did they direct it. Ideologically they saw themselves to be a political grouping at the service of popular dissent, rather than some kind of proto-Leninist vanguard directing revolutionary activities. They were democrats, and many were small businessmen with an interest in the general maintenance of civil order. These three and others were nevertheless instrumental in the estab-lishment of an 'OP Committee' which first met on 28 October, with the support of the radical newspaper *The Statesman* (Baer 1992: 121). The Committee's prin-cipal function initially was to raise funds for the legal defence of those arrested (and they raised thousands of pounds to this end). They also used their own legal expertise, and that of their friends, to provide that defence and to conduct pros-ecutions against the 'bruisers', and others including Brandon the unpopular door keeper. They also attempted, perhaps mischievously, to prosecute the patentees for 'running a disorderly house' – by providing the boxes where prostitutes could work unseen. In addition, they wrote and had published articles in the press and on free broadsheets putting the rioters' case to the public. These activities soon gained the trust of the rioters, so that eventually the Westminster democrats would be seen as competent to negotiate the final victory with Kemble. The Committee was made up of all well-known radicals, which suggests that the broad politics of the protestors cannot have been too far out of line with the democratic principles of the Westminster men.

The nightly disturbance continued, and acquired its own rituals. From the beginning the OP rioters parodically reversed the normal practice with regard to the wearing of hats in the theatre. When the curtain rose they stood and put on their hats. When the curtain came down they sat and took off their headgear. At different times they also came in fancy dress. 'On various occasions', writes Marc Baer, 'OPs sported red or white nightcaps, military hats, barristers' wigs, large false noses, and coachmen's coats. They dressed as Jews, midshipmen, Irish grooms, butchers, Welshmen, or women'. Baer suggests that the rioters were putting on their own theatrical masquerade in a theatre where the tradi-tion of audience interaction was strong (Baer 1992: 173). But it is also true that such costumes – especially cross-dressing – were also worn by economic riot-ers at other times in this period and after, such as the Welsh 'Rebecca Riots' in

1839 and 1843. In both the carnivalesque OP riots and in economic disturbances normal social rules had been suspended, and the order of things reversed. Dressing up in a similar manner to the OPs, including cross-dressing, can of course still be seen as a marker of working people in holiday mode in Britain today, particularly at cricket test matches, on the last day of the football season or on pre-marriage 'stag' or 'hen' events. Carnival dress then, as now, declares that the normal standards of behaviour are under temporary suspension. The OPs made it clear in their appearance that they would not behave until the old prices returned. But carnival is not revolution, and there was a tacit acceptance that in suspending normal behaviour in this fashion they were not making their own rules for themselves on their terms; they merely wished to keep the pre-existing conditions. The OPs were to win this battle, but not, in the end, the war to preserve a popular national theatre for all classes.

Outside and inside the theatre OP badges in silver or pewter were worn in the hat, and on 10 November an OP medal was advertised on sale in *The Times*. Symbolically prominent on the medal were the rioters' weapons, – the rattle and the horn. Amongst other inscriptions, quotations on either side alluded to Kemble as both the avaricious moneylender Shylock in Shakespeare's *The Merchant of Venice* and to the tyrannous King John. Shakespeare was theirs to use, and they defended their rights over the stage by also inscribing a much used 1757 couplet by the poet, critic and lexicographer Samuel Johnson (Baer 1992: 228, 172):

The Drama's laws the Drama's Patrons give
For we [actors, writers] that live to please, must please to live.

The pit was the centre of festivities every evening. On different evenings there were a variety of activities (Baer 1992: 63). Early on there was dancing on the benches and mimicking of the actors on stage. On 23 October the rioters fought mock-fights in parody of the swordplay on stage. Later the rioters paid less attention to the play and took to racing each other across the pit benches. On 24 November the benches in the centre of the pit were cleared and a programme of gymnastics, 'gladiator fights' and the OP dance followed. Five performances later two rattle-wielding protestors performed a new, 'rattlesnake minuet', and on the following night there was sword-fighting and wrestling. By late November the boxes had mostly emptied: the struggle was between the OP carnival in the pit and the performance on stage.

This kind of behaviour has been described as 'counterspectacle' (McPherson 2002: 237). If theatre projects a certain ideological power in its representation of the world, then the show which the OP protestors put on in the auditorium was intended to have a countervailing spectacular force. The rattle and horn were employed in hunting, and the races and mock-fights were similarly outdoor, physically energetic and even violent. If these activities had anything in common it is perhaps that racing, gymnastics, mock-fighting and ritual dancing were traditional village-green, common-land activities which were open for all to take part in and observe and which would take place in a communal space. Hunting would take place over private land but with an understanding that in such a traditional English activity the right to communal recreation would take precedence over private property rights. Thus the OP sports could perhaps be seen to be a spectacular assertion of communal rights over private privilege.

When eight rioters were indicted at the Court of the King's Bench on 27 November the management-supporting newspapers suggested that the trouble had subsided, but the pro-OP *Statesman* reported that there was in fact an upsurge in activity in response to this news. A new trial was to bring matters to a climax. On 5 December, in the Court of Common Pleas, Brandon the door keeper was found guilty of false imprisonment by a jury in answer to the civil action brought by Clifford. This was hailed as a great victory by the OPs, and that night in the theatre laurel sprigs were worn in hats, handkerchiefs were waved, placards were brandished and the OP dance was performed in triumph.

Vindicated by Clifford's successful prosecution events in the pit now took on a new tone. From 6 December, for the first time the audience began pelting the stage with objects. Such assaults had been rare before, but now 'lemons, apples, pennies, horns, sticks and pieces of pit-bench' (Doran 1865: 414) were aimed with menace at the actors. Hard peas were rolled under dancers' feet with spectacular results. It was clear that the resolve of the protestors was not wavering and that things were turning nasty. Serious fist-fights were happening in the pit now. While the OPs became more violent total audience numbers declined. Kemble and the management were giving free seats to 'NPs' who would support their cause in the pit, but to little effect. Legal fees were also mounting, but Kemble had nothing like the popular appeal of the OP cause, which enabled the OP Committee to raise so much money to back their legal efforts. Kemble was already losing £300 a night by 1 December, and was perhaps £12,000 down overall. On 14 December Kemble asked to speak to Clifford. They dined together at the Crown and Anchor Tavern, the haunt of radicals, which was located where the north end of Waterloo Bridge now stands. Kemble issued a public apology. He then appeared on stage to announce the capitulation.

One of the rioters' terms remained unmet in his statement: they had demanded the dismissal of Brandon, and so that night the disturbances continued. The following day Kemble agreed to that matter as well, undertook to end all legal proceedings against rioters and apologised on stage for having employed the boxers. There was applause and a banner was unfurled proclaiming 'we are satisfied'. The OP riots were over. Old Prices were restored in the pit – but not in the gallery – and the number of private boxes was to be reduced from the next season onwards.

When Covent Garden Theatre opened for the 1810 season the number of private boxes was larger than that agreed, and violent trouble once more broke out; but a resolution was rapidly agreed on this occasion.

Financially, the pit had won. But the political principles which the most articulate OP supporters had put forwards to justify their cause were soon to go down in defeat. Francis Place felt that the idea of expanding a theatre to accommodate three thousand people involved breaking the possibility for personal contact between the performers and the whole audience, a personal connection which would allow the former to communicate ideas and argument rather than merely present spectacle. Such a move, he later wrote

> will not be supported by the public, to whom it can never supply the rational entertainments they desire in the way which can alone satisfy them, by ena- bling them to see the countenances of the performers and to hear their voices.
> (*A Brief Examination of Dramatic Patents* (1834), p.7, cited in Baer 1992: 168)

The stark separation of different classes in the theatre, as occasioned by the new boxes in which the aristocracy could remain hidden from view from those in the pit was also held to be damaging to the idea of the theatre as a place where the whole nation would share a common experience. In James Brandon's trial in early December, Henry Clifford's lawyer argued that the nobility should not 'have places allotted to them in which they may be kept separate and distinct from those of inferior condition or from the public in general' (cited in Baer 1992: 158).

But over the following decades the theatre became even less of a national and 'rational entertainment'. The rise of melodrama and spectacle led to different social classes attending different theatres, with the aristocracy favouring opera. Perhaps the OP rioters' belief in a theatre where there was a great deal of direct commu- nication between actors and audience, where in the plays themselves secrecy was always uncovered and social harmony and due deference between classes was a feature of the denouement made early melodrama just the kind of theatre many ordinary theatregoers wanted (Hadley 1992: 529ff.). Working people still wanted serious theatre, including Shakespeare (see below, Chapter 6), but they increas- ingly watched it in their own playhouses and 'penny gaffs'. When Drury Lane reopened in 1812 it was still a huge space, seating 3,060. Covent Garden was next remodelled in 1847, when it was renamed the Royal Italian Opera House. Opera has been the core of its repertoire ever since. The present Royal Opera House is largely the building erected to replace Smirke's theatre, which burned down in 1856. The ending of the patent system for theatres in 1843 paved the way for a huge number of new theatres to be built in London. Gradually the pit benches in theatres were replaced by 'stalls', which came to be the most expensive seats in the house and where there was also most contact between actor and audience. The gallery became the location of cheap wooden benches for working people, now themselves out of sight of their betters in the stalls and circles below. The OP riot- ers had protested about the box dwellers having a separate entrance from everyone else. In Victorian theatres it became common for the gallery to have a different entrance to every other class of seat, sometimes even located around the corner in a different street from the main entrance. This arrangement still obtains today in some of these surviving theatres.

The carnivalesque behaviour of the OP rioters survived in English culture, and survives today at sporting events and other festivals, but usually divorced from any political project. Neither the rioters nor the authorities regarded the riots as an insurgency, symbolic or otherwise, even if some contemporary commentators did so, and in particular those reactionaries who called for violent suppression of the OPs. For example, Sir James Mansfield, the judge in the Clifford *versus* Brandon case castigated the jury's verdict, predicting that the 'spirit' which motivated their decision would lead to 'every species of misery; it leads possibly to the subversion of the present Government; and it leads probably to great evils, perhaps the worst a nation can endure' (cited in Baer 1992: 102). The spirit of the OPs may well have been at large in the radical movements for parliamentary reform in the years to follow, and amongst the Chartists (see below, pp.109ff.), but it was not able to preserve a national and rational theatre. The objectives of the OPs were explicitly economic – 'Old Prices' – though they were grounded in a vision of society where economics was at the service of social cohesion. They were eventually to be defeated, not for the last time, by those who put the former before the latter.

References

Baer, Marc (1992), *Theatre and Disorder in Late Georgian London* (Oxford: Clarendon Press).

Bate, Jonathan (1989), *Shakespearean Constitutions: Politics, Theatre, Criticism 1730–1830* (Oxford: The Clarendon Press).

Dobson, Michael (1992), *The Making of the National Poet: Shakespeare, Adaptation and Authorship 1660–1769* (Oxford: The Clarendon Press).

Doran, John (1865), *Their Majesty's Servants: The English Stage from Thomas Betterton to Edmund Kean* (London: W. H. Allen).

Downer, Alan S. (1966), *The Eminent Tragedian William Charles Macready* (Cambridge MA: Harvard University Press).

Emeljanow, Victor (2003), 'The Events of June 1848: The Monte Cristo Riots and the Politics of Protest', *New Theatre Quarterly*, 19, 23–32.

Hadley, Elaine (1992), 'The Old Price Wars: Melodramatizing the Public Sphere in Early-Nineteenth Century England', *PMLA*, 107 (3), 524–37.

Mackay, Charles (2011), *Memoirs of Extraordinary Popular Delusions* [1852] (Cambridge: Cambridge University Press).

McPherson, Heather (2002), 'Theatrical Riots and Cultural Politics in Eighteenth-Century London', *The Eighteenth Century*, 43 (3), 236–52.

Moody, Richard (1958), *The Astor Place Riot* (Bloomington IN: The University of Indiana Press).

Thornbury, Walter (1887), 'Covent Garden Theatre', *Old and New London: Volume 3* (no publisher), pp. 227–37 http://www.british-history.ac.uk/report.aspx?compid=45149 (accessed 2/5/15).

Wells, Stanley (ed.) (2000), *Shakespeare in the Theatre: An Anthology of Criticism* (Oxford: Oxford University Press).

Worrall, David (2006), *Theatric Revolution: Drama, Censorship and Romantic Period Subcultures 1773–1832* (Oxford: Oxford University Press).

Chapter 4

'The most important occasion of the century'
Victor Hugo and the 1830 Battle of *Hernani*

The notorious disturbances which marked the first run of Victor Hugo's tragedy *Hernani* at the Théâtre-Français in Paris in the spring of 1830 had a very different cause from the English and American theatre riots of the nineteenth century. At the root of the trouble was not class conflict about access to the theatre, nor political controversy concerning the content of the play itself. The matter in contention, according to those who contended, was the *style* in which the play was written. What they objected to was Hugo's flouting of the traditional principles and dignified tone of the French tragic theatre. There was, in short, fist-fighting in the auditorium about the play's poetic techniques. But beneath the surface of what might appear to be an abstract literary dispute simmered a larger question about what sort of country France would be, culturally and politically, after the fall of the Emperor Napoleon in 1815 and the apparent defeat of what was left of the principles of the 1789 Revolution. Culturally, the 'Battle of *Hernani*' marked the establishment of Romanticism at the heart of the nation's theatre. Politically, it announced that the days of the restored autocracy of the Bourbon Kings were numbered.

The Théâtre-Français was founded by King Louis XIV in 1680 by merging the two most prominent theatre companies of the time (Howarth 1995: 245). Originally it was not seen as the national theatre company, for its name merely distinguished itself from the company who played in Italian at that time. After 1680 both the French- and Italian-speaking companies became the servants of the King, and performance at court, in the King's various palaces, was their priority. The Bourbon Kings of France saw themselves to be absolute monarchs, whose God-given authority was not to be questioned by any of their subjects, and whose rule extended over all aspects of French life. Under such royal and aristocratic patronage of the serious theatre, seventeenth- and eighteenth-century French audiences became more noble in their make-up, more refined in their taste and more likely to include ladies. By this time French tragedy had evolved into a neo-classical form which was very different from what English audiences were used to. The style of play which developed appeared to have much formally in common with ancient Greek and Roman tragedies, although it was not simple deliberate emulation. It set out to show an idealised, dignified world of kings and nobles. It proposed itself as a more rational and elegant form of theatre than the less shapely and more popular kinds of drama which did not conform to the concept of the 'unities'. According to these rules, each play, written in rhyming verse, had only one main plot. All the action occurred in a single place, and occupied only a single day. The tone of the play was serious and poetic; there was no comedy, and there were no lower-class characters promiscuously mixing with the nobles as they struggled heroically against their tragic fates. There was very little on-stage action, or indeed stage movement, and the emphasis was on the beautiful delivery of the verse. The great founder of this mode of tragedy was Pierre Corneille, and by the time of its other great exponent, Jean Racine, it had become one of the glories of the national culture, and closely connected with French national identity, particularly in the long series of wars against the English in the eighteenth century. By 1752, the French Enlightenment philosopher Voltaire in his *Dissertation sur la Tragédie* accompanying his play *Semiramis* could denounce Shakespeare's *Hamlet* (which, like all of his tragedies, flouts all the 'unities'), as 'a vulgar and barbarous drama, which would not be tolerated by the vilest populace of France' (cited in McEvoy 2006: 30).

The revolution which began in 1789 brought a temporary end to traditional theatre in Paris. The monarchy was swept away, and many of the aristocratic audience were killed or forced into exile. For a dozen years the different revolutionary factions sought to create a republic established on the principles of liberty, equality and fraternity. There was enormous factional and counter-revolutionary bloodshed and the other European monarchies soon tried to crush the French Republic with armed force. During these years of turmoil most theatre was no more than propaganda supporting the interests of the group in power. Eventually a charismatic general, Napoleon Bonaparte, took control of the government as First Consul in 1799 and moved to establish order across all parts of French society. The Théâtre-Français had managed to reform in that year, and in 1800 Napoleon granted the company permanent possession of its building, where it stands today, on the Rue Richelieu in Paris (Carlson 1972: 15). From 1802 the company had state funding, but it had to provide a permanent box for Napoleon, who two years later became Emperor of the French. He required his court and family to keep boxes there too. He reinstated neo-classical tragedy as the main part of the repertoire, albeit with considerable government censorship. Napoleon was a dictator and no defender of liberty or equality, but he brought in a series of modernising reforms to his country, and won a series of stunning military victories which extended French rule over much of Europe. The glorious military career of this Corsican of quite humble origins made him a hero to Romantics everywhere. Romanticism was by this time the dominant artistic movement in Western Europe. For its adherents, the life of the emotions and the freedom of the human spirit were central both in art and in politics. It had many followers among the young, and many Romantics – initially at least – were supporters of the Revolution, and later admirers of the Emperor Napoleon.

When the Emperor suffered his decisive defeat at the hands of Wellington and Blucher at Waterloo in 1815, the absolutist Bourbon monarchy was put back on the throne by the victorious allies. The Théâtre de l'Empereur, as it had been known, reverted to its former title. But even as censorship remained in force, there now began to be some subversive changes to the conservative production of plays on the Rue Richelieu. Elsewhere melodrama was increasingly popular in the theatre, which made the formal restraint of traditional theatre seem old-fashioned. There began to be some breaks with tradition in neo-classical tragedy at the Théâtre-Français. In 1821 the great actor Talma lay down on a bed in de Jouy's Roman tragedy *Sylla* – such an indignity had never been seen on stage before – and there were even crowd scenes, another shocking innovation in a theatre where only nobles had previously been represented on stage (Carlson 1972: 29). Talma also challenged his royal patrons by blatantly playing the Roman military leader as the recently dead Napoleon, to great acclaim: the status of the restored monarchy remained fragile.

There were still, however, powerful and numerous opponents to any change to so culturally central an institution as neo-classical tragedy. When, in 1822, an English theatre company performed Shakespeare for the first time since the 1789 Revolution, *Othello* was drowned out by cries that Shakespeare was a 'flunky of Wellington'. Potatoes, eggs and large coins were hurled at the actors (Carlson 1972: 60). There was, however, a younger generation growing up in the 1820s who were Romantics in temperament and much more sensitive to the English style of theatre, and to British literature. The novels of Walter Scott and the poetry of Byron were becoming increasingly popular with younger people. Animosity towards Britain began to decline, and when a company put together from actors at Covent Garden, Drury Lane, the Haymarket, Bath and Dublin visited Paris in 1827 they were much more warmly received. Charles Macready (see p.92ff) arrived the following year with his Macbeth (amongst other roles), along with Edmund Kean as Richard III and Shylock. In particular, French audiences admired the unaccustomed naturalism of the movement and manner of speech of the English and Irish actors. They enjoyed the busy stage action, but most of all they appreciated what they took to be realism in the presentation of emotions. The Irish actress Harriet Smithson, playing Ophelia opposite Charles Kemble's Hamlet, became a sensation for her portrayal of Ophelia's mad scenes (Charles was John Philip Kemble's younger brother). The composer Hector Berlioz was so struck that he pursued Smithson until she consented to marry him in 1833. Alexandre Dumas, later the author of *The Three Musketeers*, wrote in his memoirs that 'this was the first time that I had seen real passions on the stage, inspiring men and women of real flesh and blood' (Carlson 1972: 60).

Another young writer inspired by the English and Irish tragedians was Victor Hugo. Hugo's father, Joseph, had enlisted as a soldier at fifteen and rose to the rank of major-general and Count of Siguenza in Napoleon's armies. In 1822, at the age of twenty, Victor made his own name as a poet with a volume that won him an audience with King Louis XVIII and a gift of twelve hundred francs

(Edwards 1971: 12, 24, 47). At this time the young man, a fervent royalist, was estranged from his father, but by 1827 they were reconciled. Victor became a principal member of a social circle of writers ('le Cénacle') who were Romantic in their artistic inclinations and Bonapartist in their politics. He resolved to write a heroic, Romantic drama in a Shakespearean mode, and he chose Oliver Cromwell as his hero. Hugo's *Cromwell* was never performed, and in its huge scale is probably unperformable, but its published preface proved much more significant.

In this Preface Hugo sets out a manifesto for the Romantic drama which he felt must replace neo-classicism in the theatre. Hugo asserts that the Christian age requires a different literature from the classical. 'Christianity', he wrote, 'brings poetry to the truth' (Howarth 1975: 129, my translation). Whereas the classical view of humanity sees only a lofty nobility, Christianity acknowledges that human beings are composed of both the physical body and the spiritual soul, and that it is natural and truthful for both to be shown on the stage. For:

> the one is perishable, the other immortal; the one is physical, the other is ethereal; the one is enchained by its appetites, needs and passions, the other is carried away on the wings of enthusiasm and dreams. The former, ultimately, is always bent towards its mother, the earth; the latter is ceaselessly soaring towards the sky, its fatherland ... The poetry born from Christianity, the poetry of our time, is then the drama; the style of the drama is then realism; realism is the result of the natural combination of two qualities, the sublime and the grotesque, which meet each other in the drama, just as they meet each other in life and in all creation.
>
> (Howarth 1975: 130, my translation)

It is not a simple copy of nature that Hugo wants on stage, but a theatre which shows the beauties of human aspiration and emotion; the sublime world of the soul, but also the ugly facts of mortal existence, what he terms the 'grotesque'. The master of this style of theatre who must be emulated is Shakespeare, 'this god of the theatre' (Howarth 1975: 132), who combined both qualities – the ridiculous and the tragic, the low and the noble – in the same scenes. Shakespeare's rejection of the restrictive unities of time and place must also be followed; but the design of the play, its sets, costumes and props must, as *Hernani*'s modern translator writes, 'be in conformity with the historical times depicted' (Schumacher 2004: xxxviii). Hugo says that plays must still be in verse, like Shakespeare's, because a play is not real life, and if its language is 'hardened in verse, [it] suddenly takes on a sharper, more brilliant quality. It is iron turning to steel' (cited in and translated by Schumacher 2004: xxxix).

Hugo had already had one Romantic history play in which he put these ideas to work accepted by the Théâtre-Français, *Marion de Lorme*, in 1829, but the state censor banned the play before performances could begin (Howarth 1975:

144–5). Both the theatre's manager, Taylor, and Hugo himself were granted audiences with the King in order to obtain a reprieve, but the King's ministers insisted that the depiction of King Louis XIII in the play was an attack on the monarchy and the ban remained in place. King Charles X, who had replaced Louis XVIII in 1824, subsequently offered Hugo a state pension of four thousand francs. He refused the transparent offer to be put on the royal payroll (Hugo 1863: 2: 254). Yet the theatre did begin to move towards the new Romantic drama. In the place of *Marion de Lorme*, the Théâtre-Français put on Vigny's *Le More de Venise*, an adaptation of Shakespeare's *Othello*. Vigny worked on the plot and characters to ensure that this version was close enough to neo-classical conventions to avoid scandal – Bianca the prostitute was removed entirely, for example – but the action and the emotional display of what remained of Vigny's version were enough to excite the hostility of the press towards this obvious experiment in Romanticism (Howarth 1975: 145–8).

When Hugo wrote *Hernani* he saw it as a chance both to strike back at the King's ministers and to stage his ideas for the new romantic theatre at the Théâtre-Français in earnest. He first read the play to his friends on 30 September 1829 before it was approved by the Committee of the Théâtre-Français on 5 October (Descotes 1955: 199). 'The play was received with acclamations' recalled Hugo's wife Adèle, 'and the parts immediately distributed' (Hugo 1863: 2: 256). *Hernani*'s overheated rhetoric and constant, passionate outbursts of throbbing emotion would probably make it unstageable for British audiences today. Hernani is the exiled aristocrat Juan of Aragon and the dashing leader of a bandit gang in Spain in 1519. He is in love with the beautiful, chaste and, it seems, emotionally incontinent noblewoman Doña Sol. Unfortunately Doña Sol is both engaged to be married to her uncle, the aged Don Ruy Gomez, and pursued by the King himself, Don Carlos. After a series of tempestuous and convoluted confrontations between the three suitors, Ruy Gomez saves Hernani from the King. Honour, the bandit leader proclaims, dictates that the old man may now kill him since Hernani now owes him his life. But Ruy Gomez spares Hernani so that the bandit-in-disguise may pursue the King, who has now abducted Doña Sol (and who has herself pledged her own suicide rather than marry the old man). Hernani promises to be Ruy Gomez's 'right arm'. 'I shall avenge you, duke' he cries. 'And afterwards, you shall kill me!' (Hugo 2004: 167). Hernani then gives Ruy Gomez his hunting horn. When he blows it Hernani must pay the debt of honour and die. But after becoming Holy Roman Emperor Don Carlos has a life-changing experience at the ancient tomb of Charlemagne: he adopts 'clemency' as his watchword, forgives and knights Hernani and gives Doña Sol to him (Hugo 2004: 190). Inevitably, at their wedding feast Ruy Gomez returns and blows the horn. Honour requires the hero's suicide, but not before Doña Sol has drunk the poison first to send her to a common grave with her husband ('Should we not lie together tonight? Does it matter in which bed?') (Hugo 2004: 207). In despair at this demonstration of true love, Ruy Gomez kills himself with the words 'Oh! I am damned to hell!' (Hugo 2004: 209). The unities of time and place are certainly flouted, but the language itself was to prove more scandalous to the audience of the Théâtre-Français.

Excitement and controversy surrounded the play both inside and outside the rehearsal room. A bitter winter delayed the first night until 25 February, principally because the scenery painters could not work on the huge set in unheated lofts (Carlson 1972: 64). The part of the seventeen-year-old Doña Sol was taken by the theatre's most distinguished actress, the 52-year-old Anne-Françoise-Hippolyte Boutet. French actors took a single professional name, and she was known as Mademoiselle Mars. Mars had made her debut as long ago as 1795 and had long been the principal tragic actress in Parisian neo-classical drama (Carlson 1972: 27). Contemporary reports, mostly partisan towards Hugo, stress her vanity and obstructiveness during rehearsals towards what she saw as unwarranted innovation in the French theatre. 'It was only her fear of leaving a possible triumph to some younger rival', snipes one early twentieth-century biographer of the great man, 'that induced her to undertake the part of Doña Sol at all' (Davison 1912: 81). In particular, it seems that she objected to the overblown nature of some of Hugo's writing. Famously, she thought it absurd that Doña Sol would say to Hernani 'Vous êtes mon lion superbe et généreux' ('You are my magnificent and generous lion'[1]) (Hugo 1863: 2: 258–63). Quite accurately, she predicted that this kind of writing would be hissed by the audience. She persisted in her suggestion that the line should be changed to 'Vous êtes, monseigneur, superbe et généreux' ('You are, my lord, magnificent and generous'). Hugo claimed that his original line raised 'the style of the verse'; and he would 'rather be hissed for a bad verse than applauded for a bad one'. He also claimed that his line was more authentic to the period and the character, but could not resist the cheap jibe that the line wouldn't be hissed if she were good enough an actress to deliver it properly. Hugo even threatened to dispense with her services if she continued to obstruct him. Yet he was not completely inflexible and did respond to the criticism of the experienced actors, most of whom he thought were against him. The exception was Joanny, who played Ruy Gomez. Joanny had lost two fingers fighting for Napoleon under the command of Hugo's father, and seemed to have embraced the project with the greatest enthusiasm (Hugo 1863: 2: 257). The continuing extreme cold weather cannot have helped matters. In that winter of 1829–30 the River Seine froze over from 20 December until the end of February (Hugo 1863: 2: 265). The actors scurried back to their warm lodgings out of the rehearsal room as soon as they could. But Mars and Michelot, who played Don Carlos, stuck with the play and in fact worked hard to ensure the audience would accept this 'ground-breaking' new drama.

Rumours of a divided cast circulated outside the theatre, where Hugo had many enemies, both artistic and political. The Parisian newspapers were powerful formers of public opinion, despite state censorship. They took a keen interest in the progress of rehearsals. Hugo was a glamorous young celebrity who was both an opponent of the King's ministers (though a favourite of the King) and who seemed to be bringing Romantic historical melodrama into the heart of

France's national theatre, to be performed, reluctantly, by the great actors of that traditionally neo-classical institution. As part of a theatrical genre associated, paradoxically, both with British culture and with Bonapartism (in the form of the cult of the dynamic and passionate patriotic military leader), *Hernani* was bound to generate controversy at that moment. A hostile critic (who was also a neo-classical playwright) was discovered lurking at the back of the theatre during rehearsals, having sneaked in without permission (Hugo 1863: 2: 263). Parts of the play started to appear in print and to be criticised in the newspapers. A scene from Act Three, set in Ruy Gomez's picture gallery, was even parodied in a satire at one popular theatre, the Théâtre de Vaudevilles, well before the first night (Hugo 1863: 2: 263). Then in early February Hugo discovered that a private reading had taken place of the whole play without his knowledge. Since there existed only two manuscript copies of the entire script, one of which was used for rehearsals and locked up every night, Hugo suspected that the source of the leaks must be the state censors – one of whom was yet another neo-classical tragedian – who had the only other copy (Descotes 1955: 264). It seems that the actors were also letting friends see copies of their parts. The play was public property even before official approval was given. Eventually the censors granted permission for performance, with some changes: for example, Hernani's line 'do you believe, then, that kings are sacred to me?' was altered so as not to suggest so direct a challenge to the divine right of kings, a doctrine still espoused by the restored Bourbon monarchy.[2]

In the nineteenth-century French theatre it was common practice to employ an organised group of theatregoers to applaud and cheer a new production to ensure a favourable reception. Hugo was aware that this *claque*, as it was known, was equally capable of also taking money from a play's opponents and sabotaging the production it was supposed to support (Descotes 1955: 125). He decided not to employ the Théâtre-Français' usual *claque* but to bring in a crowd of his friends and supporters, young men dedicated to the Romantic cause whom he could rely on. He claimed, somewhat disingenuously, that as a Romantic playwright he did not want organised applause for his play, but the spontaneous response of young artists and poets: 'free' art required a 'free' audience (Hugo 1863: 2: 266–7). Taylor, the theatre's manager, was anxious about this idea but eventually agreed. Entry to most of the pit and to the second gallery for the first night would be secured by a small red card printed with the word *hierro* ('iron' in Spanish). Soon, to possess one of these tickets became the mark of being an authentic Romantic amongst young Parisian men of culture.

Sartorially prominent amongst this group – which included the composer Hector Berlioz and the writer Honoré de Balzac – was the eighteen-year-old Théophile Gautier, who, in his own words, would on that first night attract the attention of every eye as the self-styled flamboyant scourge of the old art. He was dressed for the part (translated here and elsewhere by Daphne Wall):

> his red waistcoat flamed that night above pale grey trousers trimmed with
> black velvet, and his hair, under a flat, broad-brimmed hat, was long and

flowing. His regular, pale features were impassive and the *sang-froid* with which he was gazing at the good folk in the boxes showed to what depths of degradation and desolation the theatre had fallen.

(Gautier 2011: 133)

For Gautier, the first night of *Hernani* would be 'the most important occasion of the century, for it was to be the start of a free, young, school of thought', and he dressed 'to annoy and scandalise the philistines' (Gautier 2011: 129, 132). The dress of the group of 'young Shakespearean Barbarians' was, as Gautier recalled, designed to signal the coming of a new 'free' generation, wearing clothes that,

> combining eccentric fantasy with a feeling for colour, inclined more to paint-ing. Their satin, velvet, braiding, decorative fastenings and trimmings of fur, had every bit as much value as your lawyer's black frock coat and too-short silk waistcoat straining over his belly, his starched muslin cravat hiding his chin, and the points of his collar like blinkers on either side of his gold-rimmed spectacles.

(Gautier 2011: 136)

Gautier was keen to stress that this was a stylistic, not a political rebellion. The famous red waistcoat of which he was proud was made from a fabric with a hint of purple 'to avoid the infamous red of [17]93 … because I did not want to be accused of political leanings. I was not one of Saint-Just's and Robespierre's henchmen like some of my friends' (Gautier 2011: 132). Gautier admits that, despite his intentions, these young men might easily have been associated with the revolutionaries of the previous century, when bright red was the colour of revolutionary terror. The government-supporting paper *Quotidienne* felt the need to reassure its readers just before the play opened that its innovations were to be restricted to the realm of art: 'whatever importance *Hernani* may have for the literary republic, there is no occasion for the French monarchy to feel any anxi-ety about it' (Hugo 1863: 2: 270). Whether that was true or not, there was clearly an association between artistic and political rebellion in the minds of many who awaited the opening night of Hugo's play.

   On the day of the first performance Gautier's group of 'champions of ideas, defenders of free art' (Gautier 2011: 136) gathered outside the theatre at one in the afternoon. They had obtained permission to enter before the rest of the audi-ence in order to plan their actions for the evening. For some reason, however, they were kept waiting at the entrance in the Rue de Valois for two hours, making quite a spectacle for the passing Parisian bourgeoisie, who gazed 'stupefied and indignant' (Hugo 1863: 2: 272) at their outlandish clothes and long hair. Some of the many employees of the theatre who did not approve of Hugo or his play took the opportunity to besmirch the fine clothes of the Romantics by throwing rubbish and filth of various kinds from the roof onto them. Balzac was hit by a cabbage stump. The young men reacted angrily, but soon realised that they must not give the police any reason to remove them, and endured the bombardment with gritted teeth. Eventually, at three in the afternoon they were admitted and settled in the near-dark of the auditorium to prepare for the battle to come. They spent their time discussing the play to come, singing, eating, making animal noises and generally larking around (Gautier 2011: 140).

Their spirits remained high, and the young men grew even more excitable as the gas-lights began to be lit and the audience began to arrive. With their enemy in sight, their attack began. Gautier felt that these older theatregoers of the Théâtre-Français were 'the enemies of art, of the ideal, of liberty and poetry'. He felt a desire to 'scalp their heads with a tomahawk' – except that he would have 'run the risk of collecting more wigs than scalps'. Disgusted at the 'aspect of these hairless stumps, the colour of flesh and rancid butter', one young sculptor cried out 'to the guillotine, bald-pates!' – political and artistic revolution remained hard to separate in that moment (Gautier 2011: 133). Their response to the female members of the audience was rather different. As the young women entered, their shoulders bare in fashionable low-cut dresses, they were warmly applauded, 'which was found to be in the worst possible taste and height of rudeness by ugly old ladies', as Gautier sneeringly put it (Gautier 2011: 140). This rudeness appalled many of the actors and theatre workers, who peered out from the wings at an auditorium which bore a strong smell of garlic sausage from the afternoon's picnic. Mademoiselle Mars was furious at such events in her theatre. She sought out Hugo to confront him. 'You have nice friends!' she exclaimed, with great hauteur. 'I have performed before many an audience' she went on, 'but I shall owe it to you that I have acted before this kind of people' (Hugo 1863: 2: 273). Hugo tried to excuse his supporters' behaviour by citing their treatment that afternoon, but the hostile atmosphere to him prevailed backstage, with the exception of Joanny in the role of Ruy Gomez.

So fired up were Hugo's partisans that they were even shaking their fists and jeering at empty seats, accusing them of being bought by the Classicals and kept deliberately empty (Descotes 1955: 127). At last the moment came and there arose a grumbling roar from the factions in the audience as the curtains drew aside. On stage an old noblewoman dressed in black was drawing crimson curtains at the back of a dimly lit bedroom, and started to arrange the chairs as if expecting someone (Hugo 2004: 111). There is a knock, apparently from behind the panelled wall to the right. Doña Josefa pauses and waits for a second knock, then speaks:

> Can he be there already? (*another knock*) Yes, that's him at the stair
> Concealed. Let me open quick! Good day, fine cavalier ...[3]

This apparently harmless opening immediately caused uproar. In English verse drama there is nothing unusual about the sense of one line flowing into the following one (the technical term for this is enjambment). But in French neo-classical drama the convention had always been to keep the meaning of the line contained within the twelve-syllable line (the 'alexandrine'). Hugo was to break many conventions in *Hernani*, but he stuck to the alexandrine as his poetic measure. To break this convention in the very first line of the play was regarded, under these circumstances, as an outright provocation. Gautier, with typical flamboyance, called it an 'impudent enjambment … tweaking the nose of classicism to provoke a duel' (Gautier 2011: 141). Immediately there was a cry of protest from the Classicals, to be answered loudly, lengthily and pretentiously by a Romantic with long red curly hair:

> It isn't disrespect, it is beauty! Can't you see how the word 'concealed', carried forward like that and suspended outside the verse line, admirably depicts the secret staircase, a staircase of love and mystery spiralling up within the defensive wall of the manor! What marvellous architectonic skill! What a feeling for the art of the sixteenth century! What a profound understanding of an entire civilization …
>
> (Gautier 2011: 141)

The red-headed man was eventually hushed by a torrent of cries calling for his ejection. Through the secret door came Don Carlos, the King of Spain, who in a further innovation 'talked like a commoner and hid in a cupboard like a thief' (Carlson 1972: 165). Michelot, who played the King, had tried to persuade Hugo to rewrite a scene that failed to give a king the dignity which neo-classical drama had always provided, but in vain (Schumacher 2004: xxix). It was a further shock to the traditionalists, but also a political statement. 'Giving vulgar, commonplace speech to kings and nobles becomes a political act', writes the literary critic Jean Gaudon, 'since it tends to blur class differences and to deprive those at the top of the social pyramid of everything that distinguishes them: of, in short, their dignity' (Gaudon 1985: 175, translated by Daphne Wall).

Once Don Carlos was hidden again behind the secret door Mademoiselle Mars entered, dressed all in white. As the great female star of the Théâtre-Français she was accustomed to an enthusiastic burst of applause at her first appearance, but on this occasion she was met by complete silence (Hugo 1863: 2: 274). The Romantics suspected her of being an enemy of *Hernani* and the Classicals resented her even taking part in this production. She was uncharacteristically subdued on stage for a long time afterwards. But, as the performance went on, the explosion which the initial excitement had suggested never quite arrived on this first night. Gautier wrote much later, that 'elbows were sharp, and all that the quarrel was waiting for to burst out was the slightest contact; it was not difficult to see that this young man with long hair found this clean-shaven gentleman beside him a downright cretin' (Gautier 2011: 145), but there were to be no more than a few minor scuffles. Perhaps the presence of the large Romantic *claque* was just too intimidating.

The next flashpoint was the spectacle in Act Two of Don Carlos the King asking for the time as he lies in wait with his noblemen to intercept Hernani, who is attending a secret tryst with Doña Sol (Hugo 1863: 2: 131). For the Classicals, such a simple question was again regarded as behaviour beneath the dignity of a monarch. It caused cries of protest, soon shouted down in turn, but again no violence. In principle the idea of 'decorum' in neo-classical drama was solely a matter of dramatic theory. Characters represented ideals, since the function of art was to show a more beautiful and refined realm than the 'real' world, and to provide a more elevated, purer experience than that offered in 'normal' life. But in Paris in 1830 the representation of a king being concerned with such a mundane matter as asking the time – placing him in the workaday world and not in a timeless realm of poetry and emotion – could not but also be understood politically. The idea that a king was just a man had inspired the revolution which began in 1789, and the restoration of the hereditary Bourbon monarchy by Napoleon's conquerors in 1815 rankled with very many in the audience and elsewhere. Indeed, Hernani was being performed in what turned out to be the final days of the reign of Charles X, the last, would-be absolutist King of France. Once more theatrical riots demonstrate the continuing inseparability of the theatre and politics.

The scene in Ruy Gomez's picture gallery which had already been pilloried at the Vaudeville was the next critical moment. Would it be laughed off the stage? Don Carlos arrives at Gomez's castle and accuses the old lord of sheltering the bandit Hernani. Gomez admits that he is in the castle (at which point Doña Sol, typically, '*hides her head in her hands and collapses into a chair*') (Hugo 2004: 159). Instead of producing Hernani immediately, the old man pauses, thinks and gives the King a tour of the portraits of his ancestors hanging on the wall, identifying each in turn and listing each of his forebears' accomplishments in battle. At the end of the sequence – his own portrait – Gomez reveals that he will not betray Hernani after all. Pointing to his own picture, he cries 'Would you have those who see it say: "This last, the worthy son of a heroic race, was a traitor, and sold the life of a man he sheltered as a guest!"' (Hugo 2004: 161). The dramatic effect which Hugo is striving after is plain, but the execution is heavy-handed to say the least. Gomez gives an account of no fewer than eleven different portraits before reaching his conclusion. There were many more portraits on the wall than this which were visible to the audience. After the first eight he skips to the last three in the sequence, since the King is getting impatient, and he pleads that 'there are many more [of my ancestors], far better than I could mention'. To the audience, however, after five or six potted biographies with many more in sight the inept build-up of dramatic tension towards such an obvious conclusion by piling up so many identical accounts of heroism in battle did appear ludicrous, effectively putting them on the side of the wicked Don Carlos, who cries out 'Is this a joke?' On the first night no complaints were heard until the sixth portrait; the seventh and eighth were hissed; just in time Joanny moved on. Adèle Hugo writes that Gomez's account of his own portrait 'was received with acclamations', applause that was redoubled when his defiance of the King was then made plain; 'from that moment no-one in the green room had any doubt about the success of the piece'.

Those many partisans of Hugo who wrote in defence of *Hernani* regard audience hostility to be the product of sheer artistic reaction. But there is also a case to be made that those who were to hiss and ridicule the play, in increasing numbers as the run went on, were also reacting to the difference between the Romantic hype about the play and the poor quality of Hugo's dramatic writing. The elegant, subtle and intricate neo-classical twelve-syllable line was not well suited to the kind of emotionally charged, poetically over-elaborate utterance which Hugo gave to his characters, even if this style of poetry enjoyed such popularity off the stage. Nor did it sound right to express conversational, colloquial speech in such a verse form, carrying all the associations of a 'moderate, reasonable discourse' (Gaudon 1985: 170). When Doña Sol tells Doña Josefa in Act One to 'dry her coat' the domestic sentiment sounds absurd in this verse form (Gaudon 1985: 174). What was intended to be bold and innovative simply sounded clumsy and silly to many of the usual audience of the Théâtre-Français, and maybe they were right. *Hernani* was only Hugo's fourth adult attempt at a play. *Amy Ronsard* had failed on stage, *Marion de Lorme* had been banned and *Cromwell* was generally agreed to be unstageable. The twentieth-century critic George Steiner found *Hernani* 'intolerable', a 'vehement triviality' and in the theatre 'it is difficult to last the distance' (Steiner 1961: 160–1).

The bad construction of Act Four also got off lightly that first night. The act is expensively set in a replica of Aachen Cathedral's crypt at the tomb of Charlemagne, the eighth-century founder of the conglomeration of European states known as the Holy Roman Empire. By the early sixteenth century, when *Hernani* is set, the Emperor was elected by various princes and bishops. The first scene of the act clunkily works through the names of a group of conspirators who are planning to kill Don Carlos (none of whom have appeared in the play before), then embarks on a tedious explanation of the how the votes are stacked for and against the King of Spain in the coming election. Left alone in Scene Two, Don Carlos embarks on a 1,600-word soliloquy addressed to the hero's tomb, full of grandiloquent words as the King sets out his boundless ambitions and asks for guidance on 'how to conquer and how to rule, and which is the nobler, to punish or to pardon!' (Hugo 2004: 177). That first night at least the speech had been shortened, and Michelot in the role worked hard not to send the speech up. The Romantics worked hard to protect one of the play's weakest moments with repeated cries of 'bravo!' In future performances, however, the interminable melodramatic pomposity of the speech would bring peals of laughter. When Don Carlos had to speak lines like this,

DON CARLOS (*aside, his hand on his heart*) Be still, young heart, and douse your flame! Be ruled by those saner thoughts which you have disturbed for so long. From now on your loves, your mistresses, alas, shall be Germany, Flanders, Spain.

(Hugo 2004: 188)

The laughter 'redoubled' (Hugo 1863: 2: 284).

But some people were impressed, and others saw the opportunity to make money. Adèle Hugo recounts how a publisher, Mame ('a little man with a round belly and staring eyes'), summoned Hugo from the theatre at the end of Act Four to offer him six thousand francs in cash for the rights to the play. Hugo suggested they wait until the play was over, but Monsieur Mame pleaded that by the end of Act Five he would have to offer ten thousand for the deal to be accepted. Hugo was happy to sign the contract there and then on the counter of a nearby *tabac*, an ordinary tobacco shop. Adèle reports that the money was 'by no means unacceptable, as he had no more than fifty francs in his possession' (Hugo 1863: 2: 266).

Up until Act Five Mademoiselle Mars had not had the chance to shine on stage. When she finally appeared as Hernani's bride dressed in white satin with a crown of roses on her head, 'with her brilliant teeth and her figure, which always looked as if she were just eighteen, she produced all the effect of youth and beauty', recalled Adèle Hugo (Hugo 1863: 2: 278). But despite the reservations she had expressed about the production, as a professional she was prepared to act in the way the play demanded. In expressing her love for Hernani and her desire to die with him she produced a display of romantic passion which was quite unexpected, dying with 'the terrifying convulsions of a long agony' (Hugo 1863: 2: 278). The critic Pontmartin also called her acting 'sublime' and felt she must have learned how to die on stage from the English actresses (cited in Descotes 1955: 129). A shower of bouquets fell at her feet when the curtain call came soon after. In her dressing room she called Hugo over and permitted him to kiss her cheek. The first night of Hernani, it was agreed, had been a triumph after all.

But the hostile press were not won over. Those reviewers with less animosity, who tactfully recognised that the play's merits were 'lyric, not dramatic' (Davison 1912: 85), concentrated on praising the sets and costumes rather than other aspects of the whole production (Descotes 1955: 129). The real test of the play, and the real trouble, would come when Hugo's Romantic *claque* was no longer there to defend it from the ridicule of the general public. For the second and third performances the flamboyant young men continued to attend and to try to silence any ridicule, but they still could not prevent the gallery scene in Act Three getting, in Hugo's own words, 'rough treatment' (cited in Descotes 1955: 129). There was still some childish behaviour from the Romantics: on both nights someone dropped a swarm of tiny pieces of white paper from above onto the dress circle and into the more expensive seats, which stuck annoyingly to 'people's coats, to ladies' curls, and even fell into the bosoms of their dresses' (Hugo 1863: 2: 282). This later seems to have become a tradition at Hugo's plays. The police were concerned that violence might break out at any moment, and tried to ban curtain calls as a possible flashpoint. Nevertheless, all the actors defiantly came on together at the end, unusually, to avoid certain of them being singled out by the *claque* or its opponents.

There were certainly moments in the play whose obvious anti-aristocratic tenor would have gained Hugo powerful enemies, such as when the medal of the noble Order of the Golden Fleece is described as 'just a yellow sheep that I am going to hang round my neck', or when the King declares of his courtiers in Act Four that 'the truth is, they'd sell their soul for a title' (Gaudon 1985: 177, his translation of Hugo 2004: 128, 172). Hugo received threatening anonymous letters, one offering to 'take away your appetite for dinner' if he didn't close the play within twenty-four hours (Gaudon 1985: 290). After this Hugo had two bodyguards each evening who insisted on escorting him home from the theatre until the end of the run.

After the fourth performance, on 3 March 1830, the Romantics were limited by the management to a hundred tickets in the 1,500-seat theatre. From now on the play began to be hissed and jeered generally. The rump of the *claque* responded with personal abuse. A young woman laughing uproariously at the gallery scene was told to stop since she was showing her bad teeth (Gaudon 1985: 287). An old man who misheard Hernani's insult to Ruy Gomez, '*vieillard stupide*' ('stupid old man') as '*viel as de pique*' ('old ace of spades') and who objected to the insult, was upbraided absurdly for his ignorance by Dumas' friend Lassailly, who hadn't been listening to the play but still defended what he took to be a piece of authentic sixteenth-century invective (Dumas 1989: 1100). The insults most frequently hurled by the Romantics at those who hissed or jeered reveal their age and prejudices: 'wig-head', 'fossil' and 'grocer' are recorded. Many members of the audience, as they became bored or annoyed by the play would turn their backs, or just open their newspapers and start reading. Others cried out 'I can't stand this anymore!' and left in the middle of an Act, banging the door of their box if they had one. Nearly every line seems to have been hissed at some point in the run, but the portrait scene in Act Three and Don Carlos's monologue in Act Four remained the most barracked, with much of the audience standing on their seats at those moments. Elsewhere, a comedian gave a public reading of the play in which he succeeded in sending up every single line of it. Outrage at the flouting of traditional conventions had turned into outright ridicule.

The actors struggled on. Some even let the audience know they shared their feelings about the play, winking in complicity as they spoke a line they thought absurd. Mademoiselle Mars kept performing as required, but Hugo complained that she would laugh at the play off stage even in front of the author. He nevertheless made sure that there was a picked group of *hernanistes* in the orchestra stalls who would offer her loud applause, and give her bouquets every night. Michelot, more publicly disenchanted, took to playing his role as the King with his hands in his pockets. He started deliberately skipping over parts of the Act Four monologue, especially those most ridiculed. But one of the Romantics in the orchestra pit was keeping furious notes to check that he was delivering the text faithfully, ready to hold him to account. Firmin as Hernani did his best, and would repeat a line which had been drowned out by audience whistling up to three times in order to be heard (Descotes 1955: 130–4). Joanny kept a journal, in which he expressed his exasperation. On 5 March he wrote 'there is something of a paradox about this: if the play is so bad, why do people come. If they are so anxious to come, why do they whistle?' (cited in Roy 2003: 420). He eventually confided that he didn't feel he could keep going. On 8 March the play was jeered from beginning to end.

It was on 10 March that violence broke out. The Romantics launched an attack on the jeerers in the stalls. Joanny recalls fists flying. The play was interrupted and the police intervened. There is a contemporary illustration of the fighting by Grandville. It would appear to depict the play's last moments with Hernani and Doña Sol lying dead at the feet of old Ruy Gomez, but the picture gallery from Act Three also appears stage left. In the orchestra pit a crowd of young men with waxed moustaches and pointed beards, their long hair flying behind them, wave their arms excitedly and point at the stage. In the foreground two of them have grabbed an older, bespectacled member of the audience by the beard, toppling him backwards off his feet. Arrests were made, and there was uproar. It seems the play was performed to the end even so.

By 29 March Joanny felt that it was almost impossible to perform any more. The strain told, and he and Mademoiselle Mars later became ill. Finally the run came to an end on 22 June, after thirty-nine performances. It had taken a huge amount of money. The first night alone took 5,134 francs. After the first nineteen performances the takings stood at 76,092 francs (Howarth 1975: 15). The actors had taken a lot of criticism in the press for on-stage ranting, but they were well rewarded.

Beyond the Rue Richelieu the play suddenly became a rallying point for the young. *Hernani* was performed in at least three colleges by the company to great acclaim from the students, even if their teachers tried to restrain their pupils' enthusiasm. In Toulouse a young man named Batlam fought a duel in defence of *Hernani*, and was killed. A corporal of dragoons died that year at Vannes and asked that his tombstone should bear the words 'Here lies one who believed in Victor Hugo' (Hugo 1863: 2: 291).

Liberal opposition to Charles X's monarchy, amongst the young, but also amongst the people in general, was reaching a critical point during March and April 1830, even within the ruling class. In Restoration France there was a parliament of sorts, modelled on the unreformed British system. The Chamber of Deputies had such a high property qualification that only the very rich could be members, and only the rich could vote for them. Yet on 18 March 221 members of the chamber voted for what was, in effect, a no confidence motion in the King's government and the ministers he had chosen, the chief of whom was the ultra-Royalist Jules de Polignac. A right-wing newspaperman joked to Hugo that he and Polignac were the most hated men in France, albeit for different reasons (Hugo 1863: 2: 290). The King dissolved parliament the following day but the elections which took place in May only returned an even more liberal-minded assembly. When in July the King reacted by suspending press freedom, dissolving the new parliament and decreeing new restrictions on its powers and on the right to vote, an uprising broke out. In three days the King was swept from power in a violent insurrection and forced to flee in exile to England. In his place came a new, more liberal constitutional monarchy, with a distant cousin of Charles X, Louis Philippe, taking the throne as the more democratic-sounding 'King of the French', not 'King of France'. He was to be the first of the nineteenth-century pseudo-bourgeois monarchs, walking the streets as a private individual and drinking in cafés like any other middle-class Parisian, at least in the early years of his reign (Edwards 1971: 84). By 1832 his ministers would be banning Hugo's play *Le Roi s'amuse*.

The Battle of *Hernani* was thus taking place at a revolutionary moment in Paris, in a turbulent political atmosphere when Romanticism in art could not be kept apart from opposition politics, whether liberal or Bonapartist. An analogy can certainly be drawn between the Romantic rebellion against the neo-classical conventions of the Théatre-Français embodied in Hugo's *Hernani*, and the demands for freedom of expression both in the press and in parliament which were an important motivation for the anti-Bourbon revolutionaries of July 1830. *Hernani* might also be seen as a bourgeois theatrical storming of the palace of *ancien regime* culture. The young bohemians who championed the play were also champions of the new popular, commercial art against what they saw as stuffy and elitist (Gluck 2008: 35). It cannot be claimed that the first production of *Hernani* was a spark to revolutionary violence on the streets, as was the case with *Venice Preserv'd* in 1795 (see Chapter 2). Rather, it embodied the modern, libertarian mood of that moment of political crisis, which is perhaps why it produced such strong passions. It is also a play about a heroic adventurer in conflict with a tyrannical monarch which ends not with the foundation of a republic, but with the establishment of a better kind of monarchy; and the outlaw turns out to have been a good nobleman after all. Unlike the Old Price Riots of 1809 in London or the 1849 Astor Place massacre in New York, this was not really class conflict; nor was the right to participate in what was becoming 'high culture' at stake.

The victory won by the *hernanistes* was to establish Romantic drama securely as a respectable form of theatre in France, but it had not conquered the citadel. The Théatre-Français rarely put on Romantic drama for a long time after 1830. It carried on as it had before, albeit with considerable resentment on both sides of the dispute. As the genre gained respect and a wider following, however, *Hernani* no longer seemed so ridiculous. It also became more of a symbol of anti-authoritarianism than a play in its own right. It was staged again in 1838 with several of the old cast, including Firmin and Joanny (Descotes 1955: 135). Adèle Hugo remarks with amusement how the play's warm reception on that occasion vindicated it as having in fact been in advance of public taste, in her opinion (Hugo 1863: 2: 291). After being banned in 1852 for political reasons, it was restaged as 'a triumph' in 1877, with the great Sarah Bernhardt as Doña Sol. Hugo had become a major figure in French national life by this point. But this was the play's last hurrah. Giuseppe Verdi had adapted the play as an opera in 1844, though it is rarely performed. *Hernani* is uncommon on the French stage today (there was, however, a performance as recently as February 2012 at the small Théâtre de Deux Rêves in Paris). The Battle of *Hernani* was a landmark in the history of the French theatre, but it was also a symptom of a bigger political and cultural transformation, and perhaps it was not ultimately about the content, or even the style, of Hugo's play at all. It demonstrated how important a barometer the Parisian theatre was to the political weather in all of France. It was again to be so, in even more violent circumstances a century later, as Chapter 8 will tell.

Notes

1 In Golder's translation (Hugo 2004: 155) it is 'You are my generous, proud lion …'.
2 My translation; the new line was 'Crois tu, donc, que pour nous il soit des noms sacrés' (Hugo 1863: 2: 265).
3 Gautier 2011: 141, in Daphne Wall's translation. I have used this version to show the enjambment in the French original.

References

Carlson, Marvin (1972), *The French Stage in the Nineteenth Century* (Metuchen NJ: The Scarecrow Press).

Davison, A. F. (1912), *Victor Hugo, His Life and Work* (London: Eveleigh Nash).

Descotes, Maurice (1955), *Le Drame Romantique et ses Grands Créateurs* (Paris: Presses Universitaires de France).

Dumas, Alexandre (1989), *Mes Mémoires 1802–30* (Paris: Robert Laffont).

Edwards, Samuel (1971), *Victor Hugo: A Tumultuous Life* (New York: David McKay).

Gaudon, Jean (1985), *Victor Hugo et le Théâtre* (Paris: Editions Suger).

Gautier, Théophile (2011), *Histoire du Romantisme* (Paris: Éditions Gallimard).

Gluck, Mary (2008), *Popular Bohemia: Modernism and Urban Culture in Nineteenth-Century Paris* (Cambridge MA: Harvard University Press).

Howarth, William D. (1975), *Sublime and Grotesque: A Study of French Romantic Drama* (London: Harrap).

—— (1995), 'French Renaissance and Neo-Classical Theatre', in John Russell Brown (ed.) *The Oxford Illustrated History of Theatre* (Oxford: Oxford University Press).

Hugo, Adèle (1863), *Victor Hugo: A Life Related by One who has Witnessed It* (London: W. H. Allen).

Hugo, Victor (2004), *Hernani*, trans. John Golder, in *Victor Hugo, Four Plays*, ed. Claude Schumacher (London: Methuen).

McEvoy, Sean (ed.) (2006), *William Shakespeare's 'Hamlet': A Sourcebook* (London: Routledge).

Roy, Donald (2003), *Romantic and Revolutionary Theatre, 1789–1860* (Cambridge: Cambridge University Press).

Schumacher, Claude (2004), 'Introduction', in *Victor Hugo, Four Plays*, ed. Claude Schumacher (London: Methuen).

Steiner, George (1961), *The Death of Tragedy* (London: Faber & Faber).

Chapter 5

Theatre's bloodiest night
The New York riots of 1849

When the great William Charles Macready, the 'Eminent Tragedian', set off from London for his second tour of the United States in 1848 he seriously intended that his visit would be a prelude to settling in America for good. Macready loathed the social injustices of Victorian England and personally despised its aristocracy. As revolutions spread rapidly across Europe that year, he looked forwards to what he expected to be the imminent class conflict which might bring some freedom to England's labouring masses, but wanted to place his own family out of harm's way in a country whose democratic principles he admired, at least in theory (Downer 1966: 286–7). But the tour was to end with Macready smuggled out of the country, his life in danger from angry men who regarded themselves as true American patriots. Macready also left behind at least thirty dead and over 150 wounded New Yorkers, the result of a savage disturbance at the Astor Place Opera House on the evening of 10 May 1849, in what was the bloodiest episode of civil unrest since the foundation of the United States of America (Cliff 2007: 241).

There had been sporadic trouble throughout the tour. The strangest incident was when half a dead sheep was hurled onto the stage by a protestor while Macready was performing *Hamlet* in Cincinnati ('disgusting brutality, indecent outrage, and malevolent barbarism' fulminated Macready in his diary) (Downer 1966: 296). Yet he was also received with enormous civility. In New Orleans in the slave-owning south, after triumphing in *Othello*, he had been treated at a banquet in his honour as a conquering hero. The newspaper *The Spirit of the Times* reported that

> behind the chairman was hung an admirably executed portrait of the tra-
> gedian, and in front of him, when the dessert was spread, were placed a
> facsimile of Shakespeare's house at Stratford-upon-Avon, and a temple of
> Thespis [the legendary inventor of Greek tragedy], both in confectionery, the
> latter inscribed with the principal characters of the drama, in the personation
> of which Mr Macready excels.

> (Cited in Downer 1966: 295)

The toast was drunk to Shakespeare and Macready, 'the greatest dead poet; the greatest living actor; the former the diamond; the latter, the golden setting in which the brilliant shines'. Back in London, *Punch* suggested that there was perhaps some contradiction between the local papers praising Macready's depiction of the heroic Moor – himself an ex-slave (1.3.151–2) – and yet advertising black men and women for sale as slaves in the same pages. This was a time of considerable political friction between the two countries, a factor which was to play a full part in the riots to follow.

Macready intended to settle in America amongst the New England intelligentsia, with whom he felt most at home, but at least when he came to New York he was to perform in a theatre of some exclusivity. The recently opened Astor Place Opera House was located on one of the city's class fault lines, between prosperous Broadway and the impoverished and gang-ridden Bowery and the slums of Five-Points. The theatre served only New York's wealthier theatrical patrons. The dress code for men specified 'freshly shaven faces, evening dress, fresh waistcoats and kid gloves' (Cliff 2007: xiv). The voluminous evening dress then fashionable for women would also require a highly expensive coach to transport the wearer through the muddy streets. Unaccompanied women were not admitted, in an attempt to bar the prostitutes who generally used theatre bars to pick up clients. There was no pit, as such: this traditionally popular area of the auditorium nearest the stage had been replaced by the 'parquette': rows of armchairs similar in function to the 'stalls' which would soon complete the job of cleansing the pits of London's theatres of rowdies. The theatre itself had only been completed the previous year, financed by subscriptions from 'wealthy aspirers to fashion' (Moody 1958: 103), and had been luxuriously appointed, with gilt and white latticework on the galleries and a huge sparkling chandelier suspended over the parquette.

All of this was most congenial to Macready. He had painfully endured the discomforts and difficulties of travelling vast distances across the United States in order to earn the money he required to live in an elegant way. Macready was fifty-six years old and feeling his advancing years. He had been educated to be a gentleman at public school, but had then entered the theatre, initially as a manager, in order to save the fortunes of his bankrupt actor-father William McCready (the son's amended surname served both to distinguish him from his father and perhaps to distance him a little from his Irish origin; Downer 1966: 16). When he performed in some of the more rudimentary theatres of the American south and west, with their lively audiences, he felt that he was regressing to the times when he was little more than a teenage strolling player in the English provinces during the troubled years following the end of the war with Napoleon.

The 'stock' system of the mid-nineteenth century in Britain and America meant that each provincial theatre would have a group of resident actors who knew, or should have known, the lesser parts in a standard repertory of Shakespeare and popular contemporary plays. The touring 'star' would arrive and take the main role, accompanied perhaps by one or two touring colleagues. Macready did not hide his contempt for the insufficiency of his fellow performers on these occasions.

Even in Boston he despaired at having to act in *Othello* with 'a Desdemona
[Othello's youthful bride] of 50, patched up to 45'. When he played King Lear,
his daughter Goneril was at least sober, he remarked, but 'distressful!' in her acting; his youngest daughter Cordelia did not understand what she was saying, and
was 'as haggard and old as Tisiphone' (one of the ugly Furies who pursued mur-
derers in Greek myth). He described the unfortunate actress who played opposite
him in Coleman's eighteenth-century comedy *The Jealous Wife* as having a 'face
to make a dog vomit!' Macready's intemperate hauteur was not always found
endearing by his colleagues (Moody 1958: 73).

On the opening night at the Astor Place Opera House, however, he felt much
more comfortable, assured of the quality of his mostly British cast (Downer
1966: 297). He was also much more at ease about the likely conduct of the audience. Macready was certainly aware of the excitement which had been stirred
up in advance of his taking the stage as Macbeth in New York that evening,
Monday, 7 May 1849. Two other productions of *Macbeth* were to open in the city
that same night. Thomas Hamblin was playing Macbeth at the Bowery Theatre,
and at the Broadway Theatre Macready's great rival, the American actor Edwin
Forrest, was also about to take the stage in the same role (Moody 1958: 104).
Macready saw Forrest's choice of play as provocative, but was confident that
his playing of the Scottish usurper would clearly demonstrate his greater talent
as an actor and his superior understanding of Shakespeare's play. There was
certainly some hint of potential trouble in the air. The newspaper correspond-
ent for the Philadelphia *Ledger* wrote that 'the great theatrical warfare, which
begins tonight, is the leading topic of town conversation today. This triangular
is expected to be productive of curious incidents during the evening – and not of
the most felicitous character, either' (cited in Moody 1958: 106). And, indeed,
there was a significant body of police on duty in and around the Astor Place
Theatre, accompanied by George Matsell, the Chief of Police for the City. But
Macready was complacent enough as the curtain rose.

The actor playing Macbeth does not enter until the third scene of the first Act.
When Macready heard the audience cheering Macduff's entrance in the previous
scene, he smiled (according to his diary) and said to himself 'they mistake him
for me'.[1] But the noise came from the gallery, where the crowd gave a round
of applause and three cheers at the appearance of an American actor, Corson
Clarke. However, they were cheering because he was American, not because he
was Clarke.

Macready was disabused of his complacency as soon as he made his first
entrance. There were cheers from the parquette, and the ladies in the boxes waved
their handkerchiefs – but pandemonium broke out in the gallery, and in parts
of the parquette, and it was entirely directed at him. Potatoes, an old shoe and
a cent piece were flung at him. According to the New York *Herald*, Macready
'picked up the copper coin, and with a kingly air, put it in his bosom, bowing, at
the same time, with mock humility, to the quarter of the gallery from which the
visitation had descended' (cited in Downer 1966: 298). Much worse was flung.

The protestors had come armed with quantities of asafoetida, the gum extracted from an Indian herb which is vile-smelling when raw, and appropriately known as 'devil's dung'. This substance was 'dispensed profusely over the actors creating a most repulsive stench in the house' (Moody 1958: 109). The first of several rotten eggs landed at Macready's feet, bespattering the stage. In partial explanation for this assault two banners were strung across the front of the gallery. One read 'No apologies – it is too late!' and the other 'You have ever proved yourself a liar!' Stamping, screaming, hooting and hissing continued, with Macready's supporters attempting to cheer on their hero, chanting 'Go on! Go on!' in response to the gallery's 'Off! Off!' (Downer 1966: 298).

It was clear to Macready that these rioters were partisans of his rival, Edwin Forrest. The Eminent Tragedian was no stranger to theatrical disturbance. His first ever visit to the London theatre had been on the second night of the Old Price Riots at Covent Garden in 1809, where he had seen something similar (Downer 1966: 298; see p.56, this volume). He now approached the footlights and stood absolutely still for some fifteen minutes while he waited for a hearing. According to his diary he wanted to express the 'pain and shame which the intelligent and respectable must feel for their country's reputation', and to offer to 'instantly resign my engagement rather than encounter such disgraceful conduct' (cited in Cliff 2007: 17–18). Macready had no doubt that this riot was part of the continuing culture war between England and America, and that the gallery was scoring an own goal against the USA in that particular competition. But he was completely ignored. Eventually gave up and signalled to the actors to continue the play.

Little could be heard in the tumult. The police who were present made no attempt to intervene. In the interval at the end of Act One a gentlemen in the boxes tried to plead with the rioters, only to be mocked and then drowned out by the lusty signing of a Methodist hymn, accompanied by dancing and stamping on the red plush armchairs of the parquette. Some of the cast were not keen to go out again to face the barrage, but Macready insisted, and Act Two was got through. It was when Macready appeared as the King of Scotland at the beginning of Act Three that the calibre of the projectiles deployed caused him to give up the cause. Four chairs were hurled from the upper tier. The first landed in the orchestra pit, sending the musicians scurrying for cover. The second landed just in front of Mrs Pope, who was playing Lady Macbeth. The third and fourth just missed Macready, but smashed and splintered around him. Macready bowed to the audience, and remarked to one of the actors, William Chippendale, that that 'had quite fulfilled' his obligation to the theatre managers, and he 'would remain no longer' (Moody 1958: 110). The curtain came down to roars of triumph. Outside, a crowd could be heard beating at the doors to get in. At this point the police barricaded most of the doors but saw the ladies safely off the premises.

Macready thought of arming himself with his stage dagger in order to get safely off the premises, but in the end thought it unworthy of him to stoop to such an expedient, and threw it down again. Accompanied by two friends he simply left by the back door and calmly made his way to his hotel nearby.

In the theatre, Corson Clarke came on stage to tell the rioters that Macready had now gone. Some accused him of betrayal for associating with the Englishman, but he defended his right to follow his profession and to make an honest living. For half an hour longer the same cries went up before the crowd dispersed: 'Three groans for the English bulldog!', 'Nine cheers for Edwin Forrest!', 'Down with the codfish aristocracy!', 'Huzza for native talent!' (Moody 1958: 111).

In these slogans can be seen the reasons behind the Monday night riot, and the feelings that would lead to much bloodshed on Thursday 10 May. The rioters were drawn from the working men of the city, for many of whom Edwin Forrest was a hero. A feud had developed between the two men whereby the two actors had come to stand for conflicting political positions. Macready was lionised by New York City's Anglophile wealthy. Some of these families had originally made their wealth in trading Atlantic cod, hence their satirical nickname of 'codfish aristocracy', a term of particular contempt in a Republic which prided itself on being comprised of equal citizens, at least in theory. Class conflict was only part of the story, however. 'Native' was an emotive word in American politics at the time. The 'Nativists' were men born in America who resented the influx of new immigrants into the Republic. In particular their anger was directed against the huge numbers of Roman Catholic Irish fleeing famine at home after the failure of the potato crop in 1845–6. In the last years of the 1840s a hundred thousand or more Irish people were arriving in New York each year, and many remained in the city (Cliff 2007: 191). The Nativists felt that the rugged virtues of those born American would supply every need, economic and cultural, of the new Republic. No newcomers were needed, especially Catholics. There were older resentments at play, too. Britain and America had fought a major war in 1812–14 and periods of diplomatic tension followed, not least in 1847–8. Aristocratic, arrogant Britain, as personified by Macready, was the old enemy of the Nativists – but also, of course, of the Irish. Previously the most bloody riot on American soil had occurred when the Nativists had set upon the Irish in Philadelphia in 1844 (Cliff 2007: 241). The Militia had shot dead at least six on that occasion. Uniquely, hatred for Macready in 1849 united both the Nativist and Irish gangs on the same side.

The origins of the fighting on the streets of May 1849 lay then in the personal rivalry between Edwin Forrest and William Charles Macready, but also in the wider political situation, both in the city itself, and internationally between Britain and America at the time.

Forrest's Macbeth that night received a totally different reception at the Broadway Theatre, a mile from Astor Place. When Macbeth reached the lines in Act Five 'What rhubarb, senna, or what purgative drug/ Would scour these English hence?' the whole audience rose to their feet and cheered wildly (5.3.61–2). A New York paper described Forrest as a 'great American tragedian' who 'delineated the character of Macbeth in a style of unsurpassed beauty'. 'The bursts of applause which followed from the enraptured audience' were apparently 'truly astonishing' (Cliff 2007: 113). 'Beauty' was not, however, always the first idea which occurred to Forrest's audiences, and especially the more urbane ones. At the age of forty-two Forrest remained a physically imposing figure: broad-chested, muscular and powerful. His style of acting was marked also by its energy, volume and bursts of violent emotion. In 1908 the critic William Winter recalled Forrest in the New York *Tribune* as follows:

> He had a magnificent voice, powerful, rich, copious, various, resonant; a face of leonine strength and lowering menace; dark, piercing eyes, and a person of rugged build; and in theatrical situations of peril, suspense, or conflict, requiring the opposition of granite solidity, physical power, and vehement, tumultuous, overwhelming vociferation, he was tremendously effective.
>
> (Cited in Moses 1969: 334)

Unfortunately, notes his biographer Montrose J. Moses,

> An actor of such power could easily fall into absurd excesses, especially where physical realism took the place of spiritual insight. Winter recalls how Forrest would loll out his tongue in terror, contort the muscles of his face, pant, snort, snarl, gasp, and gurgle in the agonies of death.
>
> (Moses 1969: 334)

Macready and others felt that Forrest did not always understand Shakespeare. In *Othello*, he could not portray the Moor's jealousy and love at the same time; as Macbeth, he could not convey the horror in Macbeth's sense of remorse for his crimes (Moses 1969: 340). He was 'eloquent' but 'deficient in imagination':

> The fault of his reading was in its mannerism; he developed its virtues sometimes to an excess, and used his voice too much as if it were a musical instrument. His emphasis was occasionally too elaborate, and the way he uttered Hamlet's first words, 'A little more than kin and less than kind,' showed at the very beginning his misconception of the character.
>
> (Moses 1969: 341)

But Forrest's love for Shakespeare could not be doubted. As a fourteen-year-old he was mocked by his employer at the ship's chandlers for reciting soliloquies in the office. He secured his longed-for professional stage debut at that age in peculiar circumstances. As a volunteer at a demonstration of the effects of laughing gas at the Tivoli Gardens Theatre in Philadelphia, Forrest squeaked a speech from *Richard III* with such power that he won an influential patron. At fifteen he appeared at the Walnut Street Theatre, and at seventeen he set off as a touring performer. Performing in ramshackle and sometimes violent theatres in the south and west of the rapidly expanding United States enabled Forrest to develop the rugged style which enthused audiences in New Orleans in particular. When he returned to the East Coast in 1825 he performed with the passionate and charismatic English actor Edmund Kean at Albany in New York State. Drink and riotous living had dimmed Kean's fire somewhat (he was still only thirty-six), and he was hounded by audiences for his recent public adultery, but everything about Kean's fulminous acting validated Forrest's own style. Kean praised and encouraged the young man when Forrest played Iago to the great man's Othello. Perhaps Kean mentioned Macready by name to Forrest then, as the younger actor who had displaced him as London's leading tragedian, and whose ability he feared (FitzSimons 1976: 134–5).

In November 1826 at the Bowery Theatre in New York City Forrest established himself as a star in the role of Othello, and was hailed as 'The Native Tragedian' (Moses 1969: 87). For the first time America had its own champion actor, and did not need to import its high cultural icons from Europe. Forrest, whose own patriotism and populist, democratic politics were never in doubt, revelled in his new status. All that was left was to demonstrate American dramatic prowess to the British on home soil.

In October 1837 Forrest first played in London at Drury Lane, in one of his most famous muscular roles: the rebel Roman slave Spartacus in his countryman Robert Montgomery Bird's play *The Gladiator*. He declined to open in *Othello* because he was tactfully keen not to provoke comparison with the leading English Shakespearean, Macready. When Forrest did play the Moor soon afterwards most of the critics praised him, but John Forster – Charles Dickens's best friend, and a good friend of Macready, too – published a review stating that Forrest was 'given to little fierce bursts of passions', displaying 'no intellectual comprehension of what he was about' (Moody 1958: 36). Macready himself was currently feeling more insecure than normal, following a bad-tempered, undignified and well-publicised punch-up with Alfred Bunn, the unscrupulous manager of Drury Lane. Nevertheless, he graciously welcomed the American into his own home. Only to his diary did he confide his jealousy of Forrest's success. All too aware of his own capacity to lose control of his emotions, Macready did his utmost to avoid appearing threatened by the younger man's success (Forrest was thirty-one, Macready forty-four) (Moody 1958: 34–5).

After a tour of provincial theatres, Forrest returned to London, where he renewed his acquaintance with Macready's friend John Sinclair, and in particular with Sinclair's nineteen-year-old daughter Catherine. Catherine claimed to be smitten with the smouldering Forrest the moment she saw him, thinking him 'the handsomest man on whom my eyes have ever fallen'. The pair became engaged, but when Sinclair offered to pay a marriage dowry Forrest was grossly insulted: not only did it smack of aristocratic manners, but it suggested to his mind a lack of trust in his reliability as a husband. Catherine was distraught at this breach between her fiancé and her father. Soon her father backed down in the face of his daughter's feelings. They were married at St Paul's Covent Garden, the actors' church, in June 1837 (Moses 1969: 161–3). Forrest took his bride back to America. She, too, was to have a role to play in the events of May 1849.

When Macready in turn toured America in 1843 Forrest was the first to welcome him in New York. Even though Macready took more at the box office than Forrest during this time, Macready's jealousy now began to gnaw at him further. Macready felt a personal mission to make acting an art once again, as he saw it. In the 1820s and 1830s the status of the theatre in polite society had declined as the aristocracy began to desert the playhouses for the opera. Macready wanted to rid the theatre of what he saw as popular coarseness and make it a respectable, artistic experience for the early Victorian middle classes. To a considerable degree he was successful in this mission, despite his own pessimism about perennially declining standards. Macready's own desire to make acting artistic led him to develop a distinctive style, which strove for what would later become known as naturalism. Forrest's style of acting, with its sudden muscular bursts of highly charged passion, looked back to the romanticism of Edmund Kean, and was ideally suited to the melodramas which dominated the early nineteenth-century stage. Macready, on the other hand, was developing the style which would lead towards the naturalism of the late nineteenth and twentieth centuries. He sought to reveal the meaning of the text rather just to perform it, and he did this by living out on stage the variety of successive thoughts which the text suggests to the actor in the context of the scene. Small, familiar actions or habits such as a real person might use were deployed to build the character; meticulous attention to detail in matters of appropriate and historically accurate costume went with this. Macready also aimed at an emotional sincerity in performance, and sometimes employed a technique not unlike that of the later Russian theatre practitioner Konstantin Stanislavsky, with his notion of 'emotion memory' where the actor draws on a feeling he or she had in their own life in order to present a truthful emotion on stage. He sought to identify personally with his character (Downer 1966: 71–80). For American critics Forrest's barnstorming declamations and volcanic emotions were the stuff of great acting, but for Macready they seemed coarse, self-promoting and often ungrounded in the text: all that he was striving against in his own work. The lukewarm response of the American critics at that time prompted Macready to declare, with barely concealed animus, that his rival was '*not an artist*. Let him be an American actor – and a great American actor – but keep on this side of the Atlantic and no-one will gainsay his comparative excellence' (Moody 1958: 44–5, emphasis in original).

Macready could not hide his feelings about what he took to be the quality of American actors and audiences, and he sometimes faced hostility in consequence. He thanked an audience on the last night of his first tour in Philadelphia for their generous applause, particularly since he recognised that there had been 'some unworthy attempts that have been made to excite a prejudice against me and my countrymen engaged in this profession on the plea of being foreigners' (Downer 1966: 268).

He returned to England in November 1844. American tours were lucrative, and he had taken £5,500 at the box office (Moody 1958: 46). But he had not escaped his rival. In February 1845 Forrest was back in London, initially playing Othello at the Princess's Theatre. There were some favourable reviews again, but also, for the first time, some booing and hissing from sections of the audience. Whether this was prompted by aesthetic judgement or anti-Americanism is unclear, but Forrest saw Macready's hand in it: or rather Macready's hand hiding behind the spiteful actions of his friends and allies. John Forster was scathing in print about Forrest's Macbeth:

> Our old friend, Mr Forrest, afforded great amusement to the public by his performance of Macbeth on Friday evening at the Princess's. Indeed, our best comic actors do not often excite so great a quantity of mirth. The change from inaudible murmur to a thunder of sound was enormous; but the grand feature was the combat, in which he stood scraping his sword against that of Macduff [instead of fencing realistically]. We were at a loss to know what this gesture meant, till an enlightened critic in the gallery shouted out, 'That's right, sharpen it!'
>
> (Cited in Downer: 1966: 276)

When Forrest failed to secure engagements from a proposed visit to Paris, he claimed he had been turned down because both the manager of the English company there and the playwright whose work he wished to present were friends of Macready. Forrest left London to tour the provinces, where he was received with much more warmth than in London. He crossed the sea to Ireland, where he was a great success in Cork, Belfast and Dublin. The political dimension of his reception cannot be ignored here again. In the role of medieval rebel Jack Cade his outbursts against tyranny were roundly cheered. In Dublin, when the Queen's representative, the Lord Lieutenant of Ireland, entered the theatre in ceremonial procession Forrest, against all convention, totally ignored his presence (Moses 1969: 218–19). America and Ireland shared a common enemy.

Macready then toured Ireland himself, to less satisfaction all round. In his typically bilious view the island was the 'base posterior of the world' (Downer 1966: 278). It was in Scotland, however, where a seemingly petty incident led to the open hostility between Macready and Forrest which would culminate in the bloodshed at Astor Place three years later. Macready opened in *Hamlet* at Edinburgh on 2 March 1846. Macready's conception of the role meant that he filled it with details he felt were true to the character and the dramatic moment. At one particular point in the play the Prince is about to witness a performance at the court of *The Murder of Gonzago*, a play which Hamlet has arranged to be a re-enactment of his father's murder in front of his uncle, King Claudius, the man whom Hamlet suspects of the crime. Hamlet asks his friend Horatio to watch closely the King's reaction to the events on stage for any sign of guilt. As the court enters to watch the play, Hamlet tells his friend 'I must be idle' (3.2.76). He may mean that he will appear to be doing nothing, to give no sign of the ruse he has laid, or alternatively he may be saying that that he needs to carry on with the feigned madness, the 'antic disposition' which he has adopted since seeing his father's ghost. Macready seems to have taken the latter reading, for as the court entered he walked rapidly back and forth across the stage, bobbed his head from side to side, pulled out his handkerchief, took it by the corner and twirled it in the air while dancing a little hopping jig.

(Cliff 2007: 160)

At this point a loud hiss was heard from a box to the right of the stage, which another actor present, John Coleman, described as sounding like steam escaping from a locomotive. Macready bowed mockingly and waved his handkerchief even more camply. The audience booed the hisser, and the furious Macready, 'absolutely hysterical with rage' according to Coleman, staggered back into a chair. A voice in the gallery cried 'throw him out', but the critic rose in dead silence and solemnly left the theatre. 'Then Macready,' recalled Coleman, 'like a man possessed, leaped into the breach and took the audience by storm' (Downer 1966: 279).

A rumour immediately began to circulate backstage that the hisser had been a journalist accompanying Forrest – or even Forrest himself. At first Macready would not believe it of his rival, but as more and more corroborative identifications were made, he exclaimed in his diary how 'glad' he was that it 'was not an Englishman … I do not think such an action has its parallel in all theatrical history! The low-minded ruffian! That man would commit a murder if he dare' (cited in Cliff 2007: 163). Shortly afterwards *The Scotsman* outed Forrest as the hisser. All doubt was removed when a letter from Forrest was published in the London *Times* on 12 March. Forrest claimed that to hiss was to execute 'a right, which until now, I have never once heard questioned' to 'manifest his pleasure or displeasure according to the recognised mode'. He was clear about the reason for his critical intervention: 'Mr Macready thought fit to introduce a fancy dance into his performance of *Hamlet*, which I thought, and still think, a desecration of the scene' (Moses 1969: 221–2). Forrest did not feel that Macready's Hamlet was manly enough, and to avoid effeminacy in the performance of a Shakespearean hero was a sacred duty.

Open hostilities were now declared, and when Forrest returned home in July to great enthusiasm, he condemned from the New York stage 'that narrow, exclusive, prejudiced, and, I may add, anti-American feeling which prescribes geographical limits to the growth of genius and talent' (Moses 1969: 229). Macready for his part condemned the whole country which could produce such a man as Forrest, writing that 'I feel I cannot *stomach* the United States as a nation'. Later in the year he seemed to renounce all desire to seek his fortune or safety there: 'America!! Give me a crust in England' (Moses 1969: 226).

Yet by March 1847 he was planning to tour the USA once more, as prelude to settling there. Not only would he now have to face a potential storm of personal animosity whipped up by Forrest and his supporters amongst the press and the public, but he would also have to consider the consequences of being an iconic Englishman exposing himself to public scrutiny when relations between Britain and America were downright hostile. Although there were plenty of Americans ready to welcome an artist of Macready's stature, there were also unscrupulous political operators keen to exploit the divisions which the arrival of such a controversial figure would bring to public affairs.

American independence had originally been secured after a war against British colonial rule, and as recently as 1812–15 a war had been fought on land and sea. Britain had burned Washington DC, and a small American naval force had even landed in Whitehaven in Cumbria. When slavery was abolished in the British Empire in 1833, the persistence of the evil in the southern states of the USA rankled with many in Britain, even though the produce of the cotton plantations was a main source of raw materials for the British textile industry. Once steamships permitted rapid Atlantic crossings, British travel writers who now had easy access to the country could express their continuing resentments about the ex-colony in diatribes about the coarseness and violence of Americans in newspapers and books, which were now becoming available relatively cheaply. These accounts were distributed rapidly thanks to steam presses and steam railways.

Macready's close friend Charles Dickens was probably the most notable English satirist of America. Dickens's early novels had proved very popular in the USA, but the writer saw little profit from his sales. British copyright protection did not extend to America, and US publishers made fortunes from pirated copies of his novels, offering only token payments when they wanted to get advance proofs to steal a march on rivals, much to Dickens's frustration (Tomalin 2011: 104–6). In 1842 he travelled to the United States, but his attempts to raise the copyright issue met only hostility in the press. He was unpleasantly overwhelmed by the celebrity reception he met in New York, and felt that his guests were trying to make money from him. He met the President, and travelled widely, but as the tour went on he became more and more disenchanted with the venality of American politics and business, the superficial and humourless conversation he felt that he met everywhere, and by the inhuman treatment he saw meted out to slaves and to Native Americans. He made his feelings all too clear in his *American Notes*, published later that year, and in his depiction of the United States in his novel *Martin Chuzzlewit* in 1844 (Tomalin 2011: 134–7). Dickens became a hate-figure in America, and when Macready set off on his ill-fated 1848 tour, Dickens would not see him off from Liverpool, knowing that any association with the writer would only do the actor harm across the Atlantic (Moody 1958: 66). But Macready's friendship with Dickens was well known, as was their mutual closeness to Forrest's most outspoken theatrical critic, John Forster, who was also Dickens's most loyal lieutenant and first biographer. Forrest and others believed that Forster was no more than Macready's mouthpiece.

But the hostility between Britain and America in May 1848 also had more profound roots. Canada had of course remained within the British Empire upon the USA gaining its independence, and there remained skirmishes and border incidents into the 1830s and beyond. A major dispute now arose as the US expanded rapidly westwards over the Oregon territory, the land west of the Rocky Mountains (Cliff 2007: 142–3). Where would the border with Canada in the west be drawn? In the 1844 presidential election the Democrat James Polk campaigned on extending the US north all the way to the southern edge of Alaska, then a Russian territory. The British insisted that the province of British Columbia should border the USA on the Columbia River. When Polk won the election London informed the American envoy it was 'ready to strike great blows at the first outbreak of hostilities' (Cliff 2007: 155). Britain was also supporting the new independent state of Texas, which had seceded from Mexico in 1835. Until 1845, when Texas joined the Union, London had encouraged Texas to abolish slavery and remain outside both Mexico and the US as a favoured trading partner.

Most damaging of all for Anglo-American relations was the 'repudiation' issue (Cliff 2007: 143–7). Individual American states stood greatly indebted to foreign banks, mostly British. When a deep recession came in the US economy in the late 1830s many states which could no longer keep up the interest payments on the bonds they had issued either defaulted or 'repudiated' – refused to pay back – what they owed to British creditors. This was not just a major problem for British banks, but also for many middle-class British people of modest means who had invested in US state bonds in order to provide an income when widowed, old or infirm. There was fury in Britain at such behaviour. The London *Foreign Quarterly Review* concluded, according to the *New York Herald* in 1844, that America was merely a 'vast deposit of human dregs' (Cliff 2007: 147). Such animosity was well known in the US and the mutual loathing had scarcely diminished four years later.

Edwin Forrest's own publicly expressed political views made him a figurehead for anti-British feeling (Moses 1969: 166–80). Fiercely patriotic and democratic, he opposed all privilege (except for whites) and all aristocracy. His views were very much those of Andrew Jackson, who was President of the USA from 1829 to 1837. In America, Macready was accused of conspiring to thwart Forrest's triumphal demonstration of American superiority in Europe by procuring hostile reviews and preventing Forrest performing in Paris. Macready's denial of these charges was seen as a demonstrable lie, as the banner displayed at Astor Place that first night of rioting had claimed. He was the perfect lightning conductor for the storm of popular hatred for Britain in New York City.

Now local political forces came into play. Democracy in New York in those days was often a cynical, corrupt and violent process. There was a flourishing gang culture based in the city's slums, which amongst other criminal activities worked to deliver votes by bribery, intimidation and personation, principally for the Democratic Party, whose headquarters, Tammany Hall, became a byword for political chicanery (Cliff 2007: 189–200). Irish immigrants voted in a block for the Democrats, and the Irish street gangs such as the Plug Uglies and the Dead Rabbits fought the gangs who acted for the racist American Nativist party, and principally the Bowery Boys. The term 'b'hoy' was used for all these men, after the supposed Irish pronunciation of the word. There was a distinctive 'b'hoy' fashion on both sides of the divide, which included wearing a tall stovepipe hat, a red shirt and huge projecting sideburns made rigid with soap. Many gangs were based around the different private fire brigades which competed for business in the teeming city. Many enjoyed attending the popular theatres, and especially the Bowery, where Forrest was their hero.

Both Nativist and Irish hated the English for different reasons; both identified the city's super-rich as their class enemies, seeing them as effectively English in their effete tastes and aristocratic attitudes. The new and exclusive Astor Place Opera House, which was dedicated to the exclusion of working-class rowdies and their women was an obvious target for their hostility. For the gangs, the appearance of Forrest's underhand and supercilious enemy at Astor Place was an opportunity not to be missed. It was Isaiah Rynders, protection-racketeer, gang-leader and political fixer who led the conspirators. He managed to get hold of five hundred tickets for Macready's first night at Astor Place and handed them out to the b'hoys who succeeded in bringing *Macbeth* to a close so spectacularly. After their victory Rynders journeyed in triumph to the Broadway Theatre just as Forrest came off stage, boasting that 'we have put hell to Macready; he has never had such a reception before' (Cliff 2007: 206). Then they went on to attempt to disrupt an abolitionist meeting run by the freed slave Alfred Douglass.

Rynders had approached Forrest to get his explicit backing for the original attack on Macready. 'Two wrongs do not make a right', the actor had chided, but then added the words 'Let the people do as they please' (Cliff 2007: 207). Rynders's deputy, the rabble-rousing thug Ned Buntline, had tried once more to enlist Forrest's support for further assaults on Macready the following morning, but the tragedian was not at home. Forrest had good reason for not wishing to become involved, for this happened also to be a moment of crisis in his personal life. He had suspected his wife's infidelity the previous spring when he returned unexpectedly to their hotel to find her 'between the knees' of a young actor, George Jamieson. According to his later testimony, 'Mrs Forrest replied, with considerable perturbation, that Mr Jamieson had been pointing out her phrenological developments' (phrenology was a nineteenth-century pseudo-science which claimed to be able to read character by feeling bumps on the head) (Moody 1958: 83). Forrest had striven to believe in her innocence, but as the evidence of her amorous connections with others spread he could take no more. Their childless marriage had ended in separation on 1 May 1849, just a week before Buntline's visit. A scandalous divorce trial was to follow in December 1851 which would in fact vindicate Catherine, and award her substantial alimony (Moses 1969: 265).

On the Tuesday morning following the abandoned *Macbeth*, 8 May, Macready awoke with a headache, determined not to play Astor Place again. He requested a booking on the steamship *America* for immediate departure. But as the day progressed he was visited by a number of eminent New Yorkers who were determined not to permit what they saw as mob rule over a theatre which they regarded as their territory. There was also a clear class confrontation. The city's rich were not prepared to see their authority undermined. They were disturbed by the European revolutions of 1848 and feared that this rioting might be a harbinger of the trouble spreading to the New World. In the evening a letter was delivered to Macready's hotel signed by forty-seven notable men, including the writers Washington Irving and Herman Melville, who would publish his great novel *Moby Dick* two years later. The letter condemned Monday night's events as an 'outrage', requesting Macready to reconsider his decision, and assuring him that 'the good sense and respect for order prevailing in this community will sustain you on the subsequent nights of your performance' (Moses 1969: 116). Macready reluctantly conceded to their request. But he asked to postpone the next performance until Friday; whether he stayed or not, he was about to publish testimony from his friends in London and Paris that he had in no way attempted to hinder Forrest's career during his last tour, and he hoped that this evidence might counteract some of the grievances clearly held against him. He was of course naive in this matter: when these 'Replies' appeared in the morning papers on Thursday, they only provoked his opponents further. But Macready, having been prevailed upon, did agree to return to Astor Place on Thursday night.

Tuesday also saw the swearing-in of a new city Mayor, Caleb Smith Woodhull. Woodhull was a Whig (broadly, the antecedent of the modern Republican Party). The Democrat vote had been split, and Woodhull won easily. The Whigs were associated with the city's wealthy. The forty-seven signatories on the letter that evening were almost all prominent Whigs (Melville was an exception) (Cliff 2007: 209–10). To take a stand behind Macready would be Woodhull's chance to put the Nativist gangs and Democratic Tammany Hall mobs in their place.

Over Wednesday night and Thursday morning Rynders had two hundred posters put up all over the city (cited in Cliff 2007: 210–11):

> WORKING MEN,
> SHALL
> AMERICANS
> OR
> ENGLISH RULE
> IN THIS CITY
> The Crew of the British Steamer have
> Threatened all Americans who shall dare to express their
> Opinions this night, at the
> ENGLISH ARISTOCRATIC OPERA HOUSE!
> We advocate no violence, but a free expression of opinion
> to all public men.
> WORKINGMEN! FREEMEN!
> STAND BY YOUR LAWFUL RIGHTS!
> American Committee.

The claim that there was a threatening 'British steamer' in the port was a deceit, as were the provocative handbills signed 'John Bull' which were also distributed – they were produced on the same Ann Street press as the posters. On Wednesday and Thursday the city's newspapers noisily took sides in the dispute, and by Thursday morning it was clear that Mayor Woodhull had a powder keg on his hands.

A meeting was called at City Hall for 11am. Amongst those present with Mayor Woodhull were John Westervelt, the Sheriff; George Matsell, the Chief of Police; Recorder Frederick Tallmadge, the senior legal official; and Major General Charles Sandford, who commanded the New York State Militia, a volunteer force of army reservists (the forerunner of the present US National Guard). The managers of the Astor Place Opera House, William Niblo and James Hackett, were also in attendance. According to the statement he made at the later coroner's inquest, the Major told Niblo that he had 'no authority to interfere in his establishment', but that his personal opinion was that 'he should close his theatre on that night' (Moody 1958: 134). Niblo and Hackett claimed the right to keep their lawful business open, and expressed the view that 'the magistracy should protect them'. Woodhull and the others 'then came to the conclusion that their house should be protected'. It was agreed that if the police were unable to 'preserve the peace', then Major General Sandford was 'requested to hold a sufficient military force in readiness to meet the apprehended emergency' (Moses 1969: 188–9; Cliff 2007: 177).

It may seem strange in retrospect that the authorities were prepared to shoot people in order to protect the rights of two theatre managers to keep the takings of a full house. There seem, however, to have been other forces at work apart from an expressed belief in the right to make a profit whatever the consequences. The Astor Place Opera House was a citadel of high culture for New York's elite, whom the new city administration represented. Hackett was also a gentleman-actor and critic, and was 'a longstanding enemy of Forrest', about whom he had not always written favourably. Chief of Police Matsell was no doubt in favour of the involvement of the Militia if fighting began. His officers were appointed and paid by officials of the different city wards, many of whom were in the control of the corrupt Democratic politicians who sided with the rioters (Cliff 2007: 213). This is the most likely explanation of the failure of the police to take any action, though under his command, during Monday night's disturbance at the theatre.

Macready's supporters were much more successful at ensuring that tickets were not made available to the b'hoys, and marked the back of the tickets of those holders they knew to be friends. Some nevertheless did get into the hands of their enemies, sold on by fraudsters who claimed that they wanted to attend in order to put down any trouble (Cliff 2007: 215). As the windows of the Opera House were boarded up in anticipation, at the Broadway Theatre Forrest was asked by his friends to issue a statement disassociating himself from any violence that might occur that night. He refused.

At four in the afternoon 325 police officers arrived at the opera house (Moody 1958: 136–75; Cliff 2007: 217–31). Two hundred were stationed inside the theatre itself, and the rest in the streets outside. The Seventh Regiment of the New York State Militia, under the command of Colonel Duryea, assembled at the Artillery Drill Room at Centre Market. This unit was known as 'the Silk Stocking Regiment' because so many of its officers were drawn from the city's wealthy elite (Cliff 2007: 214fn). Only 210 of the full complement arrived for duty, more than a hundred short. Perhaps there were those amongst the rank and file with little stomach for what they might be called upon to do. Two small cavalry units were ordered to assemble at the city Arsenal, together with two six-pound cannon equipped with grape and canister shot. This type of ammunition was designed for use against concentrations of the enemy at close range. It consisted of bags or tubes of musket balls which would scatter with deadly effect when fired. Two more cavalry companies, hussars with curved sabres, were also mobilised to be kept in reserve.

A large crowd began to gather around Astor Place from late afternoon, perhaps ten to fifteen thousand strong. Many had come to riot, but a large number had also come as spectators of the promised affray. Ticket holders could only enter the theatre by passing through a double file of policemen. By 7.15pm the streets around the Opera House were packed solid. The police and theatre staff were deliberately excluding those ticket holders they thought might cause trouble, while some of the wealthy could be seen entering through the stage door. Only seven women were present among the 1,800 in the audience. Trouble was expected.

The curtain went up ten minutes late. There was little disturbance until the entry of Macready as Macbeth in Act One Scene Three. There were fewer than two hundred protestors in the house, but they had positioned themselves in the front rows of the parquette and the gallery and exploded into hissing, stamping and catcalls as soon as he arrived on stage. Macready's supporters stood and shouted back at the b'hoys, and for fifteen minutes the play stopped altogether. Then a board appeared at the side of the stage, requesting that 'the friends of order will remain quiet'. Macready's friends sat down. It was now clear who the protestors were.

Chief of Police Matsell had positioned himself in the box to the right of the stage where he could be seen to give orders. After consulting with Recorder Tallmadge he led his men into the parquette, where after a violent struggle in which some of the protestors lost much of their clothing, the ringleaders were arrested and locked in a cellar under the parquette. There they succeeded in starting a fire using a gas lamp and some wood shavings, which was soon put out by the police who then handcuffed the incendiaries to prevent further trouble. The other rioters in the parquette were marched out of the building. The play began again, with the trouble now concentrated to a relatively small number at the front of the gallery.

But serious violence now began outside the theatre. At the front of the crowd were about two hundred teenage boys, many associated with the private fire brigades. They were also gang members. Ned Buntline, keen to be the nucleus of the action, ordered the boys to collect armfuls of cobblestones. A sewer was under construction in Astor Place, and piles of stones to be used for paving were lying to hand. The Mayor had previously ordered this obvious ammunition to be cleared away, but his command had clearly not been carried out. At Buntline's command, volleys of cobblestones now crashed against the theatre building, taking out the streetlights nearby. Under this bombardment the boards which had been put up to protect the windows became dislodged, and the windows were soon smashed. The police tried to board up the windows from the inside, but soon stones and shattered boards were landing in the auditorium itself. One hit the great chandelier, scattering glass shards on those below. Outside, Buntline's boys could be heard shouting 'Fight! Fight! Tear it down! Burn the damned den of the aristocracy!'

On stage Macready carried on with the performance with cool determination. According to his diary he told a frightened actor that 'whatever the consequences I must go through with it. The audience have paid for it and the law compels me to give it'. Apparently without irony he added that 'they would have cause for riot if all is not properly done' (cited in Cliff 2007: 222).

The cobblestones were also aimed at the police who were standing outside the theatre. Each stone, mostly weighing a kilogram or more, could cause a serious injury on the unprotected officers. At least twenty were badly hurt, and they began to retreat into the protection of the building. The rioters now charged the doors and broke one down, only to be beaten back when a force of baton-wielding police sallied out to make a few arrests after a fierce struggle before returning inside. The despairing captain of the Eighth Ward Police reported to Matsell and Tallmadge that it was impossible to keep the crowd back, and that the building would be destroyed without reinforcement. The city's senior law enforcement officers and three hundred policemen, together with many of New York's upper crust, were besieged by a stone-throwing mob which appeared to be thousands strong. The smoke from the fire which had been started in the storeroom then began to permeate the building. At this point one of the Sheriff's deputies was sent to fetch the State Militia.

At about nine, just after the third act of *Macbeth* got underway, the Seventh Regiment arrived in Astor Place, dressed in white trousers, grey coats frogged in black with white epaulettes, and wearing black shakoes with white plumes. Mayor Woodhull now also made his entrance on the scene, stayed about half an hour to observe and then left for the New York Hotel without issuing any orders which might make him politically accountable for what happened next. The small detachment of cavalry which led the military advance were not apparently an imposing presence, and they were soon put out of action by a hail of stones, bloodying the riders and causing the horses to rear and shy. Most of the force dismounted, and having only sabres they played no further part in the action.

Slowly, with fixed bayonets, the Militia forced a way through the crowds in front of the theatre, then the open space to the right of the theatre, where Astor Place met the Bowery and Fourth Avenue, always under fire from stone throwers. Then they pushed their way to the centre of the rear of the building, and having formed two outwards-facing lines across the street, advanced until they had cleared the whole street of rioters. Policemen then emerged to hold the position so that the troops could be redeployed where the mass of the protestors were gathered, in front of the theatre itself. A hundred soldiers were placed to guard the Broadway end of the theatre. As more and more of his men were wounded by stones, the senior officers, Generals Hall and Sandford – the former bleeding from a head wound – requested the support of the civil authorities, whose command would be needed if they had to open fire. Sheriff Westervelt, followed by Recorder Tallmadge, then accompanied 150 troops as they set out to clear the main force of rioters from Astor Place itself.

Twice they attempted to force their way through and clear the space as they had done behind the theatre, but under a hail of cobblestones twice their formation was driven back in disarray to the pavement hard by the theatre entrance. Two-thirds of the soldiers in the front rank went down injured, and the officers were bruised and bleeding. A pistol shot rang out and wounded a captain in the leg. General Sandford was knocked down again by a stone, got to his feet amongst the wounded lying around him and ordered the men to charge with their bayonets. The crowd were so close, however, that there was no room to make the attack, and as the soldiers thrust their muskets forwards some of them were seized by the crowd. General Hall remembered Chief Matsell at this moment demanding he order his men to open fire, but he insisted that he needed a magistrate's command. The noise was deafening as the stones from the rear ranks of the crowd rained against the musket barrels. More than thirty soldiers lay injured, and the officer whose company was guarding the theatre entrance told General Sandford that unless they opened fire they would have to abandon their position.

Meanwhile the play continued inside regardless. A stream of arrested rioters kept being brought in and locked in the storerooms, including Ned Buntline, who claimed he was only a journalist and then demanded to be released because his wife was about to give birth. He was handcuffed and taken below. The dressing rooms became flooded when stones fractured the building's plumbing. Macready pressed on. The noise outside seemed all the more appropriate in Act Five when Macbeth's castle comes under siege from the English forces. He played his lines to full effect, getting a response when he stressed the word 'forest' in the lines 'I will not be afraid of death and bane/ Till Birnam forest come to Dunsinane' (5.4.66–7), and provoking laughter with the lines 'Our castle's strength/ Will laugh a siege to scorn' (5.5.2–3). The play came to an end, Macready took his curtain call, and the 'afterpiece', a farce, began. Then the audience heard what they took to be fireworks going off outside.

The Sheriff could see that the rioters had no fear of the Militia so long as their muskets remained silent. The soldiers were being battered into submission. Their lives were at risk, and a humiliating defeat for the city authorities was imminent. Westervelt and Recorder Tallmadge went bravely amongst the press of rioters, warning them that unless they dispersed the order to open fire would be given, but the magistrates could be barely heard. The Sheriff struggled back to the troops and finally gave General Hall the order to fire – but only above the rioters' heads as a warning. It was now about 9.45pm. A ragged volley went off, and the crowd scattered backwards. Some of the bullets had lethal consequences behind the b'hoys, but when the rioters saw (falsely, as it turned out) that they had suffered no casualties, a contemptuous cry went up that the Militia had only been issued with blank cartridges. A new hail of stones came crashing down on the soldiers. Once again the Sheriff and Recorder Tallmadge, as he later recalled, 'rushed into the mob and

Figure 5.1 The Astor Place riot. The front page of the *Illustrated London News*, 2 June 1849. In front of the main façade the Militia are depicted in a very regular line firing a controlled volley, quite unlike written accounts of the riot. There is no evidence that cavalry with drawn sabres saw any action at all as depicted to the right. The whole picture owes more in its composition to contemporary battle portraits. The hail of cobblestones thrown by the rioters and the smashed windows of the theatre are clearly visible, however.

invoked them to depart, as the military would fire directly upon them ... [but] I was assailed by a volley of stones, and was injured on my ankle and other parts of my body and forced to retreat into the rear of the military'. Some of the crowd began taunting the Militia to fire again. One of the b'hoys, 'a begrimed and burly ruffian with a huge stone between his knees, exposing with both hands his bare breast covered with a red flannel shirt, cried "Fire into this. Take the life of a free-born American for a bloody British actor! Do it – Ay, you darsn't."'

Westervelt ordered Hall to fire again. General Hall instructed his troops to aim at the rioters' legs to avoid fatalities if at all possible. These were the critical seconds. Three times the order to fire was given before the volley rang out. The anxious moment of hesitation may have occurred because the soldiers could not hear their orders in the tumult, but it also seems that a number were unwilling to open fire on their fellow citizens. Eventually many of them did pull their triggers, smoke and flame burst forth and men fell dying and bleeding in front of them. The rioters fell back in shock as the smoke cleared, and the soldiers now advanced to clear Astor Place in front of the theatre. The rioters regrouped in two forces. The remaining hundred soldiers reloaded, faced two ways to confront each mob, and presented their muskets once more. Again the stones rained in, and once more the Sheriff tried in vain to get the protestors to abandon their assault. The soldiers fired again, at least once, and the rioters were broken. Just at this moment military reinforcements arrived, including the two cannon, which were rapidly set up at either end of the theatre. The rioters realised the true nature of what they had got into and dispersed, shocked, cowed yet furious at what had happened.

Macready was in his flooded dressing room at the first volley. News came of the deaths outside, and he resolved that 'there was nothing for it but to meet the worst with dignity, and so I stood prepared' (cited in Moody 1958: 164). He had to make his escape somehow, and now realised the extreme danger he faced. He finally agreed to be disguised in the greatcoat of the actor who played Malcolm, and to wear the cap of another actor, split up the back so it should fit him. He then coolly joined the spectators leaving under police guard at the rear of theatre. Wisely, however, he did not return to his hotel, which was ineffectually attacked later that evening by rioters searching for him. He was saved by the lawyer Robert Emmett (nephew of the Irish nationalist rebel) who accompanied Macready to his house. The actor sat by the fire smoking cigars with Robert's brother Richard until he could be put in a covered phaeton – a fast carriage – and driven to New Rochelle station where he was put on the early morning train to safety in Boston. In this way Macready escaped the gangs searching the city for him who would surely have done him great harm. One horse bus was chased down a New York street by a mob that night shouting 'Macready's in the omnibus; they've killed twenty of us, and by God we'll kill him!'

The best estimate of those killed on the night of 10 May is thirty-one (Moody 1958: 172). At least forty-eight civilians were wounded, and at least seventy soldiers and policemen were injured before the firing started. It seems that most of the civilian casualties were amongst the bystanders standing behind the rioters, or even amongst those going about their business some distance away. An elderly woman was shot in the face lying at home in her own bed; two men were shot and killed as they got off a horse tram 150 metres away from the shooting. Perhaps many of the Militia deliberately fired over the heads of their fellow citizens even when ordered to aim at them; perhaps the part-time soldiers were simply not very skilled at using the smoothbore musket, an outdated and inaccurate weapon which was being replaced in professional European armies by breech-loading rifles. Those rioters who were killed were young: at the initial inquest into eighteen deaths, five were under twenty and most of the rest under twenty-five. Nearly half had been born in Ireland.

Eighty-six rioters had been arrested and dragged into the Opera House, well over half of them under twenty. In all there were 113 arrests, but only nineteen were eventually put on trial, including Ned Buntline. Nine were convicted. Buntline was fined $250 and given a year's hard labour. Rynders was charged with instigating the riot, but was, astonishingly, acquitted. He went on to become the US Marshal of the Southern District of New York (Cliff 2007: 224). When Buntline was released he was driven to a dinner in his honour in an open carriage with a band playing 'Hail to the Chief'.

The city remained tense on the Friday morning. The bodies of some of the dead were on public display in the streets nearby and a huge public protest meeting was called for six that evening in City Hall Park. Up to 25,000 people heard a series of fiery speeches from Rynders and others, and six or seven thousand then marched on the Opera House shouting for vengeance (Moody 1958: 194). When they arrived they faced two thousand infantry, cavalry and artillery supported by nine hundred police and a thousand hurriedly sworn-in special constables. The authorities had ensured that there was little ammunition lying around to be thrown, and after a warning to disperse the crowd did so, following no more than a few small skirmishes. A continuing show of force in the streets in the following nights brought an end to the disorder. The city was in shock.

Macready never returned to America and retired from the stage three years later. Forrest's personal reputation was damaged in the eyes of those who deplored the rioting, and further sullied by his defeat in the divorce case. In the years that followed his acting style became seen as increasingly crude, and became the subject of satirical burlesques (Cliff 2007: 250–1). Yet he had his fans, even if the working-class theatre audience in the cities now drifted away to vaudeville and variety shows. He carried on acting even when afflicted by rheumatism and gout until his death in 1872.

Michael R. Booth has identified two significant outcomes of the Astor Place riot. It ended the domination of the American stage by British actors and playwrights. It also asserted, he wrote, the rights of 'the Jacksonian "common man" against the social and cultural domination of a middle-class power structure' (Booth 1995: 312). But even if the Astor Place Opera House itself failed as a theatre, becoming a library and lecture hall in 1854, in fact the guns of the New York State Militia effectively served to exclude working people from high culture in the city. As with the Old Price riots in London forty years earlier, despite the huge level of political manipulation the root of the trouble was the determination of the 'lower orders' to defend their right of access to all theatres and to insist on a repertory which did not affront their sensibilities. The Astor Place Opera House had tried to exclude them, had moved them out of the pit and put on the stage an actor who was politically indefensible in their eyes. At Covent Garden higher prices and new boxes were similarly exclusive, and foreign opera singers were not what a patriotic working-class audience wanted to see. The violent disturbances in nineteenth-century theatres can be seen as a response to the appropriation of a high-status cultural form by the middle and upper classes, ending the seventeenth- and eighteenth-century idea of the theatre as a common space for all classes to take part in a national dialogue and to access the best writing and acting, to attend an entertainment where intellect was as valued as sentiment. By the end of the century a clear class division had arisen between theatre, and, even more so, opera on the one hand, and music hall, variety and vaudeville (in America) on the other. What working-class audience remained in the high-status theatre was relegated to galleries high in the auditorium, often with a separate entrance and social spaces from the rest of the spectators.

At Astor Place Shakespeare as a cultural icon was also being contested. The same struggle between competing social groups for the right to claim the bard as their own became part of class struggle in Victorian England. Yet again the wealthy would win.

Note

1 The acting edition of the play used by Macready at this time gave to Macduff the lines which in Shakespeare's 1623 Folio text are given to Ross (1.2.53–63, 64–8, 72).

References

Booth, Michael R. (1995), 'Nineteenth-Century Theatre', in John Russell Brown (ed.) *The Oxford Illustrated History of Theatre* (Oxford: Oxford University Press).

Cliff, Nigel (2007), *The Shakespeare Riots: Revenge Drama and Death in Nineteenth-Century America* (New York: Random House).

Downer, Alan S. (1966), *The Eminent Tragedian William Charles Macready* (Cambridge MA: Harvard University Press).

FitzSimons, Raymund (1976), *Edmund Kean: Fire From Heaven* (London: Hamish Hamilton).

Moody, Richard (1958), *The Astor Place Riot* (Bloomington IN: The University of Indiana Press).

Moses, Montrose J. (1969), *The Fabulous Forrest: The Record of an American Actor* (New York and London: Benjamin Blom).

Tomalin, Claire (2011), *Charles Dickens: A Life* (London: Viking).

Chapter 6

Stand-off at Primrose Hill

The Shakespeare tercentenary of 1864

The *Leicester Chronicle* reported some nasty trouble during a performance of *King Lear* at the Theatre Royal, Leicester, in October 1841:

> The conduct of 'the gods' was most disgraceful during the whole evening: not only were the most disgusting oaths bandied about, but several fights took place, and the police were two or three times obliged to be called in. Coats and hats were thrown into the pit: the dregs of beer-bottles were emptied on the heads of those below – and worse things than that even. We trust the management will prevent a recurrence of like disgraceful proceedings, or they cannot expect respectable people to frequent the Theatre; we trust, also, that the decent frequenters of the gallery will aid them in their attempts to do so – and this was the last time we shall have to speak on such an unpleasant topic. We understand, since writing the above, that proper steps can be taken to prevent such an annoyance in the future.
>
> (*Leicester Chronicle*, 2 October 1841)

The cause of the disturbance seems to have been the disappointment felt by the audience on the cheapest, gallery benches ('the gods') at the poor performance given by Charles Dillon in the role of Lear. The gallery was probably very full that night, for a Shakespeare play rarely performed in that city (Crump 1986: 279). Dillon came from a theatrical family, and had been a stage manager at the age of fifteen. At only twenty-one he had been well received in London as Hamlet, and now at the advanced age of twenty-two he had come to Leicester to play Shakespeare's octogenarian king. Dillon was suffering from a severe cold, and, as the *Leicester Chronicle* records, 'in the more energetic passages there was some occasional indistinctness'. But 'in those scenes requiring feeling … his acting was both skilful and touching'. Emotional sensitivity was apparently not what the working-class Shakespeare fans in the gallery had come to see, however. The anonymous *Leicester Chronicle* writer clearly desires to see their place in the theatre taken by 'respectable people' who could appreciate sentiment. The 'after-piece' which followed *King Lear* that evening was the rather fey-sounding *Wood Demon*. In between were some pretty dances, and the reception awarded by the gallery to the Misses Ellis in their 'Sailor Dance' put them off their stride so much that they had to start again. The writer, for his part, was much affected by 'the hearty kiss' which one of dancers 'snatched from her pretty sister as she was going offstage'. At any rate it 'tickled the fancy of the audience'.

Presumably lavatory facilities were inadequate for the crowd in the gallery, and their empty beer bottles were put to a practical use. The emptying of these improvised chamber pots from the gallery onto the circle and pit below can be seen as part of the continuing rearguard action, as it were, of working-class audiences as they were being driven from the increasingly bourgeois theatre by 'educated' opinion and middle-class sentimentality. 'Proper steps can be taken in the future' to prevent this kind of thing, we are ominously informed: and they were. This was part of the same struggle as the 1809 Old Price riots and would have a deadly counterpart in the events in New York eight years later. Shakespeare the national icon became a central battleground in that struggle in England, a struggle that reached a climax during the festivities to celebrate the three-hundredth anniversary of the playwright's birth in April 1864.

As London expanded along the railway lines which spread out from central termini in the middle decades of the century new theatres sprang up in the suburbs. These playhouses not only made Shakespeare their staple, but some of their Shakespearean actors even went on to make their names on the West End stage. Samuel Phelps transformed Sadler's Wells theatre in Islington from a venue noted for tawdry spectacle into a place where 2,600 working-class people would attend 'in a happy crowd, as orderly as if they were at church, and yet as unrestrained in their enjoyment as if listening to stories told them at their own firesides', wrote Henry Morley about an 1857 *Twelfth Night* (cited in Foulkes 2002: 34). Eventually the quality of the performance drew people of all classes from all over the city, but the original audience remained the dominant component. Increasingly relegated to the gallery in the 'respectable' theatres, here working people were at home in their own space. Over Phelps's eighteen years at Sadler's Wells more than half of the performances were of Shakespearean drama. Thirty-one different plays were represented, with *Hamlet*, *Macbeth* and *The Winter's Tale* the most popular shows. Inspired by Phelps, Richard Calvert produced Shakespeare for the masses at the Prince's Theatre in Manchester, which opened in 1874.

Working-class audiences wanted bold performances; they were out of tune with the sentimentality which was increasingly popular with middle-class theatregoers. Between 1840 and 1870 the proportion of Shakespeare and other classic drama in the repertoire of Birmingham's popular Theatre Royal increased from fifteen to thirty per cent. At the same time melodrama fell from fifty to twenty-five per cent of the playhouse's programme (Rose 2002: 122). Many knew the classic plays well and could both prompt and comment knowledgeably during the performances. A Birmingham reviewer in 1885 noted that 'the criticism of the pit ... if rough and ready, is formed on a sound basis. Listen between the acts to the remarks passed around you on a new exponent of a celebrated part, and you will hear comparisons drawn between the present performance and all the great ones who have trod the boards' (cited in Rose 2002: 122).

At the Britannia in Hoxton and the Standard in Shoreditch Victorian East Enders watched their Shakespeare in large numbers. Theodor Fontane, a German novelist who visited the Standard in 1856 to see *Antony and Cleopatra*, found himself seated 'between a worker from the docks and a grenadier from the Scottish Fusiliers' (Rose 2002: 51). Particularly interesting is the way that Shakespeare's characters were represented. Women frequently played male protagonists. At the Britannia Marie Henderson, Sophie Miles and Julia Seaman all played Hamlet, the latter as the 'first colloquial Hamlet' (Rose 2002: 51–2), which suggests that she spoke the lines in her own working-class accent. African-American actors denied work by racism both in the United States and in the West End were great favourites in lead roles: not only the first great black Othello, Ira Aldridge, but also Morgan Smith, who played not only the Moor, but Richard III, Shylock, Macbeth and Hamlet as well.

It seems that 'suburban' Shakespeare not only boasted cramped performance conditions, and an engaged and vociferous audience, but also an attitude towards theatrical representation which rejected the fashion for a pictorial 'historical realism' that dominated the fashionable London playhouses. This was a Shakespeare much closer to the conditions of its original production (coincidentally, the Standard stood very near the site of James Burbage's 1576 'Theatre', the first of London's playhouses). It was theatre which did not ape reality and divide its audience from the stage; it was a communal theatre, perhaps asserting in its conditions of representation that the world, with its rigid imposed boundaries of class, race and gender, need not be as it is currently constructed.

This was the Shakespeare of the Chartists and other working-class activists. The great working-class movement of the 1840s demanded that the people should be represented in Parliament. The 'People's Charter' was originally drawn up by the London Working Men's Association. It called for annually elected parliaments, with paid MPs chosen by the votes of all men over twenty-one. All constituencies were to be of equal size, and there was to be no connection between property ownership and the right to vote. These were all radical demands in a country where the right to vote remained strictly limited, even if the franchise had been extended in 1832. Millions signed petitions demanding that the Charter be implemented. Huge demonstrations were held, and public rallies were often held in theatres.[1] A prominent Chartist leader, Feargus O'Connor, hired the Standard for a series of meetings in 1849 (Taylor 2002: 371). Many radical agitators were themselves actors, and the content and style of their platform delivery owed much to Shakespearean rhetoric and to the contemporary fashion of performing it. Their speeches were full of Shakespearean quotations and allusions. Feargus O'Connor edited the Chartist newspaper the *Northern Star*, which ran from 1838 until 1852, selling 50,000 copies at its peak. From April 1840 it began a series called 'Chartism, From Shakespeare', which printed extracts from the plays relevant to the struggle for working-class emancipation at that moment (Murphy 2008: 141–4). Generally the extracts were wrenched from their contexts to produce a particular effect, but the powerful rhetoric combined with Shakespeare's authority made them inspiring messages, and proof that Shakespeare himself was on the side of the Chartists.

Shakespeare's apparently humble origins and lack of university education marked him out for radicals as a man of the people. In 1866 when the Leicester Domestic Mission men's class began their series of Shakespeare readings, one of the members opened proceedings with these words:

> I have a right, a kindred right I claim,
> Though rank nor titles gild my humble name,
> 'Tis from his class, the class the proud discard,
> For Shakespeare was himself the people's bard.
> (Rose 2002: 123)

Up to a thousand men would attend these readings. Denied a formal education themselves, many workers had learned to read from popular editions of his plays. When a survey was made of the reading of the forty-five 'Lib-Lab' and Labour MPs in 1906, the first substantial intake of working-class men into Parliament, Shakespeare held a place of honour (Rose 2002: 42).

The English nationalism with which his works had been associated since the mid-eighteenth century, and the plays' apparent roots in the English countryside, made Shakespeare a spokesman for the mythical golden past of the common people before industrialisation, what they saw as the age of the 'freeborn Englishman'. 'Above all', writes the historian Antony Taylor, 'Shakespeare's plays were seen as expressive of a pre-modern natural order and a balance within society' (Taylor 2002: 364). And, indeed, from a radical perspective, *Julius Caesar* is easily read as a defence of republicanism, in as much as it shows a dictator who aims at monarchy being assassinated. *Coriolanus*, which depicts a Roman nobleman who hates the common people while the rich hoard grain during a famine could be interpreted as an attack on aristocracy and greedy merchants alike. *King John*, whose desire to rule absolutely was curbed by his barons, can be understood as a call for constitutional restraint on the powers of monarchs. *Macbeth*, it was argued after an unsuccessful attempt on the life of the repressive French Emperor Napoleon III, clearly advocates tyrannicide. It was also claimed that the presence of strong female characters in so many plays suggested that he would have supported the notion of female suffrage. Shakespeare's plays were seen as a forum where issues of national politics were presented to the nation. Working-class radicals, who demanded participation in all aspects of political activity, considered that they had a right to Shakespeare.

As the three-hundredth anniversary of Shakespeare's birth approached a movement began to commemorate the occasion, mindful of the significance of David Garrick's belated celebration of the bicentenary, five years late in 1769. Two separate organisations went to work, one in London and the other in Stratford-upon-Avon, without ever managing to co-ordinate their activities. Neither was wholly successful in achieving the national celebration it desired. Thanks to the efforts of the radical brewer, Edward Fordham Flower, the events in Stratford were much the better organised. A large temporary pavilion seating five thousand people was built in Southern Lane, just south of where the Royal Shakespeare Company's theatres stand today (Foulkes 1984: 22–6). Over seven days, from 23 to 29 April 1864 there were concerts, a ball and three plays performed, although without the London stars the organisers had hoped to attract. A spectacular fire-work display marked the opening of the festivities.

The cost of tickets, however, precluded working people from taking part. The cheapest ticket for an event was two shillings and sixpence. For the plays themselves the cheapest ticket cost five shillings and a reserved place cost a minimum of ten shillings (*The Standard*, 25 April 1864). 'The price', wrote Richard Foulkes, 'virtually determined the social composition of the audience and was indeed a means of keeping away undesirable elements, however earnestly they may have wished to attend' (Foulkes 1984: 31). The Sunday service on 24 April at Holy Trinity Church was presided over by the Archbishop of Dublin, Dr Richard Chenevix Trench, who had been instrumental in the establishment of the *Oxford English Dictionary*. Chenevix Trench was a shy, quietly spoken man and many in the church found it hard to hear his sermon. If they did make out what he was saying they would have heard a clear statement that the lower orders should know their place and not to trespass on what belonged to their betters – Shakespeare included. According to 'God's scheme of the universe', proclaimed Chenevix Trench, men should carry on cheerfully carrying out

> in their own appointed sphere the work which has been assigned to them …
> not fiercely dashing and shaking themselves like imprisoned birds against the
> bars of the prison house, or moodily nourishing in their own hearts and in the
> hearts of others thoughts of discontent, revolt and despair.
>
> (Cited in Foulkes 1984: 29)

These were Shakespeare's own opinions too, he hastened to add. Perhaps he knew that there were already men in the town nourishing in their own hearts and in the hearts of others thoughts of discontent.

On 15 April – the Roman Ides of the month when republicans had assassinated the would-be tyrant Julius Caesar in both Shakespeare and history – a handbill had appeared in Stratford-upon-Avon (cited in Foulkes 1984: 35–6):

TIME! SHAKESPEARE THE POET OF THE PEOPLE

People of Stratford! Where are the seats reserved for you at the forthcoming festival? What part or lot have you who originated it, in the coming celebration? None! But you will be permitted to see the Fireworks, because they cannot be let off in the Pavilion; and you are promised something *after the swells have dined*. Only wait till the next week,

and see the dainty mess that shall be BREWED for you out of the cold 'wittles'. PEOPLE OF STRATFORD, who would not see your town disgraced on such an occasion, your streets empty, or blocked up only by the carriages of *profitless swells,* take counsel without delay!
Call a meeting without delay!
Form your own Committee!
Hold your own Festival!!!
Look to your own business. Lay out your own money.
Get up your own out-door sports and in-door pastimes, and let your watchword be

SHAKESPEARE the POET OF THE PEOPLE
AND HURRAH FOR THE PAGEANT

Hobbesley Hall
Kendal Green
Flowery Land
Ides of April 1864

This is a clear declaration of class conflict over the rights to own Shakespeare, but it is not a call to revolution. There is a bold statement that the desire to celebrate Shakespeare's birthday originated amongst the people, and a condemnation of the rich 'swells' who will only allow the people to peer in to the festivities from the margins, while the common streets are jammed up by the coaches of the rich. There is also a swipe at the wealthy Flower's Brewery, which was central to the event itself. But the signatories, whose aliases recall the rural people's England which Shakespeare above all exemplified, call not for a riot but for a committee to be formed and the people's own celebrations to challenge the rights of exclusive ownership of the bard. The mid-Victorian working class was getting organised and setting up structures which would eventually bring democracy, education, social welfare – and Shakespeare, if they wanted him – to the whole people.

The official organising committee refused to arrange so vulgar an event as a street pageant, so a committee was indeed formed, headed by John Talbot. Door-to-door collections raised the money required and on Monday 2 May 30,000 people arrived to see the procession brought on cheap excursion trains from as far away as Bristol and the north of England. It had to be repeated the following day, such was the demand to see the procession of characters from the plays led by representations of the ancient goddesses who inspired comedy and tragedy, the muses Thalia and Melpomene. Costumes and armour were lent by a London theatrical costumier and a troop of circus horse acrobats completed the parade. These vast crowds brought far more useful trade to the town's small businesses than the official event. On 3 and 4 May there were performances of the plays in the Pavilion, sanctioned by the official committee, but with ticket prices ranging from one to three shillings. Audiences were bigger than before:

4,000 people saw *Othello*, *Much Ado About Nothing* and the trial scene of *The Merchant of Venice*.

In London the official National Shakespeare Committee, which had taken upon itself the duty of organising celebrations in the capital, faced even fiercer opposition from organised labour – opposition which would culminate in violence in a public park. A co-ordinating committee of trade unionists, the Trades Provisional Committee, joined forces with the Working Men's Shakespeare Committee to organise a festival of labour and democratic reform which would challenge the pro-establishment and pro-empire tone of the National Shakespeare Committee. The radical and republican *Reynolds's Newspaper* attacked the Committee's 'flunkeyish servility', run by 'nobodies who monopolised its management … a large crop of titled names' who would ensure that 'the working classes were completely and contemptuously ignored' (cited in Taylor 2002: 375). The trade unionists planned to organise a huge celebratory rally in Hyde Park, followed by a march to Green Park to lay the foundation stone for a Shakespeare statue. They were, however, pointedly banned from doing so by the Chief Commissioner of Woods and Forests (*Lloyd's Weekly*, 24 April 1864). Instead they decided to stage an event on Primrose Hill, just north of Regent's Park, a stretch of ground overlooking the city and located between the houses of the wealthy around the park and the working-class district of Chalk Farm.

The political temperature was hotter than usual in London that April because of the presence in the capital of the Italian nationalist Giuseppe Garibaldi. Garibaldi had been a tireless fighter in many liberation struggles, but he still had not succeeded in his main aim of uniting all Italy as a single state, free of foreign control or the domination of the Pope. The Kingdom of Italy had been proclaimed in 1860, but the Pope still controlled Rome and the territory around it with the help of a French garrison. In 1864 Garibaldi had just been released from prison following an unsuccessful attempt to lead his forces against the city, which he felt must be the capital of a united Italy. Garibaldi was seen as a hero to many in Britain, a tireless warrior who had liberated people from foreign oppression and who was seen as an enemy of the reactionary governments of the Austrian and Russian Empires. His attack on the Pope had made him even more popular in a country where anti-Catholic feeling remained strong (except among the many Catholic Irish immigrants in the cities; see Bloom 2010: 143–5). Garibaldi was a charismatic, legendary figure who was received with honour in 1864 by Parliament, Eton College and the Prince of Wales. But he also stirred up adulation amongst radicals and reformers wherever he went. The government grew nervous, and rather than have him tour the provinces he was persuaded to leave the country under the pretext of ill-health. He left on the Duke of Sutherland's yacht on the morning of Saturday 23 April, the very day fixed for the march to Primrose Hill, Shakespeare's supposed birthday. It appeared that there was an establishment conspiracy to snub the great liberator; feelings ran high. Many of the same men who were on the Working Men's Shakespeare Committee were also on the Garibaldian Reception Committee

(Foulkes 1984: 43), and the demonstration was to end up conflating the causes of the two heroes of the working people.

There was an official 'Grand Miscellaneous Entertainment and Monster Demonstration of the Working Classes' arranged for that day in the Royal Agricultural Hall in Islington by the London Shakespeare Committee, but that event was poorly attended. The hall was less than one third full, and massively upstaged by the trade union march. The Working Men's Committee estimated that between 70,000 and 100,000 people took part (Foulkes 1984: 43). The main body set off north from Russell Square, led by George Cruikshank, the satirical cartoonist and illustrator of Dickens's early novels. The city they moved through was 'placarded with bills ... calling upon the working classes of the Metropolis' to assemble at Primrose Hill at five that afternoon to protest against 'the manner in which Garibaldi had been hurried out of this country, under pressure from the government, at the dictation of certain European crowned heads' (*Lloyd's Weekly*, 24 April 1864). The band of the Fourth City of London Rifles provided the marching music, and children carried banners bearing the names of Shakespeare's plays.

The march may have been a challenge to the establishment celebrations, but Queen Victoria, who together with other members of the royal family had declined to play any other part in the celebrations, had donated an oak tree to be planted at Primrose Hill as the centre piece of the festivities. The star of Shakespeare at Sadler's Wells, Samuel Phelps, was to perform the honours, and a special poem had been written by the popular pro-Chartist and feminist poet Eliza Cook. As the march passed through the working-class areas of Somers Town and Camden

> flags were displayed upon many houses along the route of the various processions and on many of the dwellings around the park. In every sense this celebration by working men, which was purely spontaneous ... was as intelligent as it was successful.
>
> (*Newcastle Weekly Chronicle*, 30 April 1864, cited in Taylor 2002: 377)

Once the different marches had assembled on Primrose Hill the ceremony took place at the foot of the hill facing Ormonde Terrace. There was a small enclosure nearby, where, a Tory newspaper sneered, stood the rare sight of 'several fashionably dressed people' (*The Standard*, 25 April 1864).

Just as the whole event was contesting the ownership of Shakespeare the national icon, the oak tree was also a national symbol whose meaning was being fought over. Antony Taylor points out that for conservatives the oak tree provided the traditional material for the Royal Navy, which had guaranteed English independence from foreign invasion, or it stood as a symbol of the organic unity of the nation, rich and poor in the right places (Taylor 2002: 377). But for radicals the oak tree was the place where the Anglo-Saxons used to meet as free men to rule themselves before they were enslaved by the Norman conquest in 1066. The aristocratic descendants of those foreign invaders, it was claimed, still formed

England's ruling class. The right to assemble and demonstrate on open public spaces such as Primrose Hill was a repossession of their native land. Some of the banners carried in the demonstration bore the words 'Shakespeare Nature's Interpreter'. The oak tree for many of the demonstrators stood for the state of natural freedom which their ancestors had enjoyed before the coming of the 'Norman Yoke' of privilege by birth.

That Shakespeare's excellence as a man and a writer had nothing to do with class privilege was made clear in Eliza Cook's poem on the bard. Cook herself was suffering from an attack of neuralgia, and the poem was read by Henry Marston:

> Here do we help to stud his diadem
> With Labour's sweat-drop – England's richest gem.
> Here do the people write with blazing pen,
> Shakespeare was born of England's Working Men

Even 'England's princes' must 'bend with high regard/ To swell the homage paid to England's bard' (*Lloyd's Weekly*, 24 April 1864).

The enthusiasm of London's working people for Shakespeare was evident in the huge numbers streaming onto the hill. Samuel Phelps was supposed to plant the tree at three o'clock, but it was half-past four when all the different groups with their marching bands had assembled. To great cheers Phelps thanked the organisers, and proclaimed the assembly to be 'one of the grandest spectacles that ever met the human eye'. He then planted the tree 'in the name of the working people' (*Lloyd's Weekly*, 24 April 1864). Mrs G. Linnaeus Banks sprinkled the tree with water from the River Avon in Shakespeare's home town and the poem was read. Isabella Banks was a popular poet and novelist whose best-known work, *The Manchester Man* (1876), would depict the rise of a working-class Mancunian in the first half of the century. She was a well-known campaigner for women's and workers' rights.

Observing the crowd with less delight was Inspector Stokes accompanied by a large body of the Metropolitan Police. They ignored the various illegal gambling activities and unlicensed traders who had attracted the attention of several hundred people at the fringe of the demonstration and focused on the trade union leaders (*The Daily News*, 28 April 1864). As the ceremony came to an end a group of activists gathered at the top of the hill and encouraged the rest of the crowd to gather around them. The instigator was Edmond Beales, a public-school and Cambridge-educated radical, who addressed about four thousand people who followed him to the top of the hill (Foulkes 1984: 43). He immediately raised the matter of Garibaldi's hasty departure from England that morning, and declared that there had been a conspiracy between the Prime Minister, Lord Palmerston, and Louis Napoleon of France to get the inspirational Garibaldi away from his admirers.

It is not clear whether it was at this point that the police attacked the demonstrators. At a later meeting with Lord Grey, the Home Secretary, Beales reported

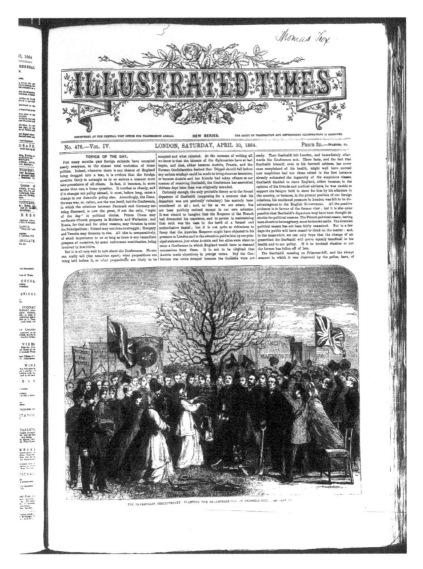

Figure 6.1 Mrs G. Linnaeus Banks Christening the Shakespeare Oak with Avon water on Primrose Hill, from *The Illustrated Times* 30 April 1864. The popular writer and campaigner for women's rights Isabella Varley Banks seems to be at the centre of a religious ceremony as an official kneels before her with a watering can of Avon water. Armed men of the local Volunteer regiments give the scene an added civic dignity. Amongst the trade union banners and placards proclaiming the names of Shakespeare's plays can be seen to the left a banner with a quotation from *Troilus and Cressida*, 'One touch of nature makes the whole world kin' (3.3.177), an apparently democratic sentiment wrenched from its actual context in the play where it refers to common human tendency to superficiality.

that there were 'many acts of personal violence' directed at the demonstrators (*The Daily News*, 28 April 1864). Beales himself was approached by Inspector Stokes, accompanied by two constables. Stokes announced that 'his orders were not to allow any political meeting to take place on Primrose Hill' (*The Times*, 25 April 1864, cited in Foulkes 1984: 43). He then made some kind of threat to Beales, and made it clear that his men were 'ready to act on a signal from the inspector' (*The Daily News*, 28 April 1864). Most newspapers make it clear that the situation was extremely tense, though they do not mention in detail the violence which Beales asserted, corroborated by the rest of the deputation to Lord Grey. *The Standard* reports (25 April 1864) that 'the prohibition [of the new meeting] occasioned some surprise and a good deal of apprehension, and at one time there was some apprehension of a riot'. The *Newcastle Weekly Chronicle* compared the conduct of Inspector Stokes with 'the brutality of the French police' under the despotic Louis Napoleon (30 April 1864, cited in Taylor 2002: 378). It does seem that blows were exchanged between those who had come to celebrate a playwright and the forces of the state, but it was the trade union activists who stepped in to avoid serious trouble. 'Had it not been for the admirable conduct of the committee and the people', Beales told Lord Grey, 'the results might have been of the most serious nature, as the conduct of the police was marked by a degree of unnecessary violence calculated to provoke resistance and create a riot' (*The Daily News*, 28 April 1864). The crowds dispersed, its leaders to assemble in the nearby Adelaide pub to pass a motion protesting against such a crude denial of political freedom.

This was not then the kind of major disturbance dealt with in other chapters of this book, but it was a public fracas where blows were exchanged that marks a major turning point: the end of the golden age of British theatre riots. As in the case of other nineteenth-century theatre riots, this was about class conflict. First of all this was not a dispute about possession of playhouse access, as in the Old Price riots; this was a contest for the rights to interpret the meaning of a playwright, a battle for possession of an iconic symbol. The Garibaldi case may have been the flashpoint on Primrose Hill, but it is clear that the thousands who gathered were making a bold assertion of their rights to an icon of liberty and emancipation. The police were there in huge numbers for the Shakespeare celebration; the impromptu demonstration at the end gave them their chance to intervene. Future riots, such as in Dublin in 1926 or in Birmingham in 2004 were also to be about the meaning of a theatrical event, not about the physical rights of different sections of the audience. Another important difference, prefigured in the Old Price conflict, was the well-developed organisation of the working-class movement, which recognised that their aims were more likely to be achieved through conventional politics rather than violence: their deputation was treated with respect by the Home Secretary on 27 April. A grievance persisted against the police action that day and there was serious violence involving Garibaldi's supporters in Hyde Park in 1866, but that was a conflict between Garibaldi's Irish opponents and his fans, rather than with the police (Bloom 2010: 143–4).

By the early years of the twentieth century Shakespeare had begun to lose his status as a working- class hero and was well on the way to becoming seen as irrelevant at best, and at worst the inaccessible possession of a social and cultural elite. Several explanations have been offered for this. The historian Jonathan Rose argues that the fashion for avant-garde Shakespeare in the theatre from about 1900 alienated working-class audiences (Rose 2002: 125). But in fact Shakespeare done in an old-fashioned way, in early modern costume and with highly dramatic delivery – the touring productions of Donald Wolfit would be a good example – continued to be performed well into the twentieth century. The literary historian Andrew Murphy points out that rather than watch Shakespeare, there developed in the late nineteenth and early twentieth centuries a whole range of alternative artistic and sporting activities where working people could enjoy the leisure time which the trade unions and the labour movement won from employers and government (Murphy 2008: 162–78). Crucial amongst these was the popularity of the cinema. But Shakespeare films remained widely popular right into the twentieth century. When Laurence Olivier's *Hamlet* was released in 1947 there were block bookings for groups of factory workers for the first showings in Birmingham (Davies 2000: 177).

But Murphy also argues that it was the presence of Shakespeare in state education in the years after schooling became universal and compulsory in 1870 that made a real difference. Perhaps the turning point was when the 'payment by results' system for schoolteachers meant that teachers' pay depended on getting students to memorise chunks of plays. School budgets were set according to the number of students passing tests of this kind at the highest levels. This was disastrous to classroom relationships, and to how Shakespeare was viewed. Shakespeare was also seen by the government as a means of countering the effects of the mass media popular with ordinary people. When compulsory lessons in English Literature were introduced into upper forms of state schools in 1871, a crucial justification for this innovation was the role which the subject would play in countering 'the corrupting attractions of newspapers, magazines and novelettes'; what a Report of the Committee on Education in 1895–6 called 'pernicious matter' (Mathieson 1975: 52). Shakespeare was explicitly deployed as a denigration of the very reading matter which ordinary people chose, and thus forcibly associated with a condescending paternalism. What is more, where once, as the Labour MP Will Crooks recalled, blacksmiths would recite Shakespeare to each other as entertainment in their lunch breaks, or a group of textile mill girls would meet at 5am to read a play before work, school recitation of Shakespeare often became a mere memory test with corporal punishment the outcome of failure (Taylor 2002: 359).

The 1864 stand-off at Primrose Hill was perhaps the last moment when the working people's claim to ownership of Shakespeare was physically challenged by their rulers. As most of them turned their backs on the 'serious' theatre in the years to come, violent conflict would be focused more on how the less powerful in society came to be represented on stage, rather than on access to the theatre and what was increasingly seen as 'high' culture.

Note

1 But the theatre was also employed by anti-Chartist, conservative activists for political ends, as in the case of the orchestrated disruption of a French touring production of Dumas' *The Count of Monte Cristo* in 1848 at the height of political disturbances and revolution on the mainland of Europe. See Emeljanow 2003.

References

Bloom, Clive (2010), *Violent London: Two Thousand Years of Riots, Rebels and Revolts* (Basingstoke: Palgrave Macmillan).

Crump, Jeremy (1986), 'Shakespeare in Nineteenth-Century Leicester', in Richard Foulkes (ed.) *Shakespeare and the Victorian Stage* (Cambridge: Cambridge University Press).

Davies, Anthony (2000), 'The Shakespeare Films of Laurence Olivier', in Russell Jackson (ed.) *The Cambridge Companion to Shakespeare on Film*, second edition (Cambridge: Cambridge University Press).

Emeljanow, Victor (2003), 'The Events of June 1848: The *Monte Cristo* Riots and the Politics of Protest', *New Theatre Quarterly*, 19, 23–32.

Foulkes, Richard (1984), *The Shakespeare Tercentenary of 1864* (London: The Society for Theatre Research).

—— (2002), *Performing Shakespeare in the Age of Empire* (Cambridge: Cambridge University Press).

Mathieson, Margaret (1975), *The Preachers of Culture: A Study of English and Its Teachers* (London: Allen & Unwin).

Murphy, Andrew (2008), *Shakespeare for the People: Working Class Readers 1800–1900* (Cambridge: Cambridge University Press).

Rose, Jonathan (2002), *The Intellectual Life of the British Working Classes* (New Haven CT and London: Yale University Press).

Taylor, Antony (2002), 'Shakespeare and Radicalism: The Uses and Abuses of Shakespeare in Nineteenth Century Popular Politics', *The Historical Journal*, 45 (2), 357–79.

Chapter 7

Representing a nation

The 1907 *Playboy of the*
Western World riot
at the Abbey Theatre, Dublin

In 1976 I attended a schools matinee of J. M. Synge's Irish rural tragicomedy *The Playboy of the Western World* at the Olivier Theatre in London, with Stephen Rea in the lead role and with the Irish folk band The Chieftains providing the music. In those days theatre tickets for such events were provided free to students by the Inner London Education Authority. The theatre was full of London teenagers, clearly unused to the theatre and over-excited to the point of near-riot. Various missiles were landing in the stalls from the circle, accompanied by quite a lot of spittle. As the play began to cacophonous hooting and whistling, interspersed with satirical catcalls, I sat squirming in my grammar school uniform wondering where this would all lead. But within a minute or two the cast had not just silenced the audience, but had them gripped, attentive and soon roaring with laughter. That engagement was sustained all the way to a tumultuous and joyful curtain call. The play and the production united with its audience, and it turned out to be a moving and memorable experience. In a curious way that afternoon, beginning in mayhem and ending in triumph, echoed the circumstances of the play's original production.

Synge's play was first produced just as the struggle for Irish independence from Great Britain was reaching a climax in the early years of the twentieth century. Apart from the nationalist political (and eventually military) struggle there was also a cultural battle for independence to be fought. Principally, writers and artists sought to foreground Ireland's own language, mythology, sport and folklore as an ancient and distinctive culture which had been overwhelmed by centuries of English domination. This movement became known as 'The Celtic Revival'. But there was also a determined and vocal resistance to the way in which Irish people were represented on stage both in Ireland and abroad, in striking anticipation of similar contests about the media representation of 'minorities' in later years. In the eighteenth century the typical Irishman on the London and Dublin stage had been a boastful and over-emotional soldier: eminent examples include Major O'Flaherty in Cumberland's *The West Indian* (1771) or Sir Lucius O'Trigger in Sheridan's *The Rivals* (1775). The playwright George Bernard Shaw summed up the stereotype as a man 'generous, drunken, thriftless, with a joke always on his lips and a sentimental tear always in his eye' (Blackadder

2003: 70). In the popular English theatre and in the music halls of the nineteenth century the depiction of Irish peasants as stupid and venal was, according to the historian of Dublin's Abbey Theatre, 'an invidious form of propaganda; not only flattering British audiences with a sense of their superiority to their second-class neighbours, but blinding them to the very real suffering of Ireland's peasants from famine and eviction' (Hunt 1979: 4). For most of the nineteenth century Ireland was a desperately poor country. To add to this situation the rural and small town population was devastated by the failure of the potato crop in 1844–6. Mass emigration followed. Those remaining suffered at the hands of profit-hungry landlords keen to evict tenants to turn arable land into more profitable pasture (Foster 1989: 168). There were a few landlords who did try to help the starving and diseased; some of whom went bankrupt in the process. There was little industrialisation outside Belfast, and therefore no mills and factories to utilise the labour that was getting on boats to Britain and America. By the time famine and disease had done their worst the population had shrunk by about a quarter. Some of those who remained became further radicalised, and fuelled by a desperate economic situation they developed skills in political insurgency against British rule, which often turned violent.

In the first decade of the twentieth century there were some disturbances in theatres in protest at representations of Irish people in Dublin, but also in Liverpool and in New York, cities with substantial Irish communities (Kilroy 1971: 6). Some felt that Ireland now needed to speak for itself. Others were less offended by stock 'Oirishry' on stage. Late nineteenth-century Irish popular theatre could be seen as manipulating the stereotypes and conventions of melodrama in subtle ways: the pugnacious and sentimental peasant-hero would often skilfully outwit his oppressor to win the day (Watt 2004: 22–8). A nationalist theatre group known as the 'Emerald Minstrels' performed a very popular play in the 1890s known as *Terence's Fireside: or The Irish Peasant at Home*, 'essentially a series of turns held together by the fiction that this was the in-house entertainment of the typical Irish home' (Cairns and Richards 1987: 226). For many nationalists, the image of the Irish peasant became iconically central to their political aspirations: honest, loyal, brave, patriotic and full of the simple virtues which contrasted strongly to their urban, sophisticated but perfidious imperial rulers. Plays like this brought together the image of the peasant and the struggle for Irish independence. At the end of the first half of *Terence's Fireside* 'The Shan Van Vocht', a nationalist song from the 1798 rebellion, was sung.

When the Irish National Theatre Society was founded in 1902 (Blackadder 2003: 71) it was with the intention that Ireland would no longer be shown on stage as 'the home of buffoonery and easy sentiment', but that the theatre would be 'primarily a means of regenerating the country'. These were the words of its founders, W. B. Yeats, Lady Augusta Gregory and Edward Martyn in their 1898 manifesto *Our Irish Theatre* (cited in Hunt 1979: 18). But that theatre company, which from 1904 made its home in the Abbey Theatre, Dublin, consequently found itself torn between the political requirements of Irish nationalism and the artistic vision both of its founders and of its best playwrights, who would not compromise their own aesthetic principles, nor their view of their country to suit the narrower political agenda of mainstream nationalism. Neither John Millington Synge nor, later, Sean O'Casey would accept constraints upon their depictions of Irish life, and in both cases trouble ensued. Riots convulsed the Abbey Theatre during the opening performances of Synge's *The Playboy of the Western World* in 1907 and subsequently at O'Casey's *The Plough and the Stars* in 1926 (see Chapter 8 below). The plays completed their runs, but the romantic nationalism and social conservatism of the protestors proved to be powerful forces that would dominate Irish political life in the decades to come. Today, by contrast, Synge's and O'Casey's detached and tragicomic view of Ireland seems to have triumphed in its own way and to have become the national style of Irish drama.

The poet and playwright W. B. Yeats was instrumental in the creation of Ireland's national theatre company. To his detractors Yeats could appear an other-worldly and cerebral figure. His devotion to mysticism, to the occult and to arcane philosophical systems added to his sombre commitment to the sacred duty of the poet made him an easy target for ridicule. Yet he proved an astute political opera-tor in establishing the Abbey Theatre and seeing it through difficult times. Yeats's idea of a theatre for Ireland was not inspired by the need to celebrate a nationalist ideal, as a beacon of national pride and as a rebuke to would-be oppressors. Yeats wanted to recreate a culture like that of ancient Athens, as he saw it, where there was a unity between art and everyday life. He wanted plays which dramatised myths in order to unify audiences in a powerful sense of national cultural identity; he sought to produce theatrical experiences which would induce the community of spectators to share common emotions. Ireland would be made one by watching 'the sacred drama of its own history, every spectator finding self and neighbour, finding all the world there as we find the bright spot under the looking glass' (cited in Flannery 1976: 65). He had allies in his vision for an Irish national theatre, not least in his patron, the tireless Lady Augusta Gregory, but he had to compromise with others in order to make the theatre a reality. Yeats came from the Protestant 'Ascendancy', the ruling class of the Anglo-Irish who had dominated the coun-try for centuries, but whose days were in fact now numbered. A national theatre which unified the nation culturally need not be a stepping stone to independence from Britain, and that was not Yeats's motive. Yeats and Gregory believed in their own artistic superiority and wanted a theatre which would educate the Irish people by making them appreciate a higher, rational, culture which found its values out-side the Catholic faith of the people. But Catholicism was also central, for many, to the nationalist project itself (Frazier 2004: 33–4; Pilkington 2004: 232–5). To the extent that the national theatre was run by people whose views could be seen as anti-democratic and anti-Catholic, it perhaps is not surprising that it should eventually run into violent conflict with its audiences.

Yeats had involved himself in nationalist politics as a means of raising Irish cultural consciousness, then, rather than out of a fervent belief in the republican

Figure 7.1 William Butler Yeats. A portrait by George Charles Beresford taken in July 1911, when Yeats was forty-six years old.

project. Yet in 1900 he worked with Arthur Griffith, the leader of the major nationalist political party, Sinn Féin, in drawing up the programme for Cumann na Gaedhal, an organisation for developing national cultural awareness. Griffith joined Yeats in the national theatre movement and in 1902 became a vice-president of the National Theatre Society. Griffith had written in 1898 that 'the Theatre is a powerful agent of building up of a nation … In the Ireland we foresee it will be an extremely dangerous thing to tell an Irishman that God made him unfit to be master in his own land' (cited in Flannery 1976: 324). Yet for funding Yeats depended on the English tea heiress Annie Horniman, who loved the theatre but hated Irish nationalism. She also had no inclination to encourage poorer Dubliners to visit the theatre, and insisted that there should be no cheap ('sixpenny') seats available as in other playhouses (Blackadder 2003: 73). In order to break even in its early days the theatre company toured England, where the laudatory reviews it received for its unfussy style of acting did not endear the company in the eyes of nationalists. It was no surprise that Arthur Griffith soon resigned from the Society, primarily over the content of a play called *The Saxon Shillin'*. In this dispute Yeats backed the director Willie Fay, who changed the play to make its conclusion less melodramatic. Fay wanted to alter the final scene, where the British army shot dead an Irish deserter protecting his father from eviction. For Griffith, the political impact must come before the artistic effect (Flannery 1976: 325).

The arrival at the Abbey of the playwright J. M. Synge precipitated open conflict between political nationalism and the national theatre. Synge, born in 1871, also came from the Anglo-Irish Protestant ruling class. After some travelling in continental Europe he spent time in the remote Aran Islands off Ireland's west coast. The peasants of the islands were later to be depicted with detached, ironic and often dark humour in his plays. Synge was a shy, introspective young man who suffered badly from asthma (he died in 1909) (Henn 1981: 6–7). His commitment was to poetry and drama in the abstract; he did not cultivate nationalist feeling in himself. He was, however, well read in the latest avant-garde artistic thinking and in contemporary philosophy, and in particular in the work of the German philosopher Friedrich Nietzsche (King 2004: 80). Synge was a European modernist rather than a Celtic Revivalist. The peasants of the west in particular, where English penetration had been least evident, had an iconic status to nationalists as honest, uncorrupted people of pure Gaelic stock: true Irishmen and women. But Synge was more interested in exploring issues of authority and sexuality through the use of myth and symbol in a language which was at once poetic and colloquial.

Synge's views on his responsibilities as a playwright are very plain in the interview he gave to a reporter from the *Dublin Evening Mail* on a chaotic stairway at the Abbey Theatre during the mayhem following the second performance of *The Playboy of the Western World* on 28 January 1907. The playwright stood 'excited and restless, the perspiration standing out in great beads over his forehead and cheeks'. 'Tell me, Mr Synge', began the reporter, 'was your purpose to represent Irish life as it is lived – in short, did you think yourself holding the mirror up to nature?' Synge refused to be drawn by the reporter's unsubtle attempt to compare himself with Shakespeare's Hamlet (3.2.22) and denied such an aim 'rather emphatically'. Having then asked a passing attendant to get the police to 'quell the row', Synge told the reporter that 'I wrote the play because it pleased me, and it just happens that I know Irish life best, so I made my methods Irish'. Far from worrying about how an audience might take his work, he added that 'I don't care a rap how the people take it'. The reporter's comment on Synge's philosophy barely concealed its disdain: 'I paused for a moment to reflect upon this new tenet in art. In idealistic quarters it has ever been the cry, art for art's sake; here it was art for the artist's sake' (cited in Kilroy 1971: 22–5).

In fact the idea of 'art for art's sake' had not been as universal as the reporter claimed – nor was it necessarily Synge's view – but it was a particular belief of the contemporary aesthetic movement. As Oscar Wilde puts in the 1891 preface to *The Picture of Dorian Gray*, 'There is no such thing as a moral or an immoral book. Books are well written, or badly written' (Wilde 2006: 3). But such views were regarded as effete and decadent by nationalists and reformers who believed in the political and moral power of art. The Europe-wide movement for the creation of national theatres was an important expression of this belief. In England, too, there was a burgeoning movement led by William Archer and Harley Granville-Barker for a publicly subsidised institution that would reflect the power and dignity of the state, and which would resist American cultural and commercial influences to 'sustain Englishness' (Shepherd 2009: 1–3). Norway's Nationaltheatret opened in Christiania (later Oslo) in 1899, and the Norwegian theatre had been seen as an important element in Norway's struggle for independence from Sweden, finally achieved in 1905 (Hunt 1979: 9–10).

Synge's first play was first performed at the Molesworth Hall in 1903. His one act drama *In the Shadow of the Glen* is a darkly funny tale of a curmudgeonly and sexless Wicklow peasant who feigns his own death to catch out his philandering wife. What really offended the audience, however, was the play's conclusion. Norah, the wife (played by Máire Nic Shiubhlaigh), decides she would prefer a life on the road with a tramp whom she has only met twenty minutes before to staying with her husband. He promises her 'the herons crying out over the black lakes … and the grouse and the owls with them, and the larks and the big thrushes when the days are warm.' 'You've a fine bit of talk, stranger', replies Nora 'and it's with yourself I'll go' (Synge 1981: 94). Arthur Griffith said the play was an example of the 'cynicism that passes current in the Latin *Quartier* [in Paris] and the London Salon'. The socialist leader James Connolly, who was to be executed by the British for his prominent role in the 1916 Easter Rising, walked out in protest and two actors resigned from the company. The writer Douglas Hyde, who went on to become the President of an independent Ireland in 1938, resigned from the Irish National Theatre Society (Blackadder 2003: 72). Griffith claimed that the play was a sheer falsehood; no Wicklow wife would ever behave in that way, since 'Irish women are the most virtuous in the world'. But there was also criticism from influential Catholics who found the play morally distasteful (Flannery 1976: 323–5). Synge's response to his critics was clear: 'the next play I write I will make sure I annoy them' (Hunt 1979: 73).

So all this was as nothing to the furore that would greet Synge's finest work, *The Playboy of the Western World*, when it opened at the Abbey Theatre on Saturday 26 January 1907. The action is set in a rough and ready pub 'near a village, on a wild coast of Mayo' (Synge 1981: 173), presided over by the publican's daughter, Pegeen Mike, 'a wild-looking but fine girl' (Synge 1981: 176). The eponymous playboy is one Christy Mahon, a stranger who suddenly comes in 'very tired and frightened and dirty' (Synge 1981: 180). When Christy reveals that he has killed his own father with a spade, he is treated with awed respect by all, is offered work as a pot-boy and displaces the feeble Shawn Keogh in Pegeen's affections. Widow Quin is soon Pegeen's rival for Christy's approval. Unfortunately for Christy, his father turns up looking for him with a heavily bandaged head. Christy is then rejected as a liar, so he attempts to regain their respect by 'killing' him again, off stage. But the villagers' disgust is only increased, and they tie Christy up with the intention of handing him over to the police. He is saved once again as Old Mahon, hilariously, enters unseen on all fours upstage. His son, '*scrambling on his knees face to face with old Mahon*' greets him with the uproarious line, 'Are you coming to be killed a third time, or what ails you now?' The father forgives the son, and announces that 'my son and myself will be going our own way, and we'll have great times from this out telling stories of the villainy of Mayo, and the fools is here.' But even after all this, Pegeen Mike is distraught. In the play's final speech she cuffs Shawn around the head, and '*breaking out in wild lamentations*' she cries, 'Oh, my grief, I've lost him surely. I've lost the only Playboy of the Western World' (Synge 1981: 228–9).

Synge claimed in his *Dublin Evening Mail* interview that he didn't care that the plot of the play was improbable ('Was Don Quixote probable? And still it is art'), but he also claimed it was a 'thing that really happened. I knew a young fellow in the Aran Islands who had killed his father. And the people befriended him and sent him off to America'. Yet his play was also 'a comedy, an extravaganza, made to amuse –', at this point all the lights failed in the Abbey and the interview was terminated. The credibility of the plot was an argument used to cover what was regarded as a slur on the national character. 'You take the worst form of murderer, a parricide, and set him up to be worshipped by the simple, honest people of the West' was the reporter's accusation (cited in Hunt 1979: 23–4). Synge may have been referring to the case of William Maley from Galway, who killed his father with a spade in 1873, hid in the Aran Islands and subsequently escaped to the United States (Grene 1999: 87–8). But the audience would also find echoes of the notorious case of James Lynchehaun, who committed arson on the estate of his English landlady and violently assaulted her. He also hid on the Aran Islands and got away to America, and his subsequent extradition case was in the news in 1904 (Grene 1999: 88–9). To foreground these stories in the plot of a drama in the Abbey Theatre was for nationalists not outlaw romance but rather a confirmation of the British imperialist stereotype of the Irishman as fundamentally lawless and in need of a firm ruling hand of a civilised master.

The critic Mary Colum recalled that even before the first night 'reports spread through Dublin that there were improprieties in the play and that the womanhood of Ireland was being slandered' (Hunt 1979: 73). The 'improprieties' included religious oaths which some might feel amount to blasphemy. But there was also the apparently shocking mention of women's underwear in both Pegeen Mike's catty remark to Widow Quin ('And you without a white shift or shirt in your whole family since the drying of the flood'), and in Christy Mahon's later protestation that he wanted only Pegeen as his lover, even if 'you brought me a drift of chosen females, standing in their shifts itself …' (Synge 1981: 198, 226). Synge grudgingly allowed only a very few excisions in rehearsal. But the Abbey's many opponents were sharpening their knives before the first night.

The opening Saturday night of *Playboy* was a social occasion for Dublin's political and artistic elite. But there were also many ordinary theatregoers from other social classes who had certain expectations of plays with settings in rural peasant life and whose vocal response to what they saw on stage tended to be unashamedly vocal for good or ill, and these patrons would make up much of the audience for the remainder of the run. An apparent but very different precursor to *Playboy* which may have been in the playgoers' minds that night was Douglas Hyde's short drama *Casadh an tSúgáin* (*The Twisting of the Rope*), which had been performed in Irish by the Gaelic League Amateur Dramatic Society at Dublin's Gaiety Theatre in October 1901. Hyde played the lead role himself. As in Synge's play, a stranger arrives in a rural community and tries to entice the beautiful Oona from her intended, Sheamus. Unlike in Synge's play, 'Hyde's peasants are intelligent and resourceful ... [and] the play closes with Sheamus' confirmation of the value of community, "isn't it a fine thing for a man to be lis-tening to the storm outside, and himself quiet and easy by the fire?"' (Cairns and Richards 1987: 226–7). Synge saw the production, and also witnessed the highly emotional reception it received from the audience, who called out encouragement in Irish to the dancers that night and sang patriotic songs during the intervals between the different parts of the evening's programme (which also featured an English company, Frank Benson's Shakespeare Company, performing a piece based on Irish mythology, *Diarmuid and Grainne*, by Yeats and George Moore) (Cairns and Richards 1987: 227).

In considering what followed, it is worth bearing in mind that the audiences for nationalist plays and popular melodramas 'regularly hissed the villain, cheered the hero, yelled advice to the characters or during the intervals' (Trotter 1998: 41). The positive representation of what they took be 'Irishness' on stage had a direct political power off stage as it sought to counter what they saw as the dominant English narrative, which had showed the Irish as childish, over-emotional and of limited intelligence. They did not see the on-stage and off-stage worlds as completely separate: what happened on stage directly affected the world beyond the footlights, so that the world had a right to intervene in the action on the stage. The Irish National Theatre Society at the Abbey Theatre, on the other hand, with its high aesthetic standards and decorous ambience 'insisted on solemn dignity in its performances ... any noises made by the audience were to be positive, polite, and at the fall of the curtain' (Trotter 1998: 46). As it happened the Abbey was also rented out to nationalist theatre groups when audi-ence behaviour would be much more raucous than when the INTS were playing. Audience members who attended Synge's play and who had been to the Abbey before had not necessarily experienced the performance etiquette which Yeats and his company expected.

It appears that for some reason on the first night *Playboy*'s abundance of joyful comedy was not so evident in the actors' work, and the play's more cruel side was on show (Hunt 1979: 74–5). Nevertheless, all went quietly enough until the final part of Act Three when Christy Mahon is captured and bound by the peasants and bites Shawn Keogh's leg. On Monday a hostile reviewer in Ireland's oldest nationalist newspaper, *The Freeman's Journal*, gave this account, and his own frank opinion:

> The audience had stood this revolting story thus far. Now angry groans, growls, hisses, and noise broke out while the pinioning of Mahon went on. It was not possible – thank goodness – to follow the dialogue for a time ... A brutal riotous scene takes place. The groans, hisses and counter cheers of the audience drowned the words, but as well as could be gathered Christy decides to part quietly with his father, and let Mayo resume its normal state of sickening demoralisation. The mere idea can be given of the barbarous jargon, the elaborate and incessant cursings of these repulsive creatures. Everything is b——y this or a——y that, and into this picturesque dialogue names that should only be used with respect and reverence are frequently introduced. Enough! The hideous caricature would be slanderous of a Kaffir kraal. The piece is announced to run for a week; it is to be hoped it will be instantly withdrawn.
>
> (*The Freeman's Journal*, 28 January 1907, p.10;
> cited in Kilroy 1971: 8–9)

While the reviewer focuses on the immorality of the play, a subconscious resentment emerges: the play represents Irish people as an inferior race, worse even than the black South Africans ('Kaffirs') with whom many Dubliners would have been familiar after service in the British army (or with their opponents) in the Boer War of 1899–1902. Pseudonymous, and probably factitious, letters were printed below the review. One, from 'A Western Girl 2', asked 'could any Irish person accept this as a true picture of Irish life?'

Special sympathy was, however, extended to Sara Allgood in the part of Widow Quin:

> Nothing redeems the general sordidness of the piece. Every character uses coarse expressions, and Miss Allgood (one of the most charming actresses I have ever seen) is forced, before the most fashionable audience in Dublin, to use a word indicating an essential item of female attire, which the lady herself would probably never utter in ordinary circumstances, even to herself.

The word 'shift', as Nicholas Grene explains, was by 1907 an archaic term for what would be politely known then as a 'chemise', with the newer term rendering the use of the older one crude and indelicate (Grene 1999: 82). Synge quite plausibly uses a word which might still be in use in farthest-flung Mayo, but the word suggested coarseness to an audience whose view of rural life was idealised and sanitised. Worse, the explicit reference to the sexual bodies of young women ('a drift of chosen females, standing in their shifts itself ...?' (Synge 1981: 226)) offended against the nationalist ideal of the Irish woman, who was 'insistently desexualised' in all representations (Grene 1999: 83). Here the playwright's romantic vision of the sensual earthiness of peasant life clashed violently with audience preconceptions: 'where the nationalists sought to project onto the peasants an idealised and asexual being, the life of the chemise rather than the shift, Synge was equally projecting from within a bourgeois consciousness in insisting on the primitive embodiedness of his characters' (Grene 1999: 84). Where Synge wanted to show the 'exhilarating otherness of the peasant milieu', the audience saw 'ugly monstrosity' (Grene 1999: 86).

Perhaps even more inflammatory was the point made more soberly in a more balanced review on the same day by *The Irish Independent*, then a recently founded cheap mass circulation daily, whose more aggressively nationalist politics were taking readers from *The Freeman's Journal*:

> His [Synge's] playboy, it is safe to say, has not his equal in Ireland. He is certainly not a type to be presented even in a farce in an Irish theatre, and under the auspices of a movement that has for its very object the destruction of such stage-Irishman types as Christie [sic] Mahon ... How would it be, say, if such a type of stage Irishman appeared in a play brought across-Channel and presented in Dublin? Wouldn't there be an uproar ...?
>
> (*The Irish Independent*, 28 January 1907, p.4; cited in Kilroy 1971: 12)

The *Independent* was playing on the unspoken suspicion that the Abbey was, in effect, a British mouthpiece, funded in Manchester by Annie Horniman and applauded by the London elite (but not, in fact, in the English popular theatres where the Abbey's style of peasant theatre soon came to be parodied) (Flannery 1976 : 346).

The hissing and catcalls were the worst that happened that first night. But word of the scandalous nature of Synge's play soon spread. The present Abbey Theatre, which opened in 1966, is much larger than its predecessor, which burned down in 1951. The 1904 Abbey was a compact, not to say cramped, venue seating only 536 people (Flannery 1976: 353). It had been adapted from two adjacent buildings, one of which had housed a small music hall and another which had once been a nationalist recruiting centre and at another time a morgue. Disrupting its proceedings would be an easy task. Ejecting troublemakers would be difficult.

On the following Monday there was a much smaller audience; as few as eighty, it seems, with the stalls sparsely populated. Some had clearly seen the Saturday performance and had come in order to protest (Blackadder 2003: 77, 81). Even though the reviews were bad, the prospect of trouble clearly put people off attending, and, apart from Wednesday night, the houses dwindled as the week's run went on (Lowery 1984: 5). The pit at the front of the stalls, however, was packed on the Monday. *Playboy* was preceded by another one act Synge drama, *Riders to the Sea*, which passed without incident. Hisses began in Act One of *Playboy* when the villagers began to admire Christy Mahon the father-killer. When it became clear that he would then be spending the night alone under the same roof as Pegeen Mike serious disruption began. A newspaper report claimed it had been carefully organised in advance (*Dublin Evening Mail*, 29 January 1907, p.2, cited in Kilroy 1971: 18). There was much booing and stamping, but many in the pit and gallery started bashing their walking sticks (a fashionable male accessory of the time) against the wooden tip-up seats. According to *The Freeman's Journal*, 'the refrain of "God save Ireland" was predominant' and 'loud shouts were also raised of "we won't have this"'. All the actors' speech was drowned out (Kilroy 1971: 10). The management of the Abbey was shocked. They did not expect such an ungrateful reaction from the people they hoped to educate. But 'an audience accustomed to reacting vigorously to melodrama simply could not manifest the passivity the Abbey attempted to cultivate' (Watt 2004: 30).

Willie Fay, who was playing Christy, came to the front of the stage and waited to be heard. Eventually he offered money back to those who objected, but insisted that the play would go ahead. He was shouted down amidst cries of 'Where is the author?', 'Sinn Féin for Ever' and 'Such a thing as this could not occur in Ireland'. But the play also had supporters. A man stood up and pointed out that some villagers in Mullinahone in Tipperary had burned a 'witch' only seven years before, but he was shouted down with 'very emphatic execrations'. Fay announced he would call the police. Fifteen minutes later, and half an hour after the trouble had started, a dozen members of the Royal Irish Constabulary entered the pit to great booing. More were stationed outside the building. Act One proceeded but not a word was audible as the sound of stamping, seat bashing and the singing of nationalist songs filled the theatre. When the interval came, however, the police marched out of the theatre – it later transpired at the wish of Synge and Lady Gregory. The protestors kept up the same din throughout Act Two, at the end of which Synge did take his seat in the auditorium, accompanied by Lady Gregory. He would not be drawn to speak to the audience (perhaps wisely, since some in the crowd were calling for his death). The play reached its conclusion unheard, but the theatre made it plain to the press that the run would definitely continue. Synge told *The Irish Independent* that 'there is nothing in it that we have reason to be ashamed of. We simply claim the liberty of Art to choose what subjects we think fit to put on' (Kilroy 1971: 14–18; Blackadder 2003: 94).

In the morning all the actors stood firm: the play must continue. Tuesday night would be even more tumultuous. Curtain up was at 8.15pm but by 7.30pm, when the doors opened, about forty young men had assembled to be admitted to the pit. At the same time a group of constables arrived to be put in waiting backstage. At 8pm another apparently organised group of about twenty men were admitted, with Synge's approval, apparently without buying tickets. One of these men, in a distinctive overcoat, and by his own admission drunk, immediately challenged the men in the pit to a fight. He was met only with laughter. Once more *Riders to the Sea* was heard in silence, but at its conclusion Yeats himself, who had been out of the country when the play opened, appeared on stage to address the audience. He acknowledged a 'difference of opinion' about the play, but offered to debate the issues on another occasion. But he asserted that 'no man has a right to interfere with another man who wants to hear the play. We shall play on and on, and I assure you our patience will last longer than their patience'. He was greeted with applause as well as jeers, and at this point the play's supporters in the audience were reinforced by the arrival of a group of students from Trinity College 'with the avowed object of suppressing all interruption of the play'. Trinity, Dublin's oldest university, was seen then as an important institution of the Protestant and Anglo-Irish ruling class.

Loud disruption began at the same point in Act One as on the previous evening. Although possibly outnumbered, the men in the pit succeeded in bringing the play to a halt. The drunk in the overcoat returned from a trip to the bar and tried to attack the pit faction. Yeats tried to stop him but the man was eventually restrained by his friends. Yeats appealed for calm again, but to no avail. The drunk was dragged out forcefully through the stage door. Again Yeats appealed vainly for quiet. Lady Gregory summoned the police from the dressing rooms, and they began to eject by force particular individuals whom Yeats and his supporters pointed out in the pit, 'amongst terrific uproar'. The provocative sight of a British police force arresting the protestors brought calls of 'Where are the militia?' – by which was meant the paramilitary anti-imperial groups which had begun to form in Dublin. As Neil Blackadder writes, this is the moment when the *Playboy* disturbances began to prefigure 'the approaching violent struggle for independence' (Blackadder 2003: 96). More police arrived and the noise began to abate. Then the orchestra played for a while, and the lights went down and the play began again. Cacophany ensued: a bugle had now been added to the protestors' armoury. Meanwhile Yeats wandered around selecting disrupters for police expulsion (Blackadder 2003: 83). Those arrested and convicted were later fined £2 or a month in prison. *The Freeman's Journal* reported that 'from start to finish not half a dozen consecutive sentences had been heard by the audience', and those that were heard were sometimes subject to heckles. When Christy described how he 'killed' his father a man in the pit called 'why not get the police to arrest him?', which elicited general laughter (Kilroy 1971: 25–31). In this mood the disturbance never quite turned to outright violence, even when the drunken Trinity College students provocatively sung 'God Save the King' at the end, reportedly with Yeats's approval (Hunt 1979: 75). The protestors answered with nationalist songs, and the contest continued in the street outside. At this point fighting broke out. The police moved in, and several arrests were made (Blackadder 2003: 85).

But Wednesday night saw fighting in the theatre itself as well as demonstrations in the streets (Kilroy 1971: 42–5). The same battle lines were drawn up again: the play's opponents crammed into the pit and the gallery, its supporters – many from Trinity College again – in the stalls, and the police ready backstage. Synge's arrival in the theatre was greeted with 'a storm of hisses, boos, and uncomplimentary epithets … there were also cries of "Take off your hat. Have manners"'. Once *Playboy* started a dozen policemen appeared at both sides of the pit, and more marched into the gallery. The shouts and bugle calls began when Christy began to be welcomed by the villagers, but for the first time there were many audible voices calling for the protestors to be quiet. When Yeats and Synge appeared in the stalls at the end of Act One they were loudly cheered as well as hissed. There were more interruptions in Act Two, as audience members called out 'That's not the West!', but even the uproar which greeted the notorious mention of women's underwear was opposed with cries of 'Shut up. We have heard enough'.

When the interval between Acts Two and Three arrived the pit and the gallery amused themselves by whistling the old nationalist song 'The Peeler and the Goat', which concerns a policeman who tries to arrest a nanny goat whom he mistakes for a prostitute. The goat concludes he must be drunk. The constabulary did not rise to the insult, however, but following an exchange of views between 'a low-sized Englishman in the stalls' and a man in the pit, the two made their way into the foyer to settle their differences, followed by 'a couple of hundred persons'. *The Freeman's Journal* only reports that 'several blows were exchanged', and that 'an animated scene ensued – there was considerable singing and commotion' but 'no one could exactly say how the incident terminated'. Good humour temporarily returned in the auditorium as Act Three began. Both factions laughed at Philly's line 'I'm thinking we'll have right sport before night will fall' (Synge 1981: 216), but the line only seemed to remind them of their intentions to bring the matter to a head. The 'inferno' of contending voices, shouts and bugle calls saw out the rest of the play, and the police began to eject people.

At the end the factions did not leave, but rather gathered in groups for a confrontation. According to *The Freeman's Journal* 'matters appeared rather critical'. A Sinn Féin leader named Monahan stood on his seat to begin a speech of denunciation and the police decided it was time to act. They rapidly cleared the auditorium. Outside the rival crowds gathered in the street, but there they met 'strong bodies of police' both in Abbey Street and in the nearby main thoroughfare, O'Connell Street. The factions marched up and down shouting, cheering and jeering, but no further violence broke out before the crowds dispersed.

At this critical moment there seems to have been no hesitation on the part of the Abbey Theatre management about whether the play should continue. The presence of such a large number of police would indicate that they had the support of the Dublin authorities. The principle they claimed to uphold was artistic freedom, and the belief that a play 'should be continued until it was made or killed by a responsible audience and not by a crowd of young men who paid their money to amuse themselves and prevent the play getting a fair hearing', as Willie Fay put it (*Dublin Evening Herald*, 31 January 1907, p.5, cited in Kilroy 1971: 55–6). But there were other forces who also wished to restrain artistic freedom. Lady Gregory also claimed that the 'Castle dinner set' – those who socialised with the King's Viceroy in Ireland at Dublin Castle – had asked her not to stage patriotic Irish plays such as Yeats's *Kathleen ní Houlihan* (1902), an allegorical drama calling for young men to sacrifice their lives for Irish freedom. She had also resisted this call, since in the end every play would offend someone and 'the management would be reduced to musical comedy' – and then just music. Severe cuts had in fact been made to the text to avoid further offence. *The Freeman's Journal* claimed that on the Wednesday, but Lady Gregory denied that there had been any significant excisions. 'It is true that a very few adjectives have been taken out, as have most of the invocations of the Holy Name' she protested, but curiously enough 'the words and phrases to which most objection has been raised have not been interfered with' (Kilroy 1971: 63–4; Blackadder 2003: 88–9).

In any case it appeared on Thursday night that the tide of battle had turned. There was sporadic disruption, but only one man was removed by the police, who were again present in large numbers. There was an orchestrated outbreak of coughing and sneezing lasting several minutes in Act Two, and during Act Three, a group of young men noisily left the pit shouting 'Rotten!' (Blackadder 2003: 94–5). But the play's infectious energy and zanily poetic language had begun to show signs of affecting the common mood of the audience on the previous night, and there was increasing evidence of this effect on Thursday. Early in Act Three 'about a dozen young men in the pit rose and left the building, booing and hissing as they went'. The protestors were starting to give up. On Friday there was almost no trouble at all. There was a short and peaceful demonstration in Marlborough Street opposite the theatre, but that was effectively the end of the trouble. The run closed on Saturday in relative peace (Blackadder 2003: 87).

Yeats held the public debate on the play which he had promised on 5 February. Correspondence on *Playboy* – mostly hostile – had continued in the weekly papers following the scheduled end of the play's run on the Saturday. Synge was too ill to attend, but Yeats defended his corner powerfully, even if he did not seem to convert his many vociferous opponents.

On the positive side, the stand which the Abbey Theatre had made secured its reputation worldwide as a serious and principled artistic institution. In perspective, however, its battle with aggressively censorious nationalist and religious feeling was a portent of Ireland's political and cultural fate in the middle part of the twentieth century. Those forces gained in strength under the Fianna Fáil governments of Éamon De Valera. The power of those ideas even then meant that the Abbey had been damaged at home. Takings were severely hit in the months ahead (Hunt 1979: 76). In March and April 1907 weekly receipts were only an eighth of what they had been in November and December 1906; but as before, financial rescue came in the form of an English tour in May and June. *Playboy* triumphed, in Oxford, Cambridge and the West End of London. It was thought too risky to stage in cities with substantial Irish populations such as Glasgow and Birmingham.

In 1909 the play was revived at the Abbey. There were no more than a few hisses on the opening night, but the press remained hostile. There was further trouble in New York and Philadelphia when *Playboy* toured there in 1911–12 (Hunt 1979: 94–5; Blackadder 2003: 103–7). In New York potatoes and stink bombs were thrown, but the show was so popular that tickets were even changing hands on the black market and opposition petered out. In puritan Philadelphia not

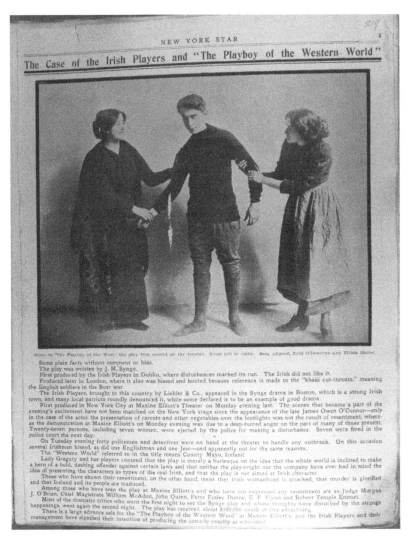

Figure 7.2 Sara Allgood (Widow Quin), Fred O'Donovan (Christy Mahon) and Eithne
Magee (Pegeen Mike), a publicity photograph in *The New York Star* for the
1911–12 American tour of *The Playboy of the Western World*. O'Donovan had
taken over the role from William Fay who took the role of the Playboy in the
original production. The original Pegeen Mike was Molly Allgood (also known as
Máire O'Neill), Sara's sister. She was engaged to Synge just before his death. *The
New York Star* reports that on the night of the Monday performance at Maxine
Elliott's theatre 'twenty-seven persons, including seven women, were ejected
for making a disturbance'. On the following day forty police were present. The
paper reports that 'on this occasion several Irishman hissed, one Englishman
and one Jew – and apparently not for the same reasons'. It also cynically and
implausibly claims that 'the play has received about $100,000 of free publicity.'

only the egg-throwing protestors but also the company were themselves techni-
cally arrested and charged with corrupting the morals of the citizens. The judge
found in favour of the Abbey and the tour continued to great acclaim and full
houses. But the script had been pruned of most of the lines and passages which
had caused uproar in Dublin.

When *Playboy* appeared in England it suffered many more cuts than ever in
Ireland, since it was subject to the Lord Chamberlain's power to censor anything
regarded offensive, particularly of a sexual or religious nature (Hunt 1979: 73).
There was no official censorship in British-run Ireland. The only power the Lord
Lieutenant of Ireland possessed was to deprive a theatre of its 'patent' – its right
to stage plays at all if it should put on 'any representation which should be deemed
or construed immoral' (Hunt 1979: 89). In some senses this bestowed a greater
liberty on the Irish theatre than that permitted in England.

The trouble at the Abbey in January and February 1907 can be interpreted as a
clash between two of the age's most powerful cultural movements: nationalist, if
not quite racial, sentiment on the one hand, and on the other the claim of aestheticism that art is self-justifying and above politics and morality. This was Synge's
view: he didn't care what the audience felt; expression must be free. Willie Fay
held a different view, seeing the market as the ultimate validation of a play, when
he argued that disruption should cease so that the audience could decide whether
the play was any good. Fay was, however, shortly to leave the company in acrimo-
nious circumstances (Hunt 1979: 79–83). The fact that Yeats deployed pro-British
students from Trinity College to shout for the play in the auditorium shows, however, that aestheticism was not above politics when the chips were down.

Yeats and Gregory saw Synge as a poet-playwright the roots of whose work lay
in a pure Gaelic peasant culture: just what they wanted their theatre to show if it
was to unite the Irish people. For them, Synge's poetic language and the deployment of quasi-legendary figures such as Christy Mahon were more important than
the content. In a sense they were right, but ultimately in a global sense: the poetic,
mythical and dramatic qualities of *Playboy* have made it one of the great plays of
the twentieth century which is still widely performed and indeed adapted glob-
ally today. But it is hard not to believe that Yeats and Gregory did not anticipate
the trouble its content would cause given the intense cultural contest over images
of Irishness being waged at that time. There is something anarchic in the play, a
sense of 'carnival' which Nicholas Grene identifies in it, where there are no rigid
polarities of morality or even identity. It came at a moment in Irish history when
a nationalist movement that scented final victory insisted on a puritan cultural
discipline that amounted to 'Manichaeanism' (Grene 1999: 108). At least they
knew that their anti-Irish nationalist English patron, Annie Horniman, would not
be offended by the play's depiction of Irish rural womanhood.

Yet the protests seemed to have subsided when audiences actually listened to
the play. Despite the authentic dialect and rhythms of the language of the West
and its many allusions to provincial peasant life, *Playboy* isn't perhaps ultimately
a play about Ireland at all. Synge claimed as much when he told the reporter from

Dublin Evening Mail, after the lights came back on again that 'I never bother whether my plots are typical Irish or not; but my methods are typical [of me]' (Kilroy 1971: 21). The wit and energy of its language, the perfection of its dramatic structure, its plot's use of deep folk-myth, not to say the Freudian resonance of its subject matter, have made it much larger than the historical circumstances in which it was first produced. To that extent *The Playboy of the Western World* is unique in this study: it was a play which, eventually, calmed a riot.

Since there was very little violence inside the Abbey Theatre itself it has been claimed that the events of 1907 cannot really be called a riot (Blackadder 2003: xii). This understates what actually happened and underplays the way the disturbances were seen at the time. But in Dublin's next major theatrical disturbance, in 1926, there was a physical battle between audience and performers for the possession of the stage space itself.

References

Blackadder, Neil (2003), *Performing Opposition: Modern Theater and the Scandalised Audience* (Westport CT: Praeger).

Cairns, David and Shaun Richards (1987), 'The "Reading Formation" of Synge's Abbey Audience', *Literature and History*, 13 (2) 219–37.

Flannery, James W. (1976), *W.B. Yeats and the Idea of a Theatre* (New Haven CT and London: Yale University Press).

Foster, R. F. (1989), *The Oxford History of Ireland* (Oxford: Oxford University Press).

Frazier, Adrian (2004), 'The Ideology of the Abbey Theatre', in Shaun Richards (ed.) *The Cambridge Companion to Twentieth-Century Irish Drama* (Cambridge: Cambridge University Press).

Grene, Nicholas (1999), *The Politics of Irish Drama: Plays in Context from Boucicault to Friel* (Cambridge: Cambridge University Press).

Henn, T.R. (1981), 'Introduction' to *Synge, The Complete Plays*, ed. T. R. Henn (London: Methuen).

Hunt, Hugh (1979), *The Abbey: Ireland's National Theatre 1904–1979* (Dublin: Gill and Macmillan).

Kilroy, James (1971), *The 'Playboy' Riots* (Dublin: The Dolmen Press).

King, Mary C. (2004), 'J. M. Synge, "National" Drama and the Post-Protestant Imagination', in Shaun Richards (ed.) *The Cambridge Companion to Twentieth-Century Irish Drama* (Cambridge: Cambridge University Press).

Lowery, Robert G. (ed.) (1984), *A Whirlwind in Dublin: The Plough and the Stars Riots* (Greenwood CT and London).

Pilkington, Lionel (2004), 'The Abbey Theatre and the Irish State', in Shaun Richards (ed.) *The Cambridge Companion to Twentieth-Century Irish Drama* (Cambridge: Cambridge University Press).

Richards, Shaun (2004), 'Plays of (ever) changing Ireland', in Shaun Richards (ed.) *The Cambridge Companion to Twentieth-Century Irish Drama* (Cambridge: Cambridge University Press), 1–17.

Shepherd, Simon (2009), *The Cambridge Introduction to Modern British Theatre* (Cambridge: Cambridge University Press).

Synge, J. M. (1981), *In the Shadow of the Glen* and *The Playboy of the Western World* in *The Complete Plays*, ed. T. R. Henn (London: Methuen).

Trotter, Mary (1998), 'Which Fiddler Calls the Tune? The *Playboy* Riots and the Politics of Nationalist Theatre Spectatorship', *Theatre Survey*, 39 (2), 39–52.

Watt, Stephen (2004), 'Late Nineteenth-century Irish Theatre: Before the Abbey – and Beyond', in Shaun Richards (ed.) *The Cambridge Companion to Twentieth-Century Irish Drama* (Cambridge: Cambridge University Press).

Wilde, Oscar (2006), *The Picture of Dorian Gray*, ed. J. Bristow (Oxford: Oxford University Press).

Chapter 8

'You have disgraced yourselves again'

The Plough and the Stars at the Abbey Theatre, Dublin, 1926

In 1926 the audience in the Abbey Theatre, Dublin tried to storm the stage itself. On this occasion the work which produced such hostility was Sean O'Casey's *The Plough and the Stars*. In many ways the disturbance was a curious reprise of the events of 1907; however, this time the struggle was not over the representation of the virtue of the Irish people, but specifically concerned the depiction of the men who had fought and died for Irish independence in the Easter Rising of 1916. Once again, a spasm of sexual hypocrisy was involved, too. But there was also a contest for control over the performance space, as well as the auditorium. The high point of this protest was a battle to occupy crucial territory, in this case the stage at the Abbey.

By 1926 the Abbey was the national theatre of a new country, the Irish Free State. A political movement to achieve 'Home Rule' within the British Empire seemed to have partially succeeded by the summer of 1914, although the Protestants in the north were ready to fight to prevent it (Foster 1989: 190–4). The outbreak of the First World War suspended the implementation of Home Rule and in 1916 there followed a military uprising in Dublin which produced a violent imperial backlash, followed by five years of chaotic guerrilla warfare which resulted in the Anglo Irish Treaty and the foundation of the Irish Free State in 1921. The Free State comprised twenty-six out of the thirty-two counties of Ireland, rather than the independent republic of the whole island that Sinn Féin had campaigned for. The new statelet of Northern Ireland had already been set up in 1920 and remained part of the United Kingdom.

The establishment of the Irish Free State was opposed by many national-ist Republicans who did not accept partition. The Abbey's failure to close in disapproval of the treaty in 1921 now led to threats from some Republicans, and the theatre remained under armed guard for some time afterwards. By 1926 the Abbey was officially subsidised with £1,000 a year by the Free State government, the first theatre in the English-speaking world to receive national subsidy (Annie Horniman had withdrawn all funding when the theatre did not close out of respect for King Edward VII's death in 1910) (Hunt 1979: 126). In recognition of the subsidy a government representative was appointed at the theatre, George O'Brien, an economics professor at University College Dublin.

It remained unclear exactly what O'Brien's role was. Given the Abbey Theatre's history, the portrayal by the Abbey Theatre of the failed insurrection in Dublin in Easter 1916 which precipitated the establishment of the Irish Free State was always going to be treated with suspicion by those Republicans; 1907 had not been forgotten.

Sean O'Casey was committed to an independent Ireland, but he was a socialist first and foremost. He had grown up in lower-middle-class north Dublin, not in poverty but in close proximity to it (Grene 1999: 112–13). O'Casey left school at fourteen and chose to work as a manual labourer, on the railways and in newspaper distribution. An active trade unionist in the Irish Transport and General Workers' Union under James Larkin's leadership, O'Casey had joined the Irish Citizen Army in 1914 at a moment of great crisis. As Home Rule for Ireland seemed increasingly likely, the Protestants and Unionists in the north armed themselves with German-supplied weapons. The nationalists in response formed their own paramilitary organisations and also secured Mauser rifles. One such force, the Irish Citizen Army (ICA), was a socialist and Republican militia, and much smaller than the purely nationalist Irish Volunteers. O'Casey left the ICA when it agreed to allow dual membership of both forces, since he did not think Ireland could be free and not socialist. He took no part in the Easter Rising, nor in the Anglo-Irish War (1919–21) that followed, nor the Irish Civil War of 1922–3 between forces for and against the 1921 Treaty.

The Plough and the Stars takes place in 1915 and during 'Easter Week' of 1916. There was only limited support for the insurgents in 1916 amongst the people of Dublin during the rising itself. At the time O'Casey admired the courage of those who fought, but mistrusted the motives of their leaders, and in particular Pádraic Pearse, who felt that some kind of blood-sacrifice was needed in the cause of Ireland. The cussed revolutionary streak in O'Casey can be seen in his later comments. He decried the tactical ineptitude of trying to take on the British army in open combat, rather than fighting as guerrillas who could blend back into the community ('take off your uniform … and keep them for the wedding', he advised) (O'Connor 1989: 91). He also took delight in the spectacle of the looting that took place during the chaos of battle ('a brave thing to do, for the streets sang songs of menace from bullets flying about everywhere') (O'Connor 1989: 95). As a known nationalist, O'Casey was himself arrested and held in custody for two nights in 1916. His biographer, Garry O'Connor, nevertheless felt that he was haunted by his failure to take part in the Easter Rising, and only 'exorcised' that feeling by writing *The Plough and the Stars* ten years later (O'Connor 1989: 95).

O'Casey's first two full-length plays, *The Shadow of a Gunman* (1923) and *Juno and the Paycock* (1924), were huge box-office successes (Hunt 1979: 121–2). Both were set in working-class Dublin at specific moments in the recent troubles. *The Plough and the Stars*, which opened on Monday 8 February 1926, was eagerly anticipated. From the start rumours began to spread about salacious content, and the original director and one actress had already resigned from the production. *The Plough and the Stars* was a formally challenging work in as much as it did not follow many of the traditional narrative conventions of the time. It appeared superficially to be a series of snapshots of dramatic moments, rather than a 'well-made play'. Its prospects were uncertain. At the dress rehearsal O'Casey was reported to be restless and anxious (Lowery 1984: 20), not least because he had antagonised many of the actors by being harshly critical of their performances in the previous production, Shaw's *Man and Superman* (O'Connor 1989: 185). Gabriel Fallon, who played Captain Brennan, remembered that rehearsals had begun in an 'atmosphere of tension, suspicion and distrust'. Some actors objected to the words they had to say. Eileen Crowe switched roles after her priest had supported her objection to speaking one particular line about her character's reputation for chastity (Blackadder 2003: 113). But apart from the objections to the play's sexual references, O'Casey also knew that there were many people who regarded the men of 1916 as holy martyrs whose sacrifice had brought freedom to most of Ireland. The near-summary execution of the leaders of the Rising, such as Pearse and James Connolly, together with some of O'Casey's old ICA comrades, such as Tom Clarke, had turned the men of 1916 into heroes and transformed their defeat into a symbolic turning point in the struggle for Irish independence. *The Plough and the Stars* deliberately set out to cast a cold eye on that heroism.

The Free State government's man at the Abbey, Professor O'Brien, did his best to stop the play reaching the stage. Having first objected to its profane language and the presence on stage of the prostitute Rosie Redmond in Act Two, O'Brien then wrote to Yeats, who was still at the helm of the Abbey, with darker threats. He said he was worried about 'the possibility that the play might provoke an attack on the theatre of a kind that could endanger the continuance of the subsidy'. But Yeats refused to sanction major cuts to the play that 'have nothing to do with dramatic literature' as contrary 'to all our traditions'. 'Our position is clear', he replied. 'If we have to choose between the subsidy and our freedom, it is freedom we choose.' Nevertheless, O'Casey agreed to cut Rosie's bawdy song from the end of her scene, about a sailor 'as strong an' as wild as th' sea' whom she 'cuddled an' kissed with devotion, till th' night from th' mornin' had fled' (O'Casey 1966: 179). 'Yes, it's a pity', said O'Casey. 'It would offend thousands. But it ought to be there' (Blackadder 2003: 112–13).

The play's people are working-class Dublin tenement dwellers. Nora Clitheroe is a passionate young wife whose bricklayer husband, Jack, is an officer in the Irish Citizen Army. Her fear of losing him causes her to conceal and burn a letter which appoints him commandant of the 'eighth battalion of the ICA' (O'Casey 1966: 157). The deception is revealed to him by his comrade Captain Brennan, who himself has designs on Nora. Jack offers violence to her and storms off to parade. Shortly afterwards a regiment of Irish soldiers in the British army on the way to fight on the Western Front is heard marching by, singing 'It's a Long Way to Tipperary'. Much of the comedy in this act is provided by the remorseless teasing of Nora's uncle, Peter, by a young socialist, 'the Covey'. Peter, a gaunt old man, appears, ludicrously, in the full dress of the Irish Foresters (*'green coat, gold-braided; white breeches, top boots, frilled shirt. He carries the slouch hat with the white ostrich plume'*) (O'Casey 1966: 150). The Foresters were a mutual welfare society, not a cavalry regiment. O'Casey shows an impoverished society where delusions of military glory are rampant. In the final line of the first act, Mollser, a tubercular girl with no apparent plot function asks 'Is there anybody goin', Mrs Clitheroe, with a titther o' sense?' (O'Casey 1966: 160). Yeats regarded the play as 'simply' depicting 'the effect of war upon the lives of people by a man who has lived the lives of these same people' (Hogan and Burnham 1992: 305).

It was the play's second act, however, set in a pub, that was to prove most provocative. Another young female character with no conventional plot function appears, the prostitute Rosie Redmond. The volunteers of both paramilitary forces have assembled on parade outside the pub, and the voice of a speaker is heard addressing the crowd outside, using words which echo those of those of Pádraic Pearse:

> Comrade soldiers of the Irish Volunteers and of the Citizen Army, we rejoice in this terrible war. The old heart of the earth needs to be warmed with the red wine of the battlefields … Such august homage was never offered to God as this: the homage of millions of lives given gladly for love of country. And we must be ready to pour out the same red wine in the same glorious sacrifice, for without shedding of blood there is no redemption!
>
> (O'Casey 1966: 164)

Talking of red wine outside a pub can only work to undermine this kind of heroic rhetoric. As Nicholas Grene puts it, 'it is real whiskey not sacramental blood/wine which the people in the pub are drinking, and the link between the political rhetoric and the thirst for alcohol is made directly' (Grene 1999: 143). This chilling off-stage speech is also the background to the Covey failing to interest Rosie Redmond, a young prostitute, in 'conthrol o' th' means o' production, rates of exchange an' th' means of disthribution'. Her response is to throw off a shawl 'which reveals a good deal of white bosom', and to reflect that it is 'heartbreakin' to see a young fella thinkin' of anything, or admirin' anything, but silk thransparent stockin's showin' off the shape of a little lassie's legs!' (O'Casey 1966: 165).

'*The Voice of the Man*' speaks extracts taken verbatim from a speech made by Pearse and published in 1915, *Peace and the Gael*. O'Casey regarded this talk of 'blood-sacrifice' with obvious repugnance. The first night reviewer from *The Irish Times* saw straight away that O'Casey

> hates human suffering … [and feels that] one drop of the milk of human kindness is worth more than the deepest draughts of the red wine of idealism. Time and again, that thought is forced home, now in the lines of broad comedy, again in biting sarcasm, and finally in racking tragedy.

The same reviewer, anonymous as was the practice then, astutely observed that *The Plough and the Stars* is 'a woman's play, a drama in which the men must fight and the women must weep' (Lowery 1984: 21–2). The play's focus on women's experience in the Easter Rising was answered, paradoxically, by a protest led by women, and uncovered what looks to the modern observer like a strain of misogyny amongst both sides of the contention.

Not long after the altercation between the revolutionary and the sex-worker, the banner of the ICA, showing the symbolic plough and the stars, was carried into the drunken scene of the public bar, accompanied by the Irish Tricolour. The two ensigns are themselves intoxicated on the speaker's rhetoric (*'their faces are flushed and their eyes sparkle; they speak rapidly, as if unaware of the meaning of what they said. They have been mesmerized by the fervency of the speeches'*) (O'Casey 1966: 177). To the Republican protestors in the Abbey Theatre this was a provocative desecration of holy icons of the nationalist struggle, and a betrayal of their sacrifice which could only succour Ireland's enemies. They may not have known that O'Casey had himself paid for the deep-blue fabric that formed the grounds of the real ICA standard of 1915–16 (the flag's eventual fate, according to one report, was to become a trophy for a British officer) (O'Connor 1989: 82, 93). The final two acts were equally provocative in that they showed the Dublin tenement dwellers using the uprising as a cover for looting, and even engaging in banter with British soldiers engaged in fighting the rebels. But it was Act Two which would provoke an attempt to seize the stage by force.

The Plough and the Stars was scheduled to run for a week, and the first night sold out in advance. On the day of the opening people began to queue in the streets at four in the afternoon in the hope of getting a standing place at the back of the pit. There was nothing but applause after each act, that first evening, and at the end, O'Casey was summoned on stage for an ovation. The first reviews found little to object to. *The Irish Independent* found 'no hint of polemics, no question of taking sides' (Lowery 1984: 26).

But at the second performance half a dozen women in the pit called out in protest at the flags appearing in the pub in Act Two. One was the sister of the iconic Kevin Barry, an eighteen-year-old IRA volunteer hanged by the British in 1920 despite international protests and who subsequently became the hero of a popular nationalist song. Barry had refused to reveal the names of his comrades under interrogation despite the brutal treatment of his captors. Two policemen were present in the pit that night, and little came of the altercation. On the Wednesday night 'a sort of moaning was to be heard tonight from the pit' at the same point in Act Two. O'Casey was in the balcony signing autographs, but 'only … for young and pretty girls' (Lowery 1984: 29). Word seems to have spread about the play, however, and plans were laid, since on Thursday a riot broke out.

The protest was organised by prominent members of the Republican women's group, Cumann na mBan. Its leaders were also mothers and widows of men who died at Easter 1916: Mrs Pearse, Mrs Clarke and Mrs Sheehy-Skeffington. Francis Sheehy-Skeffington had not in fact been amongst the rebels. He was a pacifist who

Figure 8.1 Ria Mooney (Rosie Redmond) in the 1926 production of *The Plough and the Stars*, with the author Sean O'Casey. O'Casey autographed the picture on 21 June 1926. The set is that for the bar-room scene which caused most offence. Mooney was in her early twenties, but was a veteran of twenty productions. She continued to perform and later direct at the Abbey until 1963.

had been out in the streets trying to prevent looting and even rescued a wounded British officer. He was unfortunate enough to be arrested by the deranged Captain Bowen-Colthurst, who had him summarily executed. Bowen-Colthurst was later locked up in Broadmoor asylum for the criminally insane. O'Casey had later written about Sheehy-Skeffington in glowing terms, calling him 'the soul of revolt against man's inhumanity to man', but this did not stop his widow appropriating her husband to the Republican cause as she led the attack on *The Plough and the Stars* (O'Connor 1989: 194–5).

The first hint of trouble came when a student approached the conductor of the orchestra and advised him to move the valuable instruments (O'Connor 1989: 198). The advice was taken. There was stamping of feet and hissing in the first act, but not enough mayhem to bring the play to a halt. That came after the first interval.

Ria Mooney, in the role of the prostitute Rosie Redmond, was a beginner for Act Two. There had been pressure on her from other members of the company, who disapproved of the play, not to take on the role. But she was so committed to the part that she went so far as to observe the behaviour of the young sex-workers in the lane behind the Abbey Theatre. She later admitted that at the age of twenty-three she was still not completely clear what the term 'prostitute' meant. At any rate, she would channel her sympathy for these girls into her performance to the point where O'Casey would later claim that her acting saved the play (Blackadder 2003: 114). As she came on stage that Thursday night Redmond heard raised voices. Suddenly lumps of coal and pennies fell noisily on the stage around her. 'Shocking epithets' were thrown at her. Several times the name 'Honor Bright' was called out. Honor Bright was the working name of Elizabeth O'Neill, a Dublin prostitute who had been abducted and shot dead the previous summer. The case had become a media sensation. A doctor and a police officer had stood trial but had been acquitted just eight days before the night of the riot. The jury had deliberated for just three minutes and there had been accusations of an establishment cover up. 'It was not clear', wrote Robert Lowery, 'whether or not the protestors wanted Rosie Redmond to meet the same fate', but the use of the name certainly carried some menace. She later reflected that 'it was not until that night that I ceased to become an amateur and became a professional in the truest sense of the word' (Hogan and Burnham 1992: 297). Stamping, shouting, hissing and singing continued throughout Act Two such that the play could not be heard. There were also 'counter-demonstrations of applause by the majority of the audience' (Lowery 1984: 33). Stink bombs were let off. Some shouts claimed the government was subsidising the Abbey to encourage it to produce anti-Republican propaganda (O'Connor 1989: 198). Hanna Sheehy-Skeffington tried to make a speech from the gallery: 'we have not come here as rowdies. We came here to make protest against the defamation of the men of Easter Week' (Blackadder 2003: 116). O' Casey later wrote that

> the high, hysterical distorted voices of women kept squealing that Irish girls were noted over the whole world for their modesty, and that Ireland's name was holy; that the Republican flag had never seen the inside of a public house … There wasn't a comely damsel amongst them.
>
> (Cited in Hunt 1979: 125, 127)

In Hugh Hunt's 1979 history of the Abbey the 1926 riot, in contrast to that of 1907, is presented as a comic incident told through a collage of voices (Hunt 1979: 124–9). There is a depressing stereotyping of Irishwomen either as virtuous paragons or hysterical termagants in narratives of the riot. The violence hinted at the cries of 'Honor Bright' was not far beneath the surface of this language. Some critics later claimed that the play lied because there were no prostitutes in Dublin; or, at least, 'there were none in Dublin until the Tommies brought them over' (Hogan and Burnham 1992: 299).

   This time, Yeats, who was present, was well prepared. He rapidly wrote the speech with which he wanted to harangue the protestors and nipped out of the theatre to let *The Irish Times* have a copy in advance (O'Connor 1989: 198). He didn't expect to be heard in peace.

As Act Three began about fifteen protestors, mostly women, tried to rush the stage. They were flung back into the orchestra pit as the rest of the cast rushed on stage to defend their territory ('O'Casey was our hero and we were prepared to fight' wrote Shelah Richards, who played Nora Clitheroe) (Hunt 1979: 126). A young woman was pinned to the floor by two actors sitting on her chest (O'Connor 1989: 198). The curtain came down, was grabbed by the attackers, went up again, then down again. It was reported that someone tried to set fire to the drapes. An actress was set upon by two young men, who were in turn hurled off the stage. One man hit Maureen Delaney (Bessie Burgess) in the face and then went after May Craig (Mrs Gogan). Barry Fitzgerald, who took the role of Fluther Good, came to her aid and sent him flying into the stalls with a punch on the jaw. Shelah Richards recalled throwing a shoe at one of the rioters, but it missed and was thrown back at Yeats when he made his appearance. Meanwhile many of the audience started to flee the theatre (Lowery 1984: 33; Blackadder 2003: 117).

There was one curious moment that occurred amidst the on-stage battle. Kitty Curling was the young actress playing the pallid consumptive Mollser. One of the men who rushed onto the stage caught her in his arms then folded her into a cloak so as to carry her to safety. Yeats described this in a letter to a friend as 'one curious effect of fine acting' (Lowery 1984: 43), but it rather demonstrated how good theatre is never merely fiction, but is also part of the real world of history and politics in which it plays a part. Perhaps subconsciously, this Republican protestor symbolically showed how the on-stage and off-stage worlds can merge into one: theatre is never pure creative expression, but always an act in the 'real' world which should not be surprised if it receives a real response of some kind. In this case it was a literal-minded one. But it is significant that it was the arrival of the two Republican standards in the pub in Act Two that was the spark to the explosion which followed. The 'pub' was of course a stage set, but the 'property' Plough and the Stars and Tricolour would be indistinguishable from the 'real' flags if they were to appear in the street outside the Abbey. The off-stage world contains powerful representations which do not lose that power when transferred into a 'fictional' context. The protestors might well be seen as respecting the power of the theatre as historical event, rather than as 'pure' work of art, as Yeats at this time might have wished it to be.

Neil Blackadder argues that the attempt to seize the stage by the Republican protestors modelled itself, even unconsciously, on the seizure of the General Post Office and other public buildings in the 1916 Easter Rising: 'just as the insurgents occupied buildings in Dublin and proclaimed their repudiation of the foreign government, the protestors occupied the stage, however briefly, and proclaimed their repudiation of O'Casey's depiction of the events of 1915–16' (Blackadder 2003: 127). The behaviour of any group of protestors is shaped by their culture and history. This may well be the case, but the attack can also be seen as part of the typical battle for ownership of the locus of authority common to theatrical disturbances. In this case the struggle can be seen to be for ownership of space in the theatre itself (as in the 1809 Old Price riots), and primarily the stage. In this way the 1926 Abbey riot was backwards-looking, almost pre-modern. The 1907 Abbey riot was forwards-looking and modernist: it was over the right to interpret the meaning of symbolic capital, not physical space itself (as in the 2004 *Behzti* disturbances).

Once the stage was cleared the actor playing Jack Clitheroe, F. J. McCormick, managed to get some kind of hearing from the play's opponents in the audience, but at this point the divisions in the cast themselves about the play became clear. McCormick pointed out that they were only acting O'Casey's words. 'Don't mob us', he pleaded, 'we have our rights as human beings and as players.' This incensed the actors who believed in the play and they brought the curtain down on him (Blackadder 2003: 118). Gabriel Fallon, who played Brennan, later suggested that McCormick was a naturally timid man who was apprehensive about appearing in such a controversial play, and who consequently ended up playing the rebel fighter Jack Clitheroe as even more of a coward than the text might suggest. To see a martyr of Easter Week portrayed in this way 'helped in no little way to increase the anger of the protestors' (Blackadder 2003: 119). If this is so, then it is yet again a telling example of how off-stage and on-stage worlds became significantly confused in the *Plough and the Stars* riot. When writing about the *Playboy* riot Nicholas Grene cites the opinion of the anthropologist Mary Douglas in her 1966 book *Purity and Danger* that 'impurity arises from a confusion of categories' (Grene 1999: 86). Could it be that a heightened sense of disgust, which is more likely to produce violence, will emerge in a theatrical situation where the on-stage and off-stage are confused? At any rate, O'Casey never forgave McCormick (Hogan and Burnham 1992: 297).

There are two versions of what O'Casey himself was up to at this point. It seems he was off-stage surrounded by a crowd of women trying to put their case. According to Shelah Richards, who played Nora, he was 'charming them like a blackbird singing to them. And they were all twittering "Yes, yes, Mr O'Casey. Yes, we see!"' (Hogan and Burnham 1992: 298). Another witness, Arthur Daley, reported that he was not quite so lionised, but 'surrounded by a crowd of questioning women, and his answer to one of them was, "I want to make money!"', which the rather jaundiced Daley felt 'sums up his attitude towards art' (Hogan and Burnham 1992: 299).

The actors were determined to start Act Three again, but there was immediately another attempt to storm the stage (one account, in *The Irish Times*, suggests that this was when the major fist-fighting took place). Scuffles and fighting now broke out throughout the theatre and Hanna Sheehy-Skeffington began to address the crowd again. Off stage, Yeats turned to Gabriel Fallon. 'Fallon', he declared, 'I am sending for the police, and *this time* it will be *their own* police!' (he meant that it would be the Garda Síochána of the Irish Free State who were summoned, and not the Royal Irish Constabulary, as in 1907) (Hunt 1979: 127). Fallon was worried that O'Casey would oppose this move. In the playwright's own self-dramatisation:

The police! Sean to agree to send for the police – never! His Irish soul revolted from the idea … No, no, never! But a wild roar heard in the theatre seemed to shake the room where they all stood, told him to make up his mind quick; and swearing he could ne'er consent, consented.

(Cited in Hunt 1979: 127)

The stage had now been cleared of protestors by the actors, and the curtain came down. Yeats knew the police were on the way. They arrived at ten o'clock and placed themselves at strategic points in the theatre (Hogan and Burnham 1992: 301). It was time for Yeats to make his entrance. He paced up and down behind the curtain while chaos raged in the auditorium. He placed himself at the curtain entrance and chose his moment to give the signal to raise it. Up it went, and he advanced to the footlights slowly, as Fallon remembered, 'with flashing eyes and upraised arm'. Then, his long hair waving, legs wide apart and one hand above his head, he raged powerfully at those before him:

I thought you had got tired of this, which commenced fifteen years ago. But you have disgraced yourselves again. Is this going to be a recurring celebration of Irish genius? Synge first and then O'Casey. The news of the happening of the last few minutes here will flash from country to country. Dublin has again rocked the cradle of a reputation. From such a scene as this theatre went forth the fame of Synge. Equally the fame of O'Casey is born here tonight. This is his apotheosis.

(Cited in Hunt 1979: 128)

Not a word of this was heard amidst the mayhem until the last few words. Half a dozen plain-clothes members of the Garda Síochána then appeared followed by uniformed gardai who cleared the demonstrators from the pit by force, physically carrying some out of the theatre. The curtain came up again for Act Three to a roar of applause that drowned out the remaining cries of protest. The last few demonstrators were soon ejected. Mrs Sheehy-Skeffington's last words before she was forced out were to accuse the play of treason to the cause of Ireland's struggles for independence:

This play is going to London soon to be advertised there because it belies Ireland. We have no quarrel with the players – we realise that they at least have to earn their bread. But I say that if they were men they would refuse to play in some of the parts. All you need to do now is sing 'God Save the King'.

(O'Connor 1989: 199; Hogan and Burnham 1992: 301–2)

There were no arrests. The curtain was slightly torn, two footlights had been broken, and there was some minor damage to the musicians' equipment.

The Plough and the Stars continued to its conclusion. Once all the audience had gone and the doors of the theatre were locked, Yeats gathered together the whole cast in the green room and congratulated them on their conduct. The run would continue, he declared, since 'their theatre had got an advertisement of the utmost value in the eyes of the whole world. Such an incident could not take place in the commercial theatre'. The run did indeed go on if under police guard, with the house lights on during Act Two. On Friday the worst that happened was one man stood up and walked out crying 'this is an insult to the memory of Pearse' (Blackadder 2003: 122).

There was also a worrying, if half-hearted attempt, by three young men armed with revolvers to kidnap Mooney, Richards and Fitzgerald on Saturday morning. In the latter case they went to his parents' house by mistake. Barry Fitzgerald's mother came out of the house bawling at the would-be abductors and they ran away in terror. That day the actors were taken to the theatre by car, and kept in the building between the matinee and the evening performance (O'Connor 1989: 200).

The final performance of the play's first run, on Saturday night, was triumphant. There were four curtain calls. O'Casey was summoned onto the stage for an ovation lasting five minutes (Blackadder 2003: 122–3).

In the following weeks correspondence raged in the papers between the play's supporters and detractors, and O'Casey agreed to a public debate with Hanna Sheehy-Skeffington on 1 March 1926 at Mills Hall in Dublin. But he was not well, and created a poor impression after an eloquent speech from his opponent. At the end of the evening, however, Hanna Sheehy-Skeffington came and shook his hand with tears in her eyes: she had recently read the tribute which O'Casey had published to her dead husband, and could no longer bear him any personal animosity (O'Connor 1989: 203–4). When the play was revived for a week in May she protested by holding up placards outside the theatre. The worst that happened inside the theatre was the letting off of a few stink bombs (Blackadder 2003: 129). Disheartened by the reception which his play had received – many of the Abbey company remained cold towards him, and the Irish literary critics were also dismissive of what he thought his best work – O'Casey soon left Ireland altogether for England, where a new production of his play *Juno and the Paycock* was scheduled to open in London (Hunt 1979: 130).

Yeats was only the first of many to make an obvious connection between the events of 1907 and 1926. There might be a tendency to see the latter disturbances as a near-farcical re-run of the more profound conflict occasioned by the first production of *The Playboy of the Western World*. But O'Casey's subsequent self-exile was a symptom of a closing down of any cultural critique which did not accord with an ever-narrowing view of Ireland's history and nationhood in the years to come. Yeats claimed that only a state-subsidised theatre could put on as outspoken a play as *The Plough and the Stars*, but his own aesthetic view of theatre would not acknowledge the principle that theatre is a place of genuine political confrontation, not merely a place for the exchange of ideas in a safely fictional realm. That confrontation may always turn violent when so much, symbolically, is at stake, and in a nation struggling for real independence the symbols which represent a fragile national identity are high-value objects – and real objects when they appear on stage.

Elsewhere in Europe in 1926 fascists were making self-conscious political use of theatricality, and of flags and costumes in particular. In twentieth-century politics, the divide between the fictional and the real would become ever narrower when it came to creating powerful narratives which could be deployed to great effect in the mass media of democratic states.

References

Blackadder, Neil (2003), *Performing Opposition: Modern Theater and the Scandalised Audience* (Westport CT: Praeger).

Foster, R. F. (1989), *The Oxford History of Ireland* (Oxford: Oxford University Press).

Grene, Nicholas (1999), *The Politics of Irish Drama: Plays in Context from Boucicault to Friel* (Cambridge: Cambridge University Press).

Hogan, Robert and Richard Burnham (1992), *The Years of O'Casey, 1921–1926: A Documentary History* (Newark DE: University of Delaware Press and Gerard's Cross: Colin Smythe).

Hunt, Hugh (1979), *The Abbey: Ireland's National Theatre 1904–1979* (Dublin: Gill and Macmillan).

Lowery, Robert G. (ed.) (1984), *A Whirlwind in Dublin: The Plough and the Stars Riots* (Greenwood CT and London).

O'Casey, Sean (1966), *The Plough and the Stars*, in *Three Plays* (London: Macmillan).

O'Connor, Garry (1989), *Sean O'Casey: A Life* (London: Paladin).

Chapter 9

The French Republic under siege

Coriolanus in Paris, February 1934

On the night of 6 February 1934 the French lower house of parliament, the Chamber of Deputies, was attacked by large numbers of right-wing political activists. The police opened fire, killing fourteen demonstrators (McMillan 1992: 106). Rioting continued all night. In the morning the Prime Minister, Édouard Daladier, resigned. It was widely believed that a fascist *coup d'état* had been narrowly averted. There were of course many causes of the bloody events of that night, but a good case can be made that the pro-fascist production of Shakespeare's tragedy *Coriolanus* at the Comédie-Française (as the Théatre-Français had become known) was a significant factor.

Shakespeare's final tragedy, originally written in 1608, had been rarely performed on the French stage. There had been a notable production by the great classical actor François-Joseph Talma in 1806. There had been political controversy on that occasion, too: the play was removed from the stage after four performances because it was felt that the autocratic Coriolanus was a hostile depiction of the Emperor Napoleon (Schwartz-Gastine 2008: 124–5; Shakespeare 2013: 19). More recently, there had also been a production at the Paris Odéon in 1910 (George 2008: 74). *Coriolanus* tells the story of the fifth-century BC Roman nobleman Caius Martius, as found in the writings of the Greek historian Plutarch. Martius is a heroic military leader, whose victories over the Volscian city of Corioli earn him an extra surname, the Roman *cognomen* 'Coriolanus'. Caius Martius is the leader of the armies of the Roman Republic, a city depicted by Shakespeare as riven with class conflict. As the play begins the ordinary people of Rome (the 'plebeians') are rioting because of a food shortage in the city, accusing the nobles (the 'patricians') of hoarding grain in a time of famine to keep prices high (1.1.14). Martius despises the common people, abusing them to their faces, and accusing them of meddling in political affairs which are not their business. If he had his way, he says, he would put them down with great bloodshed (1.1.145–83). But he cannot do so: the Republic's constitution has given the people a say in matters of state.

Following his victory over the Volscians, the patricians put Coriolanus (as he is now called) forwards for the office of consul, one of the two posts of supreme political power in the Roman Republic, an honour which was tenable for a year.

But in order to secure the consulship he must gain the votes of the plebeians. Knowing that Coriolanus would be an implacable enemy of the masses – but also a danger to their own position (2.1.186) – the two constitutional leaders of the people, the Tribunes Sicinius Velutus and Junius Brutus, succeed in provoking Coriolanus's impatient nature. In the midst of the election process Coriolanus loses his temper, cursing and threatening the plebeians (3.1.108ff., 3.3.84ff.). Accused of treason, he is banished from the city by the Tribunes (3.3.123). Coriolanus stalks off, claiming that he is banishing the people, for 'there is a world elsewhere' (3.3.189). He makes his way in disguise to Corioli, where he forms an alliance with his old enemy Tullus Aufidius, and leads a Volscian army against a Rome which is now defenceless without his leadership. Only the pleas of his mother Volumnia dissuade Coriolanus from sacking his native city (3.3.189). He turns back, inevitably to be murdered by Aufidius and the Volscians for betraying their cause.

Coriolanus is a dark, intense and passionate play, lacking humour and offering the performers little opportunity for audience contact, qualities which are so important to the effect of many other Shakespearean tragedies. But its portrayal of class conflict spoke clearly to those on the political right in the 1930s. From that perspective Coriolanus could be understood as a heroic and charismatic military leader; a man assured of his own destiny pitched into conflict with a fickle working-class mob who are easily manipulated by unscrupulous and selfish demagogues. It was not difficult for them to see Shakespeare's protagonist as a would-be Mussolini, or even a Hitler, a heroic and unique individual attempting to save his country from communist agitators who were leading the people into servitude for their own ends.

In the 1930s there were plenty of people in France, as elsewhere in Europe, whose response to economic recession and political paralysis was to condemn democracy and to seek a new kind of politics. Elected politicians from mainstream parties seemed to have no answer to the mass unemployment and sharp decline in living standards in Europe which followed the great American stock market crash of 1929. For many on the left it seemed to portend the last days of capitalism. This was a fearsome prospect for those of a more conservative and nationalist disposition. Much of France was still strongly Catholic and agricultural, and less than twenty years on from the Russian Revolution of 1917 there was widespread fear of godless Soviet Communism. Democracy was seen by many traditional conservatives to have failed, since it produced timid leaders governed by paymasters in big business or organised labour. The Fascist dictator Benito Mussolini gave the impression that he had restored national pride and was running Italy efficiently. Adolf Hitler, who became German Chancellor in 1933, seemed to some to be in the process of achieving the same national transformation. Nazi anti-Semitism was not necessarily unattractive to many in France, where the divisions caused by the Dreyfus affair had not yet been forgotten. For many on the right what was needed was a strong military leader who would put national glory and honour before the sectional interests of any group in society, and who would put the venal and cowardly leaders of the working class in their place.

That was precisely the political line taken by the production of *Coriolanus* by René-Louis Piachaud which opened at France's national theatre in Paris on 9 December 1933. Piachaud was a Swiss journalist, poet and critic who had already translated and adapted six Shakespeare plays including *Othello*, *A Midsummer Night's Dream* and *The Merry Wives of Windsor* into French prose (Cohn 1976: 11). He had begun his version of *Coriolanus* four years earlier. He claimed that his 'free translation' of the play was adapted 'to suit the taste of the time' (Schwartz-Gastine 2008: 126–7). He abandoned what he called Shakespeare's 'serene impartiality'; he sought rather to present Caius Martius as 'the hero', 'the One in his duel with the Many'. Shakespeare's Coriolanus does indeed duel with the masses, and he is never shy of coarsely venting his opinion of the people. He calls them 'scabs' (1.1.164) in his first meeting, and wishes 'boils and plagues all over them' (1.4.31). But in order to render his hero more attractive, Piachaud cut much of this undignified invective, and in production such lines were further reduced in number, as the Comédie-Française's promptbook records. The promptbook's stage directions also required the two hundred extras who played the people in the crowd scenes to be in masochistic thrall to the leader's charisma. At Coriolanus's first entrance '*the Plebeian crowd makes a backward movement: in some there is repressed hatred; in others, those who like to be mastered, a naive exhilaration at the sensation of the leader's authority over them.*' Piachaud's Coriolanus, unlike Shakespeare's, does not petulantly turn his back on the Roman people. In Shakespeare, once the people have rejected him, the world for Caius Martius starts where Rome finishes ('there is a world elsewhere', he sneers); Piachaud's unfailingly patriotic Roman hero bids a more wistful 'adieu!' for 'Rome is not the world' (Cohn 1976: 12–16, her translation). Unlike in Shakespeare, both the Roman people and his enemy Aufidius show their respect for Coriolanus – who betrays them both – right to the end. When Shakespeare talks of 'insurrection' and 'rebellion', Piachaud used the loaded term 'anarchy' in his translation (George 2008: 72). When Coriolanus talks of the 'general ignorance' of the people leading to 'unstable slightness' in the state, Piachaud had a 'stupid mob' creating a situation where 'disorder reigns'. A great concern for the need for 'order' is everywhere (my translation of a passage cited in Hardison Londré 1986: 124). In this version the Tribunes of the People are also presented as much more devious than in Shakespeare's text, roaring with cynical laughter as they claim to be completely innocent and ignorant of how it was that the people had turned against Coriolanus at the end of the first election scene (Act Two Scene Three). The identification of the Tribunes with the leftist politicians of contemporary France was evident when, at Coriolanus's exile, the people cry 'Long live the republic and the tribunes!' (George 2008: 73). In Shakespeare's text the people merely call on the gods to bless the Tribunes (4.6.30). Shakespeare's Coriolanus is an outdated aristocratic warrior struggling against a new political dispensation, as was the case for some backwards-looking noblemen in Jacobean England. Piachaud's *Coriolanus* is a man of the future, a fascist visionary whom a corrupt state fails to acknowledge with near-disastrous results. There is certainly no hint of any homoerotic feelings between him and his enemy Aufidius, unlike in Shakespeare (4.5.103–11).

Piachaud was already something of a literary celebrity. His new version of *Coriolanus* was published, alongside some photographs from the Comédie-Française production, in the conservative monthly magazine *L'Illustration*. A review of the production quoted in that magazine did not hesitate to play up the political significance of this *Coriolanus*:

> It is a great day for the Comédie-Française … [and] perhaps a great day for France. Every time our country finds itself at a crossroads, when it hesitates and does not really know where truth originates, one has seen either from literature or from the theatre that one of these calls appears to direct timid or uncertain spirits.
>
> (Cited in George: 2008: 76, his translation)

Piachaud must have been aware that the choice of repertory at France's national theatre could have considerable impact in such febrile political times. A short comedy, *La Carcasse*, had recently been withdrawn from the stage of the Comédie-Française, having been accused of insulting the French army. It had merely portrayed a general with an unfaithful wife in a comic fashion. Émile Fabre, the theatre's administrator but himself an author of social and political satires for the theatre, warned the *sociétaires* (members) who governed the theatre and the Undersecretary of State for the Arts, Jean Mistler, that 'certain lines' in the play 'could give some ideas to seditious individuals' (Pelissier 2006: 92, my translation). But Mistler gave the production the go-ahead nevertheless. Mistler had entered politics as a radical socialist, but only seven years later, in 1940, he was to introduce the bill before the French parliament which was to dissolve the Third Republic and hand supreme power to Marshal Pétain following the defeat of the French army by Nazi forces. Pétain surrendered to the Germans and became the leader of the Vichy regime in the unoccupied part of France, a regime which collaborated with the Nazis and featured many of the leaders of the anti-democratic right who were active in the February 1934 riot. Mistler was also a writer and a cultured man, and knew exactly what the political import of Piachaud's *Coriolanus* would be.

The play's historical setting was also significant for French politics. *Coriolanus* takes place during the time when Rome was a republic. In its earliest days Rome was ruled by kings, but the monarchy was driven out late in the sixth century BC by the nobility. After much struggle a republican constitution was established where power was shared between the common people and the aristocracy and where the chief officers of state were elected. It was during the days of the Republic that most of the conquests which established the Roman Empire were created, and later historians who wrote when Rome had become a monarchy again, under the

Emperors, looked back on the days of the Republic as a time when virtue and liberty flourished. The French revolutionaries of 1789 explicitly looked to the Roman Republic as a model. They too were overthrowing a tyrannical monarchy and were laying the foundations of a new France where liberty would flourish and national glory be re-established. Pro-revolutionary artists such as Jacques-Louis David painted heroic scenes from Roman Republican history which made explicit the identification between the new French Republic and its glorious predecessor. Shakespeare's *Coriolanus* is a play which shows the Republic in crisis, and Piachaud's version makes it clear that it is a failing, complacent and corrupt state which needs a strong military hero to save it. Just as the Roman Republic gave way to the rule of the Emperors in the first century BC, so the first French Republic of 1792–1804 gave way to the rule of the Emperor Napoleon I, whose armies carried as standards the eagles of the Roman legions. Napoleon himself wore ceremonially the golden laurel wreath of the Roman Emperors. Napoleon, the conqueror of Europe, remained a hero to many in France, especially to those on the far right. Piachaud's *Coriolanus* is an anti-Republican play, and to stage it at the French national theatre in 1934 was a clear provocation, and a call to arms for the anti-republican, fascist-leaning enemies of French democracy.

That *Coriolanus* was intended to be a production that made a contemporary political statement is evident from the unusual features of its scenic design. The Comédie-Française was famous for its elaborate sets and complex scene changes. The designer, André Boll, broke with tradition by putting on stage a single, immovable set in the modernist style:

> The back wall of the stage was simply covered with a painted cloth representing undistinguished bare Roman buildings, in a gradation of soft pink shades, as if the aspect of the stones were changing under the light of the setting sun, and receding toward the outline of a river (probably the Tiber) at the horizon. An imposing row of temples, with their triangular porticoes supported by regular columns, presented their dark fronts to the audience and added to the general verticality of the staging. An atmosphere of dignity and nobility prevailed. The softness of the light colours used gave an impression of quietness but could also signify the end of an era and ominous deeds to come, with the strange abnormality of a setting yet unchanging sun painted on the decor.
>
> (Schwartz-Gastine 2008: 128)

The most salient feature of the set was a wide flight of steps in the centre of the stage giving access to various levels of the acting area. When Coriolanus made his return to Rome after his victory in Corioli, two hundred extras thronged the stage of the Comédie-Française in a carefully arranged tableau either side of this staircase. As René Alexandre in the title role made his way through their midst, sword in hand, the senators and the people all raised their arms and thrust them out straight and at an angle of forty-five degrees to their bodies, booming out 'Coriolanus' as one. The historical justification was no doubt that this was the 'Roman' salute, but to everyone present it was clear that this was a direct evocation of the ceremonial behaviour of the German Nazi Party, and of their public method of acclaiming their leader, Adolf Hitler.

Coriolanus was presented as the virtuous hero of the play, and Alexandre ensured that the audience were in no doubt of this fact. At forty-seven years old on the opening night, he may have been considered too old for the role, but in the Comédie-Française the most senior actors could choose which part they played. Stocky and muscular in physique, he dominated the stage, delivering Coriolanus's rhetorical denunciations of his enemies with great energy and emphatic bravura. In Shakespeare's text his aged mother Volumnia is a similarly towering and monumental presence in the play, but she was not in this production. Gabrielle Colonna-Romano had been a famous silent-film actress, and was a former model for the artist Auguste Renoir, but she was still only forty-six, younger than her on-stage son. She only had four days to rehearse the role (Schwartz-Gastine 2008: 133). Rather than the force of nature who turns Coriolanus back from destroying Rome when no-one else can, she was very much in Alexandre's shadow.

Fabre himself directed the production, which opened on 9 December 1933. Every ticket had been sold for the first night, unusually for such a 'difficult' tragedy, but it soon became clear that it was word of the play's right-wing politics which had drawn many of the audience to the theatre. Immediately *Coriolanus* became the focus for anti-government demonstrations, and for media comment and interpretation.

Fascism, as an anti-rationalist political ideology, relied heavily on a theatrical use of symbolism and spectacle. The uniforms, the banners and the exaggerated rhetorical delivery of its leaders' speeches were all part of its strategy to appeal to atavistic emotion and nationalist sentiment, both in 'live' performance and also on cinema newsreels. But highly theatricalised spectacle was also central to fascism's own emotional and heroic conception of itself. The subject matter of Shakespeare's *Coriolanus* – class struggle, military heroism and self-sacrifice, the concept of the man of destiny – was immediately attractive to fascist ideologues, and in Piachaud's interpretation, which ironed out the political ambiguities, complexities and ironies of Shakespeare's text, the tragedy became an inflammatory intervention in a moment of political crisis. It was not new that a political outlook should attempt to appropriate the cultural capital of Shakespearean drama to enhance its status; this was also the matter of dispute in the New York *Macbeth* riots of 1849. But the fascist *Coriolanus* of 1934 exploited Shakespeare to stage what became a media 'event', as the right-wing press used the very presence of the production in Paris's cultural life to present a pro-fascist message. Piachaud's *Coriolanus* was an early example of what today we would recognise as a politically effective media event, where a work of fiction enters the public discourse and successfully establishes the authority of a wider political narrative, of a political group taking control of power-laden if ephemeral cultural symbols in a manner more familiar in 'post-modern' politics. But in 1934 the bloodshed which ensued, and the huge trade union counter-reaction to far-right insurgency which followed, was far from modern so-called 'virtual' politics.

Although France had initially not suffered as grievously as other Western nations in the Great Depression, by the winter of 1933–4 there was no doubt that the country's economic problems were becoming more acute and that the main political parties were incapable of working together to arrest the decline. Unemployment was mounting, especially amongst workers in textiles and metalworking, but the government would not devalue the currency to make French exports more competitive, as had happened in Britain and the USA (Kedward 2006: 158–9). In 1932 a 'Cartel' of left-wing and left-leaning parties won the general election, but soon fell apart over fundamental economic policy. The Radicals wanted to cut spending and deflate the economy, but their coalition partners, the Socialists, opposed these policies. By December 1933 there had been four different prime ministers in just over a year, the latest being the Radical Camille Chautemps (McMillan 1992: 104–5). At that point a new scandal broke out which suggested that the centre-left government was not only incapable of effective rule but also morally corrupt.

Sacha 'Serge' Stavisky was a Ukrainian Jew who had been a café singer and a night-club owner before moving into pawnbroking, then fraud and embezzlement, selling worthless bonds. Having already spent some time in jail he had been put prosecuted for fraud in 1927, but the trial was postponed nine times while Stavisky was bailed. His criminal activities continued. In December 1933 he was wanted for questioning in the case of some fraudulent bonds involving the deputy-mayor of the town of Bayonne and the local bank manager. French town councils offered credit to local people at a time when banks were not very willing to lend. In Bayonne the operation was based on a pawnbroking business, run by Stavisky and secured by a collection of jewellery which he claimed to be emeralds of the former Empress of Germany (George 2008: 19). The jewellery turned out to be non-existent or worthless, and those who invested in the project lost all their money. Stavisky's personal fortune, on the other hand, amounted to nearly 300 million francs by December 1933 (Kedward 2006: 164). Newspaper investigations then revealed that Stavisky had friends amongst the political elite, including the Paris Prefect of Police, Jean Chiappe; Minister for the Colonies in the Cheautemps government, Albert Dalimier; and some other members of parliament and senators in the Radical Party. The fact that the public prosecutor was Chautemps's brother-in-law made the failure to bring Stavisky to justice for such a long time look like straightforward cronyism, bribery and corruption. The fact that Stavisky was a foreign Jew made the whole business even more of a juicy target for the right-wing, routinely anti-Semitic press.

From the very first night the audience were quick to seize on any lines in *Coriolanus* that might apply to the venality and corruption of the Tribunes, those elected representatives of the people who, in this production, claimed to espouse progressive politics but were entirely driven by selfish motives. With some understatement, Fabre later recalled that first night:

Bad luck would have it that at that very moment a scandal broke out: the case of a crook named Stavisky in which a number of MPs and senators were involved and in which the police and the prosecution had apparently taken a rather soft approach. Then the outcry rose high at the Comédie-Française; all the phrases which could be turned against the MPs were caught up at once by the audience and acclaimed.

(Cited in Schwartz-Gastine 2008: 130, her translation)

At the end of the performance an anti-government demonstration took place in the street outside the theatre. As the run continued, applauding and chanting at the lines which could be given a contemporary right-wing political spin grew more riotous. One evening when the two Tribunes appeared on stage a voice in the gallery loudly identified them as Léon Blum and Paul Boncour, respectively the leader of the Socialist Party in parliament and the Foreign Minister (Shakespeare 2013: 21). The demonstrations outside the theatre grew larger. The press exacerbated the situation, contrasting in editorials the patriotic virtue of Piachaud's Coriolanus with the venality and nepotism of the governing politicians. On 27 January, following one of Coriolanus's tirades against the Republic in Act Three, the whistling and uproar grew to the extent that there had to be a pause in performance. Some of the audience were shouting 'Bravo Hitler', and others shouting back in defence of the Republic (Hardison Londré 1986: 126). The house lights were turned on until the actors were able to carry on with the play (Schwartz-Gastine 2008: 131).

On 8 January 1934 Stavisky had been found by the police in a chalet in Chamonix, in the Alps. As they entered through a half-opened window they heard two shots. They found Stavisky stretched out on the floor. He was taken to hospital but died that night without regaining consciousness (Pelissier 2006: 32–3). The police claimed it was suicide, but suspicions persisted in the right-wing press that Stavisky had been killed to prevent his testimony from incriminating his friends in high places. It was claimed that the police had waited for a suspiciously long time before calling for medical assistance. It was also thought strange that he had apparently held the pistol in his left hand but shot himself in his right temple. And where had he obtained the firearm?

From 9 January there were violent street demonstrations against the government (Pelissier 2006: 38ff.). A series of non-parliamentary political organisations representing different shades of right-wing opinion had grown up in France. The group of longest standing, Action Française, had been founded in 1899. It called for the return of an authoritarian monarchy, but was also fiercely anti-socialist, xenophobic and anti-Semitic in particular (Kedward 2006: 47–8). The young men who sold their newspaper, *Action Française*, were known as the Camelots du Roi, a thuggish royalist youth organisation. They were mostly students who were as keen on street-fighting as they were on disrupting lectures whose subject matter they found uncongenial. On 9 January two thousand Camelots du Roi rioted in

Paris against 'foreigners and thieves'; twice that number, two days later. Action Française accused the Prime Minister himself of having Stavisky murdered (Kedward 2006: 164–5). The headline on their paper read 'Camille Chautemps, boss of a gang of robbers and assassins' (Pelissier 2006: 40, my translation). As other right-wing groups joined in, the Paris Prefect of Police, Jean Chiappe, appeared sympathetic to the rioters, not attempting to restrain their violence despite his men being injured. An anti-cuts march of public-sector trade unionists on 22 January, on the other hand, was dealt with harshly by Chiappe. Despite everything, Chautemps would not allow a full public inquiry into the Stavisky affair, and was forced to resign. The Socialist Édouard Daladier became Prime Minister on 31 January 1934.

The following morning the right-wing newspaper *Le Figaro* published a front-page article attacking every member of the new government and suggesting that France needed a man like Coriolanus to take power and cleanse its corrupt politics. It directly compared Coriolanus with Hitler, and suggested that fascism might be the answer to France's problems. The paper, owned by the perfume magnate François Coty, had been even more pro-Nazi in the recent past (Kedward 2006: 165). On 8 March 1933 it had called for concentration camps to be set up in France to detain 'Jewish Bolsheviks'. *Le Figaro* was demanding internment for the thousands of Jewish and left-wing refugees who fled over the border from Hitler's Germany following the Nazis' rise to power.

Daladier reacted swiftly to this attack. He moved Chiappe to a position of responsibility in French Morocco, but also demanded the resignation of Fabre at the Comédie-Française. On 3 February Fabre, who had run the theatre since 1915, was replaced as administrator of France's national theatre by Georges-Paul-Maurice Thomé, previously head of the Sûreté Générale, the national police force dealing with internal subversion, a man whose credentials for the job were not entirely evident (though it has been claimed that he was 'a man of literary tastes') (Hardison Londré 1986: 127). On the evening of Sunday 4 February the audience was tense, fractious, disturbed by the news. There had been trouble in the streets during the day, as right-wing gangs protested against the removal of Chiappe. Newspaper kiosks were set on fire and the police were attacked with pickaxe handles. Their chant was death to Jews, foreigners, socialists and Daladier (Kedward 2006: 165). Fabre and Chiappe appeared to be martyrs for the same cause. As soon as the curtain went up in the theatre there was an impromptu speech delivered from the dress circle: 'Ladies and gentlemen, I know I can speak for you all in deploring the departure of a man of such integrity and great talent as Emile Fabre …'. But the government also had its supporters, and contending shouts for Fabre and Thomé rang across the auditorium, together with some threats of violence. When the interval came some blows were exchanged. One man, who had a physical resemblance to Thomé, was forced to flee the theatre to avoid being severely beaten.

When the play continued, the different lines in the play which had previously brought out a loud reaction were again loudly applauded:

> You are tired of the government – well it can be changed …
> Farewell, poor shepherds of the working-class herd …
> It's the inevitable collapse of the state …

Alexandre, in the title role, felt he had to step forwards and plead for some order. 'I speak now as a theatre employee', he began, 'it is not Coriolanus who is addressing you – I beg you to let us act'. He managed to get himself heard, and continued: 'You are turning this performance into a demonstration which is going to get the play banned. You're not serving Monsieur Fabre well in perhaps provoking a ban on a piece of work which shows him at his best.' But the mass of the audience chanted back at him, 'Shout down Thomé, shout down Thomé, shout down Thomé …'. The curtain came down at that point. The audience responded by changing their chant to 'We want Fabre! We want Fabre! We want Fabre!' Eventually Alexandre reappeared from the wings, still in costume. He began in a conciliatory tone, suggesting his sympathy with their demands; he said that the actors hoped that their wishes, 'just like ours, will be granted'. But then he asked them all to evacuate the theatre. There had been a power cut, he declared. They were using their emergency power supply, but soon there would not be enough light to continue the performance. It was true that there had been a brief interruption to the power supply earlier in the evening for about a minute, but no-one believed Alexandre (Pelissier 2006: 90–1). At any rate, there was no more acting at the Comédie-Française that evening.[1]

The audience did not go home, however, and a pro-Fabre demonstration continued in the street outside the theatre. The Prime Minister, Édouard Daladier, took it upon himself to address the crowd. He arrived about midnight, but he failed to calm their anger. The police made little attempt to restrain the demonstrators and Daladier was forced to retreat (Schwartz-Gastine 2008: 131). The following day Fabre was reinstated as administrator and Thomé was dismissed. The theatre was closed that night, and following the serious rioting on 6 February and on 9 February all performances of the play were suspended indefinitely. *Coriolanus* was replaced by a revival of the previous year's production of Molière's comedy *The Hypochondriac* (*Le Malade Imaginaire*). The right-wing press trumpeted that the play had been exiled from an unappreciative city just like its hero, to be replaced by the deluded and the sickly.

On Tuesday 6 February Daladier was to present his new government before the French parliament, the Chamber of Deputies. The forces of the far right announced that they would mount a huge demonstration in protest. It was clearly a threatening move. By early evening there were between twenty and thirty thousand demonstrators gathering on the routes around the Palais-Bourbon, the Chamber of the Assemblée Nationale. There was an array of right-wing groups, and even a large group of communist ex-servicemen who had also come to demonstrate but were unsure of their role given the huge presence of their political enemies. In the lead was Solidarité Française, led by Jean Renard. This group wore blue shirts in imitation of Mussolini's Blackshirts and were funded by the perfume manufacturer François Coty, and by Mussolini himself. The champagne producer Pierre Taittinger was behind the Jeunesses Patriotes, who possessed ninety thousand members nationally. Action Française was also there in huge numbers, and its members were to suffer the highest casualties of any of the far-right groups that night: four out of the fourteen who were killed and 42 per cent of the injured. The largest group was the Croix-de-Feu, commanded by Colonel de la Roque. Originally a veterans' organisation founded in 1927, it claimed 450,000 members by 1936. The Croix-de-Feu had its own paramilitaries (*dispos*) who engaged in street-fighting with communists, but although present in large numbers they remained aloof from the action that night. They had already staged their own token siege of the National Assembly the previous evening. It seems that de la Roque had already been involved in some negotiations with the government in the hope that he might be the Coriolanus-like strong man to whom France would turn in her hour of need. There was also the self-avowedly fascist group Francisme, led by Jean Bucard, and a very large number from the right-wing veterans' association, the Union Nationale des Combattants. Historians have disputed the extent to which the UNC came with violent intent, but there is no doubt that they were involved in the fighting (McMillan 1992: 106–7; Vinen 1996: 12, 14).

Having assembled in military fashion the different groups marched on the Place de la Concorde, just across the River Seine from the Palais-Bourbon. The police, both mounted and on foot, and the anti-riot *gendarmes mobiles* were positioned behind barriers on the Pont de la Concorde to defend the National Assembly. Only the bridge would stand between the demonstrators and parliament itself. The police were ordered to defend their position 'by all means' (Pelissier 2006: 129, my translation), a phrase which was later used to justify their conduct. The bridge behind them was blocked with police vehicles (Pelissier 2006: 124). As more and more demonstrators arrived the police became fearful and jittery. Random pedestrians crossing the Place de la Concorde were attacked by the *gendarmes mobiles*. At about 6pm Count Jean de Maupas was set upon on his way to his club, and Marius Brun, a restaurant worker waiting for a bus, was attacked by five policemen who dismounted from bicycles to beat him senseless with their truncheons. By half-past six the demonstrators had assembled and the first barricades went up, made from the debris of demolished street kiosks (Pelissier 2006: 123). Ammunition for throwing began to be gathered from the Tuileries Gardens just to the east of the square. A bus which found itself caught up in the action was attacked. The passengers fled. The driver was dragged from his seat, and a flaming piece of newspaper put in bus's petrol tank. The driver later testified that the newspaper was an edition of *Le Nation*, the paper of the Jeunesses Patriotes. Members of the mounted Republican Guard made five charges to clear the square so that the Fire Brigade could get to the bus. Eventually they succeeded, and just after seven the fire was out. But it was at that point that the demonstration became a full-scale riot; the anti-foreigner chants gave way to a determination to storm the police barriers and attack parliament itself. It was at about this time that the police later reported hearing gunshots from the crowd.

First missiles rained down on the police lines. The firemen, who had come to extinguish the bus, turned their hoses on the crowd. The *gendarme mobiles*, under bombardment from the huge crowd, charged their assailants to drive them back. Again the rioters attacked the police lines, but each time they were repulsed. The violence spread over a wide area as the rioters sought to find other routes towards the Palais-Bourbon, but the police resistance stood firm.

More and more demonstrators arrived to confront the police at the Pont de la Concorde. It was at about half-past seven that the killing began. Some reports say that some of the rioters had brought firearms, and that at this point shots were fired towards the police, and towards the firemen, some of whom abandoned their hoses, which were being used as water cannon. It was when the rioters seized the hoses and turned them on the police that the first order for the police to fire seems to have been given. It was a moment of crisis. Stung by the bombardment of rocks, wood and rubble some police horses bolted through their own lines causing chaos, and a few young rioters managed to get amongst the police vehicles on the bridge with the intention of setting them on fire. Some of the officers fired their pistols into the air, but many shot directly into the crowd. At least one of those who got amongst the vehicles on the bridge, a student called Gilbert Ecorcheville, was shot and wounded at close range. The firing went on for fifteen or twenty seconds and then ceased (Pelissier 2006: 142–4). The violence was chaotic; one shot (but not, it was established, from a standard police firearm) hit and killed a maidservant, Corentine Gourland, in the nearby Hôtel Crillon (Pelissier 2006: 148). There are some reports of automatic weapons used. This did not stop the rioting, however. The shooting was the source of most of the fatalities that night.

Elsewhere the Union Nationale des Combattants marched on the nearby President's Palace, L'Elysée. One member later gave this account of a police counter-attack that night:

> The flags are torn and trodden underfoot. Our old soldiers beaten, knocked to the ground, and trampled on by men and horses – I was one of those, with Lamoureux and others. Cries of terror ring out, the wounded howl and groan, those at the back push harder, shouting angrily at the men crushing their comrades. Policemen on foot and on horseback advance redoubling their blows. What can bare fists do against sabres and truncheons? We retreat, trying to parry the blows. They hit us about the head, deaf to our cries. Blows strong enough to fell an ox rain down on us and we try to protect ourselves with our heavily bruised arms or shoulders, but as for our poor standard-bearers, trying to stop their flags from being wrenched from them, their faces are battered and bloody.
>
> (Pelissier 2006: 169, translated by Daphne Wall)

Beaten back, the UNC made their way to the Place de la Concorde where the crowd facing the bridge were more subdued following their shock at the shootings around 7.30pm. The UNC column arrived just before 10.30pm. Reinforced, the right-wing insurgents then made one last attempt to cross the bridge to attack parliament. Some shots seemed to have been fired at the police at this point, but no firearms were used by the defenders this time, and the attackers very nearly forced their way through police lines. Just in time the fire hoses, spraying high-pressure icy water on a cold February night, drove the rioters back. The attackers launched one last heavy barrage of whatever missiles they could find against the police, but then the mounted officers launched a charge which drove the protestors back, albeit at considerable cost to men and horses. The moment of crisis had passed. Soon the army would arrive to reinforce the police. Many of the demonstrators, both at the Concorde and all over the city, started to drift away to catch the last Metro home. Then, at 11.30pm the police attacked in a pincer movement and cleared the Place de la Concorde, but at the cost of some more deaths amongst the rioters. It seems as if more shooting took place at this point (Pelissier 2006: 177–8, 190).

There was widespread disorder that night all over the city centre, some of it also involving communist demonstrators in conflict with the police. Fourteen civilians were killed and about 2,200 were injured. Of the security forces, one *gendarme mobile* died, and 270 policemen were injured (Anderson 2011: 100); 270 police horses were also so badly injured they had to be destroyed. Some had been slashed with razors; the others were victims of marbles and ball-bearings rolled beneath their hooves (Pelissier 2006: 178). The fighting went on until 1.30 in the morning, but the Palais-Bourbon remained safe from attack. As the riot raged outside, inside the parliament building Daladier's government finally received its vote of confidence, but not before there had been fist-fights between deputies of the left and the right.

Yet in the morning, after visiting the injured policemen in hospital, Daladier was prevailed upon to resign. The Radical Party deputies claimed that if he did not leave office the army would have to be deployed to defend his government against its enemies outside parliament. To keep the military out of political life Daladier agreed to go. In his doing so the right-wing insurgents seemed to have achieved their objective.

But in fact the fall of the Daladier government worked in the opposite way. It served to mobilise the left, who interpreted the events of that night as a pre-planned violent attempt to seize power by fascists. The far right was probably too divided and had no obvious charismatic leader to be able to take over the state, but the anti-fascist reaction was swift. In the short term a wave of strikes in protest against what was seen as the attempted coup took place on 12 February, demonstrating in turn the massive strength of the trade union and socialist movement. In the longer term the fascist threat evident on 6 February provoked the Socialist and Communist Parties to overlook their historical differences and in 1936 a 'Popular Front' government of the united left was elected to power. The government only lasted two years, but it was the first successful check on the momentum of fascist politics in Western Europe.

Coriolanus did return to the Comédie-Française on 11 March and continued to run until 30 November, this time without further disturbances (Shakespeare

2013: 22). Soon after the riot a commercial theatre, which was free of government control, offered Piachaud a large sum to transfer the play, but the Comédie-Française was desperate to keep in repertory what had been a very lucrative production (Hardison Londré 1986: 130). When the play closed, however, *Coriolanus* was banned until 1956, when Piachaud's translation was revived, but at that point in a very different mood and style of performance (George 2008: 75). In the meantime Piachaud was awarded the Légion d'Honneur in 1935. The records offer no reason why this official distinction was conferred upon him (George 2008: 78). The next notable production of the play in France was in the version by Gabriel Garran at Aubervilliers in 1964, for a working-class audience. On that occasion the play's ideological polarities were reversed, at a time when left-wing politics were in the ascendance in Europe (Schwartz-Gastine 2008: 134–5).

The 1934 distorted version of *Coriolanus* resonated powerfully within a particularly combustible political situation, and was exploited as a part of right-wing media political narrative, a cultural phenomenon which was to become more common later in the century. But it was also testament, again, to the power of live theatre to inspire and inflame public action, even of the most regressive and reactionary kind.

Note

1 Hardison Londré, less plausibly citing an 'undocumented clipping', claims that the show continued that night and received twenty curtain calls (1986: 126).

References

Anderson, Malcolm (2011), *In Thrall to Political Change: Police and Gendarmerie in France* (Oxford: Oxford University Press).

Cohn, Ruby (1976), *Modern Shakespeare Offshoots* (Princeton NJ: Princeton University Press).

George, David (2008), *A Comparison of Six Adaptations of Shakespeare's 'Coriolanus', 1681–1962* (Lampeter: The Edwin Mellen Press).

Hardison Londré, Felicity (1986), '*Coriolanus* and Stavisky: The Interpenetration of Art and Politics', *Theatre Research International*, 11 (2), 119–32.

Kedward, Rod (2006), *La Vie en Bleu: France and the French since 1900* (London: Penguin Books).

McMillan, James F. (1992), *Twentieth-Century France: Politics and Society 1898–1991* (London: Routledge).

Pelissier, Pierre (2006), *6 Février 1934: La République en Flammes* (Paris: Perrin).

Schwartz-Gastine, Isabelle (2008), '*Coriolanus* in France from 1933 to 1977: Two Extreme Interpretations', in Dirk Delabastita, Jozef De Vos and Paul Franssen (eds) *Shakespeare and European Politics* (Newark DE: University of Delaware Press).

Shakespeare, William (2013), *Coriolanus*, ed. Peter Holland (London: Bloomsbury).

Vinen, Richard (1996), *France 1934–70* (Basingstoke and London: Macmillan).

Chapter 10

Dishonour and the sacred space
Behzti in Birmingham, 2004

On the evening of Saturday 18 December 2004 a crowd of eight hundred people 'stormed' a studio theatre, according to the local paper (*Birmingham Evening Mail*, 22 December 2004, p.8).[1] The performance of the play against which they were protesting, Gurpreet Kaur Bhatti's *Behzti*, was abandoned, and the production was never performed again. The demonstrators were Sikhs who believed that *Behzti* was insulting their religion because it depicted scenes of rape and murder in a gurdwara, the Sikh temple. Subsequently a furious controversy broke out in the local and national media about a dramatist's right to free speech being silenced by a 'mob' motivated by religious intolerance. But whatever actually happened that night, and whatever the rationale for the cancellation of the production, the events in Birmingham in December 2004 seem to have something to say about the idea of the sacred in contemporary Britain, and about where the theatre stands in relation to that idea. Perhaps the power of the theatre to incite violence sometimes comes from its close relationship with religion, a field of human activity which is also no stranger to destruction and bloodshed.

What is particularly remarkable about the *Behzti* controversy is the fact that almost none of the controversialists had seen the play itself. Hardly any of the Sikhs in Birmingham's Centenary Square that December night had seen the play, and indeed very few of the play's defenders had been in the audience of the 112-seat studio theatre during its nine performances. Rather than a battle between Asian religious fundamentalism and Western liberal principle, what followed can perhaps be better understood as a contest over the idea of the sacred space in both secular and in religious Britain. This was a contest provoked by the setting of Bhatti's play, rather than by the text or by the performance of the play itself.

Since the play had opened on 9 December there had been a week of small, peaceful demonstrations in the square outside the Birmingham Rep, a concrete and glass modernist edifice in the city centre. On the evening of Saturday 18 December there was undoubtedly some violence, but it is not clear that 'hundreds of demonstrators stormed the theatre' as the *Birmingham Post* reported, even if there were 'chaotic scenes in which windows were smashed and three police officers suffered minor injuries'. The paper does not seem to have had a reporter present, since the front-page story the following Monday merely reads, 'it is reported that the demonstrators attacked security guards, threw missiles at the police and destroyed a foyer door while attempting to enter the building' (*Birmingham Post*, 20 December 2004, p.1). Three arrests were in fact made, but the detained men were bailed and charges were never brought. Ian Findlay, a photographer from a rival paper, the *Birmingham Evening Mail*, was actually present. He was jostled and his equipment was damaged by protestors. Findlay was surprised at what happened to him: 'I had covered the protests earlier in the week which were very peaceful and 95 per cent of the crowd were very friendly'. But this was not an out of control mob that night, either. Findlay pointed out that the 'community organisers were so upset when they heard about the "isolated" incident that they made those responsible apologise and offer to pay for a replacement' for his equipment (*Birmingham Evening Mail*, 20 December 2004, p.2).

Some Sikh women interviewed later that week in the *Birmingham Post* had a different view of the incident from that reported on the newspaper's front page on the Monday morning. 'How did we "storm" the theatre?' asked Manpreet Kaur:

> I was there and I didn't see that happen. We were praying but nobody reported that. We were making a peaceful protest but no one was listening to us. We were open to negotiation. We wanted a dialogue. We demonstrated peacefully all week. Just at the end there was violence and we were written about as violent people not open to negotiation.

Another woman, Amarjit Kaur, said 'I'd like to know how much violence there actually was … all I know about is a smashed window but I haven't seen any blood. We don't know what happened. We don't know who pushed who' (*Birmingham Post*, 22 December 2004, p.8).

Inside the theatre that night, however, there was genuine fear. In the 800-seat main theatre Birmingham Rep's family Christmas show, Roald Dahl's *The Witches*, was about to begin. A playgoer at that theatre, Mark Cowan, described how

> we had only been in the foyer a few minutes when we heard the smashing of glass and the staff ushered everyone up the stairs to the first floor. From the windows we could see police running in every direction. Then the theatre announced that we should all leave the building at our nearest exit. There were children crying as we all left the building in a volatile situation.
> *(Birmingham Evening Mail,* 20 December 2004, p.2)

The breaking glass also included damage done to the stage door. Having smashed their way in, some of the demonstrators managed to get onto the stage itself. The play's director, Janet Steel, in an interview in Ireland in 2006, described what happened:

And what actually happened was, you know, there were people drumming, it was quite a sort-of carnival atmosphere I guess. And then I think, I think, I don't know because I wasn't there but I think a few young guys took it upon themselves to take some action. And they smashed in the front of the Birmingham Rep, which is glass-fronted, and that was scary in itself, but the worst thing they did, which was total violation as far as I'm concerned, they smashed in the stage door and went in where the actors were. The actors had to lock themselves in their dressing rooms out of fear. And they went into the theatre itself and they, you know, pulled stuff and, you know, started to destroy the set, basically.

(Steel 2006)

The performances of both plays that evening were cancelled.

Reporters from *The Times* in London put the blame for the violence on 'extremists' linked to the Sikh Federation; the group formed after the International Sikh Youth Federation was banned under the Terrorism Act 2000 for 'being involved in assassinations, bombings and kidnappings' in India which aimed to create an independent Sikh state. A member of the Federation, Kulwinder Singh Johal, was quoted as claiming disingenuously that 'there was no violence, it has been exaggerated. A window was smashed, but we don't know if that was done from the inside or the outside' (*The Times*, 22 December 2004). Demonstrators had come from London, Leicester and Manchester as the story had started to appear in the national and then the foreign press, and international awareness of the story grew: 'Britain's Sikh community is under fire from all sides for violently forcing the premature closure of a play they said mocked their religion', reported *The Times of India* later that week (*The Times of India*, 22 December 2004). Clearly a group of demonstrators did get into the theatre through force and frightened many people inside. But they were not ruthless international terrorists. A Sikh elder, and chairman of the Sikh Gurdwaras in Birmingham, Sewa Singh Mandla, was jostled during the demonstration, then, as he told the *Evening Mail*, 'they called me a sissy and told me I should resign' (*Birmingham Evening Mail*, 22 December 2004, p.7).

On the following Monday morning, 20 December, a meeting was held between Birmingham Rep, the West Midlands Police and Sikh community leaders. Yasmin Wilde, who played the character of Min in the play, thought that the police position was supportive of the theatre. Senior police officers said Birmingham Rep 'had every right to put a play on', but offered the opinion that the situation 'was just going to get worse and worse now that it has become an international issue' (*The Guardian*, 29 December 2004). The decision was made that *Behzti* had to come off. Stuart Rogers, executive director of Birmingham Rep, told the BBC that 'When one stands in the foyer with 800 women and children and sees stones being thrown and police officers injured, then security and safety issues come to the fore. They have to'.[2] For the author, however, the worst was just beginning. Death threats forced her into hiding under police protection for some months.

Gurpreet Kaur Bhatti was an experienced writer for the stage, cinema and television. She scripted nine episodes of the popular soap opera *Eastenders*. Bhatti had worked with *Behzti*'s director, Janet Steel, before, and gave her an early draft of the script. When Steel first read the play it was the setting of scenes of rape and murder in a gurdwara which made her feel there could be a problem straight away. She raised the issue directly with Bhatti, but after much discussion it was agreed that this must not be altered since they both felt very strongly that 'the temple is another character in the play' (Freshwater 2009: 150–1).

Bhatti's theme is sacrilege in the holy place itself. For Sikhs, the presence of the book of scripture renders a building sacred; indeed, the Guru Granth Sahib is not just a holy book but the physical embodiment of God's teaching. Since the action of the play would apparently take place in the representation of such a presence there was nervousness about the reception of the production from the very start. On the second day of the three-week rehearsal period Steel 'was told' that some elders from the Sikh community had been invited to hear a reading. In fact two young men came because their fathers were unavailable. Steel recalls that 'one of the gentlemen said that he thought it was a great play, it was a very important play, but he didn't feel it should be set in a gurdwara. And the other guy, who was a lawyer, kept very quiet and didn't really say very much' (Steel 2006). The fact that the stage would only be a representation of the gurdwara was not the point as far as the Sikhs were concerned. Even a represented temple somehow shared the aura of the real thing.

During the rehearsal process a sustained attempt was made to recognise the offence that might be caused to local Sikhs. Naturally, Steel and Bhatti made some of the changes to the script which are usual when a new play is produced for the first time in order to clarify the text and to sharpen its dramatic impact. But other changes were also made. To avoid upsetting the feelings of 'the Asian community', the majority of the swearing was removed. Out of respect for Sikhism some symbolic objects, and, in particular, the sacred scripture, the Guru Granth Sahib, were not represented on stage, even though Bhatti's published text calls for it to be present (Bhatti 2004: 97). According to Yasmin Wilde, a number of jokes and some swearwords were taken out 'after interventions by members of the Sikh community'. Wilde told *The Guardian* that many of the cast were 'disappointed that compromises in the script had been made'. Wilde was clear that responding to the particular feelings of the sections of the audience should not be 'part of the creative process' (*The Guardian*, 29 December 2004). By allowing some local elders to have a say in the development of the play a signal was being sent that the content of the play was not the final decision of the writer, director and actors.

On the second day of the technical rehearsal Steel discovered that 'some members of the local Sikh community had gone to the council and wanted to get the play stopped on the grounds that it was inciting racial hatred, which was a great shock to us'. It was decided that the dress rehearsal should take place in front of some local councillors, some representatives of the Arts Council of England and 'local members of the Sikh community'. Janet Steel recalls a very difficult evening:

We did the piece, and we sort of sat there and I hugged the shoulders of the designer sat in front of me. And what happened was three members of the Sikh male community went up to Gurpreet [Kaur Bhatti] and almost, almost physically attacked her. I stepped in, and Jonathan Church [Artistic Director of Birmingham Rep] stepped in, we sort of, had to sort of stand in the middle, because the hatred from these people towards Gurpreet was so intense you could see it. They were speaking to her in Punjabi so I couldn't understand what they were saying, but they were threatening, pointing fingers, and the threatening continued out into the foyer.

(Steel 2006)

The Sikh leaders asked for the scenes that were set in the gurdwara to be relocated in 'a community centre or similar place'. The request was refused. This decision turned out to be the crucial issue in what was to follow.

Behzti opened on 9 December 2004. There were protestors outside the theatre from the beginning. Each member of the audience at The Door, the studio theatre at the Birmingham Rep, was given a printed statement which was also read out in the auditorium before every performance. This statement had been written by 'the Sikh community … expressing its views on the play' at the invitation of the theatre. As Janet Steel recalls:

The Front of House manager would get up and read this statement which would say, 'This play is not based on fact', I can't remember the exact words, 'The Sikh community are very angry about this piece, this doesn't represent us', and so on … and it was like the weirdest thing. So if people come to the theatre waiting to enjoy a play, and the opening scene, the prologue, is a very hard-hitting but very funny piece, you get this statement. There's this silence for a long time. It's like 'What are we going to see?' It was the bizarrest, weirdest, kill – how to kill the opening of a play.

(Steel 2006)

Thus the violence was not incited by the events of the play, or its power as theatre. It was the mere report of the events of the plot being set in a representation of a gurdwara, the Sikh temple, which was the spark that set off the eventual trouble.

It should, however, not be overlooked that the play puts violence on stage itself. An enthusiastic review of the play published just after the riot calls *Behzti* a 'searing comedy' which 'features rape, abuse, murder, violence – while still managing to be hugely funny, touching and tremendously important' (*The Independent*, 21 December 2004). This was not the view of the *Birmingham Evening Mail*, however, whose critic felt that the play 'lacks any apparent aim', since 'Bhatti is not actually looking at these issues in any depth'. Diane Parkes wrote that, 'Where the play could really have taken the issues of women's rights, family responsibility, faith and hypocrisy by the horns, instead it descends into a messy knot of dead bodies and crying women' (*Birmingham Evening Mail*, 20 December 2004).

Reviews of the play took sides. Those who felt that it had become a liberal *cause célèbre* found an artistic quality in the play that those who felt it to be unnecessarily provocative could not see.

Behzti apparently begins as comedy but moves towards a bloody and lurid conclusion. In the long prologue scene Balbir Kaur, a disabled Sikh woman in her late fifties, is prepared for a visit to the gurdwara on the birthday of Guru Nanak, the founder of the religion. Her daughter and carer, Min, '*a faithful lump of lard ... dressed unfashionably*' is excited by the prospect since it is many years since she has had the chance to worship God (Bhatti 2004: 21). She is also eagerly anticipating an opportunity to escape the routine squabbling and mutual abusive violence that constitutes her relationship with her mother. We see Balbir pull her daughter's hair and Min tape her mother's mouth shut (Bhatti 2004: 28, 40). Min possesses an eclectic piety and a thirst for authentic spiritual experience which delights both in Sikh ritual and in ecstatic dancing to Michael Jackson songs. The mother has none of her daughter's religious feeling. In fact Balbir is hoping to employ the services of the gurdwara matchmaker to find a husband for Min, the 33- year-old virgin. Balbir's home carer, Elvis, '*a skinny young black man ... gawky and gormless, but with razor-sharp edges*', accompanies them on their visit (Bhatti 2004: 31).

Bhatti's judgemental and prescriptive attitude towards her characters sets the tone for what follows in the scenes in the gurdwara. In her Foreword to the published edition of the play, Bhatti explains that she seeks in her work to restore 'the great ideals' of the Sikh religion. She wishes to depict how 'the simple Sikh principles of equality, compassion and modesty are sometimes discarded in favour of outward appearance, wealth and the quest for power ... I wrote *Behzti* because I passionately oppose injustice and hypocrisy' (Bhatti 2004: 17–18).

At the gurdwara Balbir seeks out Mr Sandhu, the Chairman of the Renovation Committee and a respected elder. Balbir hopes Mr Sandhu will act as matchmaker for Min, but he turns out to have been the secret homosexual lover of her dead husband, Tej. It also emerges that Min had seen her father with Sandhu, and that Tej subsequently killed himself out of shame. Instead of offering to find Min a husband, Mr Sandhu rapes her in his office. When the distressed and bleeding Min approaches her mother for help, Polly and Teetee, the old friends whom Balbir had housed when she first came to Britain, accuse Min of polluting the temple with her menstrual blood. They then gag and beat her. Teetee, however, knows what has really happened: she admits that she suffered the same outrage from Mr Sandhu when she was young. The respected elder Mr Sandhu turns out not to have been a matchmaker at all, but merely to have pretended to be one 'so that girls go up and see him. So that he can force them ... And boys sometimes. He likes to rape people' (Bhatti 2004: 125).

Sandhu is fittingly murdered by Balbir with his own kirpan, the dagger which all male Sikhs carry. It symbolises the duty of Sikhs to protect the weak from tyranny and slavery and to safeguard the universal right to live life in peace. But the play ends with Min returning the love of Elvis, her faithful admirer, who had earlier resisted the approaches of the lustful then subsequently vengeful Polly.

The Prologue, set in Balbir and Min's home, takes up a fifth of the published text. The rest of the play comprises fifteen short scenes set in different parts of the gurdwara: the shoe rack, the kitchen, the toilets, Mr Sandhu's office and the worship area where the sacred text, the Guru Granth Sahib, is displayed, according at least to the text published before the Birmingham production. The action cuts between these locations in the manner of television drama. Bhatti writes of the staging of these fifteen scenes that the play requires '*a vast dimly-lit space. This whole space may give rise to several areas, but the significant action takes place centre stage. There is the sense that parts of the space can be, or might turn into, anything*' (Bhatti 2004: 47). This is Bhatti's description of the space that represents the gurdwara, the act of representation that was to cause so much offence: not the depiction of corruption and hypocrisy on the part of a Sikh elder.

Writing in *The Guardian*, Dr Jasdev Singh Rai, Director of the Sikh Human Rights Group, argued that

> For the Sikhs, the Guru Granth Sahib, the text in complete form, is sacred. The Granth Sahib is the embodiment of the Sikh gurus and is treated as our living spiritual guide. The gurdwara is where the Guru is in residence ... *Behzti*'s theme is sexual and financial abuse using Sikh characters. Most Sikhs could not care less about this. But by setting the play – unnecessarily – in a gurdwara, Bhatti disrespected the sanctity of the Guru. An offended Sikh can of course stay away from the play, but most Sikhs feel they have to maintain the gurdwara's sanctity. This may not make sense to non-Sikhs – just as chaos theory is beyond classic scientific logic, the sacred is beyond the discourse of human reason.
>
> (*The Guardian*, 17 January 2005)

Bhatti's use of television-style short scenes, each set in a different place, on the one hand might seem to suggest that she was perhaps thinking of what an audience might see on a screen rather than in the privileged, demarcated space of the stage; the location of the action rapidly changes from place to place without developing any sense of being on a stage. On the other hand, her stage direction does indicate that she sees the area depicted on stage as a place where ritual transformation is possible, a place where the everyday rules of conduct and identity are replaced by the conventions of theatre: '*There is the sense that parts of the space can be, or might turn into, anything*' (Bhatti 2004: 47). This is a good definition of the stage itself, where mere representation (what the stage *can be*) can give way to real presence through the transformative power of art (where the stage *might turn into, anything*). In this way those who sought to close down the play and those who defended its right to speech were both agreed on the significance of the special nature of the location, a location unlike any other.

An obvious response to the Sikh objection to the play's setting is the fact that the rape was not a real rape, and that it did not take place in a real gurdwara, and thus no sacrilege occurred. In a letter to *The Guardian* in response to Jasdev

Singh Rai, Randir Singh Bains made precisely that point: 'the play was indeed set in a Sikh temple, but it was not played in a real temple. To claim that it violates the sanctity of a Sikh temple is, therefore, nonsense' (*The Guardian*, 18 January 2005). But there is nevertheless some kind of parallelism at work here.

Liberal defenders of the right of theatrical free expression would argue that inside the boundaries of the stage area a space exists where the normal rules of life are suspended so that an imaginary world can flourish. To impose some limit on what can be said and done in this space is to deny artistic freedom and to succumb again to a censorship which the stage took so many centuries to shake off.

What happens in this space is indeed a fiction, but it is not a fiction in the sense that it is a self-contained fantasy. It is a fiction which can and often does produce genuine feelings and thoughts about the real world beyond the stage boundary. Indeed, that is the stated aim of the writer of *Behzti* and perhaps of almost all serious dramatists in the Western tradition. The Sikhs who protested against the play also recognised that *Behzti* was more than pure fiction, that what is represented on stage is not an event in some fantasy land which we can only gaze upon from afar but which we cannot imagine having any relevance to our lives. The stage is a special location marked off from the rest of life, but which through the power of theatrical art has a significant impact upon how we think and feel about the off-stage world: what is represented is also real.

The gurdwara for Sikhs is indeed only a building until the presence of the Guru Granth Sahib makes it, by a leap of the religious imagination, a sacred place. As Helen Freshwater puts it:

> we might imagine that these beliefs can expect to find little sympathy in a predominantly secular society. But I would suggest, on the contrary, that cultural beliefs which allow us to conflate the real and the representational, or to distinguish between the two, are at the heart of the conflict over *Behzti*.
>
> (Freshwater 2009: 153)

The analogy here is imperfect, but both the theatre and the gurdwara are sacred spaces created by an act of the will and the imagination. Interestingly, the director of *Behzti*, Janet Steel, when interviewed in 2006, made a direct assertion of the sanctity of the theatrical space to explain her outrage at the protestors: 'How dare they? I think you've got a right to protest, everybody has. But that is total violation. I'm not a religious person, you know, I'm not, so for me the theatre is my religion. That is where I practice what I like to preach' (Steel 2006). For Steel, the theatre is a holy space from which to pass comment on the world and to affect the world.

The American philosopher Paul Woodruff is quite clear that the stage is a sacred space indistinguishable from those areas marked out for religious ritual. 'A place or an object or a person is sacred' he writes, 'if it is held to be untouchable except by people who are marked off, usually by ritual, so as to be allowed to touch it'. In the case of the theatre, a tradition based on ritual 'defines the space and calls for penalties against those who violate it. All theatre … is the heir of a long line of spaces made sacred for religious ritual' (Woodruff 2008: 111). There is perhaps a liberal assumption that the untouchable spaces of Western culture are superior to those of some other cultures because they are seen as part of a rationalist, secular way of life at odds with the superstitions of religion. But as Woodruff's definition makes clear, it is practices, not beliefs, which render a space sacred. Those who enter the stage during performance without authorisation (or indeed a sporting arena while the contest is in process) incur the same sort of social condemnation in our culture as those who disrupt religious ritual in others. The sanctions may well be more extreme in some cultures, but it is a matter of degree, not of kind.

It is also interesting to note that the Western liberal right to offend through imaginative representation has been called 'sacrosanct', the word used in this very context, for example by Darcus Howe in *The New Statesman* on 10 January 2005. Interviewed on BBC Radio 4 on 21 December 2004, Hanif Kureishi argued that 'destroying a theatre is like destroying a temple: without our culture, we are nothing. Our culture is as crucial to the liberal community as temples are to the religious community' (cited in Freshwater 2009: 145). But the Sikh protestors might also claim a 'sacred' right to defend themselves against an act of appropriation by a playwright and director whose imagination creates a fictional gurdwara in order to make some comments on the real Sikh community. Bhatti and the Birmingham Rep, by her own admission ('I believe that drama should be provocative and relevant', Bhatti 2004: 18), were using the imaginary space of the stage to produce a political impact on the real world of British Sikhs. On the other side the real feelings of some British Sikhs, even if they had not seen the play, sought to make a physical intrusion on the imaginary space of the stage. In ending the play's run, they returned the stage to a mere piece of floor. The stage is never absolutely part of non-theatrical reality, but neither is what it represents ever simply fiction.

There is then perhaps a sense in which the *Behzti* incident reveals the way in which the liberal theatrical tradition attempts to have it both ways. On the one hand it triumphantly proclaims the power of the theatre to change the way people think and feel in the real world. On the other hand it becomes very upset if the real world takes it sufficiently seriously to try to hold it responsible for affecting that world and acts accordingly, whether justified or not. As I began this book by saying, the director of the Oxford Stage Company at the time, Dominic Dromgoole, amplified this point in an article on the events in Birmingham. Writing in *The Guardian* on 20 December 2004, Dromgoole was absolutely right to point out that 'theatre asks for this trouble. It has to'. He was also right to ask

> When was the last time we had riots and arrests at the unveiling of a spring schedule for a television channel? … Many of the new media have a flat, cold deadness about their methods of distribution. Theatre doesn't. It is live and chancy and hot. It creates rumblings.

The theatre is not a 'medium'; it is indeed real life and affects the world. Even if Dromgoole qualified these opinions by writing that 'violence of this sort inevitably leaves a sense of awkward loss behind it', he was right to proclaim that the theatre should be fully engaged with the world, taking responsibility for its actions. Civil order is a police matter; as for the theatre, it needs to find 'various ways of saying no to the various blind yeses that are so ardently promoted. It's what it does'.

The debate about the theatre and free speech in the *Behzti* affair continued for some years afterwards. Perhaps the most robust defence of the stage's right to offend was voiced by the playwright David Edgar, who also pointed out that ethnic communities are not monolithic entities, but divided, for example, by age and gender. It therefore needs pointing out that

> the protests against *Behzti* were overwhelmingly male and … the sexual abuse of a young Sikh woman by an older Sikh struck a chord among young Asian women from all faiths. In this reading, *Behzti* and other Asian plays *are* being sensitive to the feelings of a marginalised and silenced community.
>
> (Edgar 2006: 73)

An opposing point of view has been put by the philosopher Monica Mookherjee. Steel and some cast members felt strongly that the play was articulating an Asian woman's sense of oppression: 'for us it was the first time that you actually saw strong Asian women on stage being wonderful characters, multi-dimensional. And we were exploring really big themes, and small themes, and love and hate and religion'. Steel points out that it was Asian men who closed the play down and silenced that voice (Steel 2006). But it is possible, Mookherjee argues, that protecting the right of minority women to speak out about 'community injustice' might work to undermine 'the ethos of receptiveness to difference in multicultural societies'. In these cases 'such speech may be informally restricted in civil society' (Mookherjee 2007: 30). By allowing Bhatti's play to present Britain's Sikhs in such a negative light, Mookherjee suggests, there is a danger that such 'representation of minorities as morally deviant, even in jest, might deepen existing ethnic cleavages in society, making it harder for minority group-members to enjoy their basic rights' in the future (Mookherjee 2007: 32). On balance, without advocating legal censorship, she considers the Birmingham Rep should not have staged Bhatti's play as written.

The Birmingham theatre academic Brian Crow is broadly in agreement with this, finding fault with Bhatti's choice of dramatic method. In choosing to write in a harsh, satirical mode, apparently attacking the hypocrisy and corruption of the entire community, she had not chosen 'a method which squares comfortably with Bhatti's stated aim of engaging members of the wider Sikh community in debate and discussion' (Crow 2007: 218). Crow also suggests that it is likely that the protestors had seen little or no theatre at all, and that 'there was an oversensitive reaction in which the necessary distinction between artistic representation and actual reality was not taken into account' (Crow 2007: 216–17). Edgar's answer to this would be that what was wrong with these young men is just that they hadn't been exposed to the theatre, to the humanising effects of art and the capacity for empathy and understanding which fictions of all kinds produce. For, 'by enabling us to imagine what it is like to see the world through other eyes (including through the eyes of the violent and murderous), artistic representation develops capacities without which we cannot live in societies at all' (Edgar 2006: 74). But the theatre, as this book has argued, is not like other kinds of fiction. Through its very nature, sometimes the distinction between the 'real' and the 'fictional' cannot be simply demarcated. When two notions of the sacred space, seen from two different perspectives, become entangled, the humane function of the art becomes harder to discern, and it is harder to find empathy with the views of others. Violence can then become more likely.

The identity of the Sikhs who clashed with the police on the Saturday 18 December is unclear. There is some evidence that younger Sikhs, who felt that the older community leaders were not being assertive enough, came to the fore in the protests. Equally there were huge numbers of Sikhs in Birmingham and elsewhere who deplored the violence, and others, including many young Sikhs, who felt that the play should have gone ahead (Freshwater 2009: 155–7).

The immediate consequences for Bhatti were most distressing. Neal Foster, who ran the Birmingham Stage Company at the time, initially offered to restage the play at his theatre and then to organise a series of readings around the country as an act of resistance. He too faced death threats, and was eventually persuaded not to go ahead with either project. In 2005 *Behzti* was translated into French and was performed in Brussels on 16 November, and again in both Belgium and France in the autumn of 2006. All of these performances passed without incident. Bhatti turned her own experiences into a new play, *Behud* ('Beyond Belief'), which played in Coventry and in London in 2010 (*The Guardian*, 15 March 2010). But that play did not connect with the provocative power of the ritual sacred space in the minds of both secular liberals and the traditionally religious.

The *Behzti* incident became significant for the national and international media because some journalists wished to interpret what happened as part of a wider cultural conflict between the (intolerant) values of Asian religion and the (freedom-loving) principles of secular Western society. This mistaken interpretation was part of a wider political narrative promoted during the ill-fated 'War on Terror' launched by the Bush administration in the United States and its allies following the terrorist attacks on New York and Washington in September 2001. The real significance lies elsewhere. Yet again, the ability of live theatre to produce a particular resonance in a political situation which will inflame feelings and lead to violence was amply demonstrated. In this particular case the very heart of that ability, the fact that the stage can somehow embody both the real and the fictional at the same time, was a crucial issue. What happens on stage doesn't just stay on stage. The age of theatre riots is not yet over.

Notes

1 According to *The Independent*, 20 December 2004, there were only 400 (Kirby *et al.* 2004).
2 http://news.bbc.co.uk/1/hi/england/west_midlands/4112985.stm (accessed 23/5/15).

References

Bhatti, Gurpreet Kaur (2004), *Behzti (Dishonour)* (London: Oberon Books).
Crow, Brian (2007), 'The 'Behzti' Affair Revisited: British Multiculturalism, Audiences and Strategy', *Studies in Theatre and Performance*, 27 (3), 211–22.
Edgar, David (2006), 'Shouting Fire: Art, Religion and the Right to be Offended', *Race & Class*, 48 (2), 61–76.
Freshwater, Helen (2009), *Theatre Censorship in Britain: Silencing, Censure and Suppression* (Basingtoke: Palgrave).
Kirby, Terry, James Burleigh and Helen McCormack (2004), 'Sikhs Storm Theatre to Demand Closure of Play that "Violates their Sacred Space"', *The Independent*, 20 December 2004.
Mookherjee, Monica (2007), 'Permitting Dishonour: Culture, Gender and Freedom of Expression', *Res Publica*, 13, 29–52.
Steel, Janet (2006), interviewed in http://www.theatrevoice.com/audio/asking-for-trouble-13-the-theatre-forum-ireland-2006/ (accessed 9/5/15).
Woodruff, Paul (2008), *The Necessity of Theater* (New York: Oxford University Press).

Chronology

	The Theatre and Theatre Riots	Other Events
1576	First English professional playhouse opens	
1595	Shakespeare, *Richard II*	
1599	Globe Theatre opens	
1600	Shakespeare, *Hamlet*	
1601	*Richard II* revived at the Globe	Essex Rebellion
1603		Death of Elizabeth I
		Accession of James I
1606	Shakespeare, *Macbeth*	
1608	Indoors theatre opens at Blackfriars	
	Shakespeare, *Coriolanus*	
1613	Apprentices attack the Phoenix Theatre	
1616	Death of Shakespeare	
1625		Charles I crowned
1642	Theatres closed	English Civil War begins
1649		Execution of Charles I
1660	Theatres reopen	Restoration of the monarchy
	Two 'patent' theatre companies established under Charles II	
1666		Great Fire of London
1676	Otway, *Don Carlos*	
1678		The 'Popish Plot'
1679		'Exclusion Crisis' begins
1680	Comédie-Française founded	
1682	Otway, *Venice Preserv'd*	

1685	Death of Otway	
1732	Covent Garden Theatre opens	
1737	French actors driven from the Haymarket Stage	
1740	Dublin four-day theatre disturbances	
1760		George III crowned
1769	Garrick's 'Jubilee' for Shakespeare at Stratford-upon-Avon	
1775	Sheridan, *The Rivals*	
1776		United States Declaration of Independence
1789		French Revolution begins
1793		Britain and France at war
1794	*Venice Preserv'd* at Covent Garden	George III's coach attacked at state opening of Parliament
1799		Napoleon Bonaparte made First Consul in France
1801		Act of Union between Britain and Ireland
1809	Old Price Riots at Covent Garden	
1812–14		War between Britain and USA
1815		Napoleon defeated at Waterloo
1822	British actors tour Paris for the first time since the Revolution	
1830	*Hernani* at the Comédie-Française	Revolution in France; last Bourbon king, Charles X, abdicates
1837		Accession of Queen Victoria
1838		'People's Charter': beginning of Chartist Movement
1841	Disturbances during *King Lear*, Theatre Royal Leicester	
1843		Theatre Regulation Act: abolition of two-company monopoly; Lord Chamberlain's powers to censor the theatre extended nationally
1848		Revolutions in Europe
1849	Astor Place Riots, New York	

1864	Shakespeare tercentenary celebrations at Stratford-upon-Avon and London	
1877	*Hernani* revived	
1895	Henry James's *Guy Domville* disrupted	
1896	Jarry's *Ubu Roi* at the Théâtre de l'Oeuvre	
1904	Abbey Theatre Dublin opens	
1907	Synge's *The Playboy of the Western World* at the Abbey	
1914		First World War begins
1916		Easter Rising in Dublin
1917		Russian Revolution
1918		First World War ends
1921		Irish Free State established
1926	O'Casey's *The Plough and the Stars* at the Abbey	
1929		Wall Street Crash; Great Depression begins
1933		Hitler becomes German Chancellor
1933–4	*Coriolanus* at the Comédie-Française	French parliament attacked
1939		Second World War begins
1940		Defeat of France
1945		Second World War ends
1963	National Theatre opens at the Old Vic	
1968		Abolition of stage censorship in Britain
2003	*Venice Preserv'd* at the Citizens Theatre, Glasgow	
2004	*Behzti* disturbances at Birmingham Rep	

Index